TOWARD JUST TRANSITIONS

TOWARD JUST TRANSITIONS

VISIONS FOR REGENERATIVE COMMUNITIES IN APPALACHIA

EDITED BY
SHAUNNA L. SCOTT
AND
KATHRYN ENGLE

Copyright © 2025 by The University Press of Kentucky

Scholarly publisher for the Commonwealth,
serving Bellarmine University, Berea College, Centre
College of Kentucky, Eastern Kentucky University,
The Filson Historical Society, Georgetown College,
Kentucky Historical Society, Kentucky State University,
Morehead State University, Murray State University,
Northern Kentucky University, Spalding University,
Transylvania University, University of Kentucky,
University of Louisville, University of Pikeville,
and Western Kentucky University.
All rights reserved.

Editorial and Sales Offices: The University Press of Kentucky
663 South Limestone, Lexington, Kentucky 40508-4008
www.kentuckypress.com

Cataloging-in-Publication data is available from the Library of Congress.

ISBN 978-1-9859-0318-0 (hardcover: alk. paper)
ISBN 978-1-9859-0319-7 (pbk.: alk. paper)
ISBN 978-1-9859-0320-3 (epub)
ISBN 978-1-9859-0321-0 (pdf)

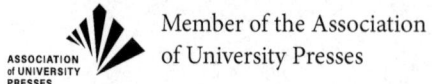

Member of the Association
of University Presses

This book is dedicated to the memory of the following individuals, whom we lost while working on this book and will mourn forever: Helen Matthew Lewis, the "grandmother" of Appalachian studies; Doug "Scutch" Scutchfield, founder of the *Journal of Appalachian Health*; bell hooks, feminist pioneer and advocate; Tammy "Tambone" Clemons, friend and colleague, and fierce advocate for Appalachian youth and the environment; David Whisnant, a pioneering thinker in Appalachian studies; Michael Burawoy, ethnographer, theorist, advocate for public sociology, and Shaunna's mentor; Phill Scott, Shaunna's beloved father, who taught her to think critically and seek justice; and "Granny," Ella Sue Engle Hoffman, Kathryn's maternal grandmother, a coal miner's daughter who modeled caring for people and place.

Contents

Introduction 1
Shaunna L. Scott and Kathryn Engle

Democratization and Equity: Meaningful Participation for All

1. What Would Make a "Just Transition" Just? Democracy, Class Justice, and a Green New Deal   17
   Dwight B. Billings

2. There Are No Black People in Coal Country: Race Formation and Just Transitions in Central Appalachia   37
   Frances B. Henderson

3. Stopping the Bad, Building the New, and Telling Our Story: An Indigenous Perspective on Rematriation as Just Transition   55
   Taysha DeVaughan

4. Community-Controlled Philanthropy: Toward a Just Reinvestment Strategy for Appalachia   66
   Lora Smith-Tovar

5. STAY Statements   81
   Stay Together Appalachian Youth

Regeneration: Land, Food, and Health

6. The Land and Us: Possibilities for Building Equitable Land Ownership in Post-Coal Appalachia   85
   Tom Hansell and Julie Shepherd-Powell

7. Seeding Just Transitions through Local Food and Agriculture Systems   96
   Kathryn Engle, Elyzabeth W. Engle, Candace Mullins, Martin Richards, and Maggie Smith Mosley

8. Health in the Quest for Appalachia's Just Transition   115
   Rachel E. Dixon and F. Douglas Scutchfield

Strategies for Advancing Just Transitions

9. Building Networks for Just Transitions   147
   Ivy Brashear, Peter Hille, and Betsy Whaley

10. "Prisons Are Not Innovation": Abolitionist Interventions for a Just Transition   160
    Sylvia Ryerson and Judah Schept

11. Appalachian Transition Fellowship: Supporting Youth Leadership for a Long-Term Vision   175
    Alice Beecher, Abby Huggins, Mae Humiston, Caitlin Myers, Susan Williams, and Elizabeth Wright

    Conclusion: Strategies for a Regenerative Region and World   186
    Shaunna L. Scott and Kathryn Engle

Acknowledgments   195

Contributors   197

Index   205

Introduction

SHAUNNA L. SCOTT AND KATHRYN ENGLE

As scholars, activists, and citizens of Appalachia, we seek to build a more equitable, sustainable, and regenerative future for the land and people of Central Appalachia. We come from various academic disciplines as well as nonacademic professions, contributing different viewpoints and styles of writing. We have written this together because Appalachia and the world are in ecological, political, and economic crisis. The Central Appalachian industries (coal, natural gas, and timber), which have contributed to this crisis, either are already in decline due to market forces (coal) and tariffs (timber) or should be phased out to reduce greenhouse gas emissions (coal and natural gas). Though this transition away from fossil fuels is almost as daunting as it is necessary, we concentrate primarily on the opportunities that such a transition provides us to make positive changes. We envision a future very different from our past and present, a future in which people can thrive without harming their health and destroying the environment, where local communities meaningfully participate and create change, where diverse constituencies are welcomed and heard, and (last but not least) where greenhouse gas emissions are reduced, climate change is mitigated, biodiversity is nurtured, and life can flourish. It stands in contrast both to Appalachia's past and to current right-wing authoritarian trends, which have been characterized by dangerous, unhealthy, and exploitative work, natural resource extraction and export, economic and political dominance of corporations headquartered outside the region, oligarchic rather than democratic governance, and systems of inequality that simultaneously privilege and marginalize. In short, we are seeking just transitions.

Transition Is Inevitable, Justice Is Not

Despite stereotypes of Appalachia as a "backward" place "frozen in time," the region has experienced considerable change—change that has brought many injustices, from appropriation of land, timber, and minerals to forced removal, and from company-owned towns to industrial disasters. Many Appalachians are pursuing "just transitions," even if this is not a phrase commonly used in local communities. In this volume, we use "just transitions" in the plural to indicate the multiplicity of ways in which justice, equity, and regeneration may be pursued and practiced, though it is not common to do so. Around the world, "just transition" means different things to different people. In this volume, we follow the Just Transition Alliance's definition: "A vision-led, unifying and place-based set of principles, processes, and practices that build economic and political power to shift from an extractive economy to a regenerative economy." Justice, in this volume, refers to a state in which societies (or communities) have robust institutions and networks that ensure equitable and fair outcomes for their citizens, not only in the cases before criminal and civil courts but also in all realms of society. The just transition movement emphasizes the importance of locally based solutions and democratic decision-making, recognizing that there are many perspectives, strategies, and transitions that will help "build thriving economies that provide dignified, productive and ecologically sustainable livelihoods, democratic governance and ecological resilience." Unlike our current extractive, capitalist economy, a regenerative one would *not* deplete the materials needed to sustain life. Rather, it would conserve resources and maintain the biosphere for future generations by keeping ecosystems healthy, reproducing, and evolving.[1]

The most recent iterations of capitalism—sometimes referred to as "neoliberal capitalism," "racial capitalism," and more recently as "predatory capitalism" and "disaster capitalism"—are environmentally destructive and socially unjust, producing an increasing gap between the "haves" and the "have nots" as well as corporate domination of government while reinforcing white supremacy and cisheteropatriarchy. Capitalism, generally, is an economic system based on private ownership and commodification of property, goods, and services necessary to sustain life. It is a system that is inherently exploitive, because profit depends on paying labor less than it is worth, using up resources that future generations will need to survive, and displacing the costs of production on others. Because this system exploits people of color by paying them even less than white labor and by siting dangerous and toxic industries near communities of color, it is sometimes referred to as racialized capitalism. Neoliberal capitalism emerged in the 1980s; it is defined by globalization, deregulation of industry and the environment, welfare and social spending cuts, deunionization, tax cuts for the wealthy, increasing economic dominance of financial institutions and markets, and policies aimed at reducing government deficits. Predatory capitalism is the product of the neoliberal era (beginning around 1980); predatory capitalism refers to a political economy revolving around financial capital based on an extreme form of market fundamentalism that has produced global economic oligarchies strong enough to determine the policy of governments. The term "disaster capitalism," coined in the early 2000s by Naomi Klein, refers to the ways in which profiteering corporations and their collaborating neoliberal states either engineer or take advantage of crises—financial crises, natural disasters, human-caused disasters, and so forth—to increase their wealth and appropriate devalued resources from communities in crisis. It is characterized by a cycle of disaster, exploitation, and privatization of public and common resources. Scott and Engle take up the question of whether capitalism in these (or any) forms is compatible with a just, regenerative society in the conclusion of this volume.[2]

By focusing on the "coal fields" and "mother forests" of Central Appalachia—eastern Kentucky, West Virginia, southwestern Virginia, and eastern Tennessee—we have chosen only one of many disaster-ridden regions that have been defined as a "sacrifice zone" because its land and people have been seen as expendable in the name of progress and profit. Others include the Mississippi Delta and "cancer alley" areas of the US South, Native American reservations, and the Global South (earlier known as the "Third World")—especially Africa, South America, and the Middle East—whose natural assets combined with weak, underfunded, or corrupt government have resulted in poverty, inequality, poor health, and climate catastrophe. Industrial and then neoliberal capitalism have created many such regions around the world.[3]

Long before Europeans colonized the region, Appalachia was home to Indigenous people with communal access to land, rivers, and forests—the sources of their livelihoods. These groups did not privately own the hunting land, forests, streams, and mountains that provided them sustenance; they shared them as a commons. The commons refers to shared resources that are nurtured and regulated by the people who rely on them; we define the climate that sustains human (and other) life as a commons. As Europeans colonized the area, they privatized Indigenous commons areas; they killed Native residents, either purposefully by murdering them or indirectly by exposing them to viruses to which they had no immunity. Some Indigenous people allied with larger neighboring chiefdoms for protection, such as the Cherokee, Shawnee, and Creek. Eventually, many Indigenous peoples assimilated into European American society and became successful farmers, business owners, and holders of enslaved people. Nevertheless, from 1831 to 1850, US troops force-marched Indigenous Appalachians west to Oklahoma on the "Trail of Tears," so called because so many died along the way. Some, however, eluded capture and remained in the mountains to continue their cultural legacy, which is now represented in the Qualla Buondary and town of Cherokee, North Carolina.[4]

The colonizers of Appalachia learned how to survive in the mountain environment from the Indigenous people, and they exploited the forced labor of enslaved individuals from Africa. Appalachian food, music, culture, and lifeways were, thus, forged in a fraught encounter between European, Native, and African peoples, structured as it was by colonialism, slavery, and white supremacy. Following Indigenous, African, and European traditions, Appalachian residents of the eighteenth and nineteenth centuries maintained a forest commons, a locally shared space for hunting, foraging, and grazing livestock. However, such commonly held lands and resources were eventually appropriated by railroad, land, coal, and steel companies from outside the region during the late nineteenth and early twentieth centuries. They not only enclosed the forest commons but also created a repressive company-owned town system that stripped employees of many American citizenship rights. The companies owned the housing and stores, hired the "law enforcement," and sometimes paid workers in company-issued currency, called scrip, which could only be used at the company-owned stores. The companies also brought in Black Southerners and imported workers from around the world to work in the mines and on the railroads. This authoritarian endeavor fueled the industrial revolution in the United States, providing energy and steel for railroad construction and manufacturing (while further emitting greenhouse gases). It also produced poverty and cyclical unemployment, environmental devastation, biodiversity loss, a weakened democracy, low levels of social trust and civic engagement, and persistent poor public health in Appalachia, issues that continue to plague the region in the twenty-first century.[5]

Global Climate Change as Existential Threat and Transformative Opportunity

According to the 2022 UN Emissions Gap Report, our fossil fuel–driven, growth-oriented, capitalist economy increasingly pollutes the planet, erodes biodiversity and threatens our existence on this planet. The report observes that none of the nation's pledges from the 2021 Glasgow COP26 conference will avert global climate disaster by 2050; it recommends *rapid social transformation* to decarbonize the power grid and transportation sectors, redesign and insulate buildings and cities, localize the food system and create a more regenerative agriculture system, eliminate fossil fuel subsidies, and revolutionize global and national financial systems in order to direct more funding to renewable energy and to marginalized populations, especially women. Technological innovation under the conventional capitalist framework, with its private property regime, profit motive, and growth imperative, is insufficient to address our current challenge, the report concludes. So it seems that the United Nation's Intergovernmental Panel on Climate Change (IPCC) envisions a future beyond or outside of capitalism.[6]

Appalachia is only one of many marginalized regions with vulnerable populations whose economies are collapsing while they contend with rising temperatures and the disasters that accompany them; the July 2022 floods, killing at least 32 people in Kentucky and Virginia, and the 2015 wildfires in eastern Tennessee and western North Carolina, which killed 14, are recent examples. In September 2024, Hurricane Helene claimed 100 lives and caused $59.6 billion in damages in North Carolina. This is not to mention the many mining-related disasters that have plagued the region, from the 1968 Farmington explosion in West Virginia (78 dead) to the 1972 Buffalo Creek, West Virginia, coal ash dam failure (126 dead), the 1976 Scotia disaster in Kentucky (26 dead), and the 2010 Upper Big Branch disaster in West Virginia (29 dead). Nor does it include the death toll of violent labor struggles in the region, from the West Virginia mine wars from the 1910s to 1921 (16 dead) to the Great Depression–era unionization struggle in Harlan and Bell Counties in Kentucky (13 dead); nor regional, race-based violence and oppression, such as the aforementioned "Trail of Tears" in the nineteenth century as well as lynchings and race-based expulsions in the early twentieth century. Indeed, the region's history of commons enclosure, the tension between Indigenous, European, and African populations, the oppressive treatment and violent removal of Native and Black populations, ongoing class exploitation, racism against all people of color (including also Asian and Latinx Appalachians), and regional experiences of disaster (both environmental and industrial) form the bases of this book, because they inform regional knowledge and inspire the legacy of resistance that we draw on here.[7]

Obviously, Appalachia has already undergone several dramatic transitions, many of them unjust. To guide us in pursuit of just transitions, we draw from the work of Elinor Ostrom and her colleagues, who, based on decades of empirical and experimental research, have identified eight principles for governing the commons necessary to sustain life, such as the climate. These principles are: (1) establish clear boundaries of the commons in question; (2) make rules to fit local circumstances; (3) use participatory and inclusive decision-making to determine the rules; (4) monitor the commons; (5) employ graduated sanctions when rules for governing the commons are violated; (6) ensure that conflict-resolution mechanisms be easily accessible, straightforward, and free of charge; (7) ensure that those managing and benefiting from a local commons be recognized by higher authorities; and (8) integrate local communities' commons into larger networks of other commons.[8]

To restate the principles in a narrative form, the people who rely on the commons must be the ones who make rules (to fit local conditions), monitor it, and enforce (graduated) sanctions. The local people must be respected by powerful institutions and individuals from outside their area and must also be in contact and collaboration with other community commons regulators and users; after all, we are connected into one planet, one biosphere, and one commons. Everyone must participate in decision-making, including youth, people of color, women, people of differing abilities, people with chronic health conditions, and LGBTQIA+ folks. Finally, we need robust, free, and transparent conflict-resolution institutions with understandable rules so that problems can be identified and resolved, rather than ignored and denied.[9]

Historically, in Appalachia and "resource cursed" regions, Ostrom's seventh principle is routinely ignored: corporations and government officials from outside the communities ignore and override the rights and preferences of (relatively powerless, poor) local and Indigenous people. A recent Appalachian example is the ongoing struggle over the construction of the Mountain Valley Pipeline (MVP), a 303-mile stretch of pipe running from the Marcellus and Utica shale formations in northern West Virginia to Pittsylvania County, Virginia. Approved by the Federal Energy Regulatory Commission in 2017, the project has significant opposition from local residents and a coalition of environmental and community groups, who maintain that the pipeline was improperly permitted. Furthermore, they argue, the pipeline will accelerate climate change and detrimentally impact water, soil, forests, and public health and safety (e.g., the commons). Three hundred landowners have sued the project; scores of citizens have protested it. Nevertheless, corporations initially succeeded in appropriating both publicly and privately owned *family* farmland for this purpose. Ironically, the doctrine of eminent domain was applied in this case, even though this doctrine is supposed to protect the public good over private (profit-extracting) interests.[10]

The local response to the MVP pipeline was similar to the Standing Rock Sioux protests of the Dakota Access Pipeline, where opponents to the project also sued for improper permitting and environmental impact studies. In April 2016, hundreds of Sioux and their Native and non-Native allies, called Water Protectors, set up a camp in the path of the proposed pipeline in protest. According to the American Civil Liberties Union, over 140 protesters now face felony charges for that protest. On Bent Mountain in Roanoke County, Virginia, a mother and daughter climbed and inhabited trees in the pipeline right-of-way until a judge held them in contempt, threatened to fine them, and sent US marshals to remove them from the land. A man who chained himself to a piece of construction equipment in West Virginia was charged with "felony terrorist threats." In Montgomery County, Virginia, authorities removed and jailed two tree-sitters after their eight hundred–day protest. Energy-rich states, including Wyoming, Kentucky, and West Virginia, have passed oil-company-backed legislation designating oil and gas pipelines as "critical" infrastructure and, thereby, criminalizing pipeline protests as acts of "terrorism." In August 2022, it appeared as if US

Introduction   7

senator Joe Manchin (WV) had succeeded in reviving the MVP when he traded his vote for the Biden administration's Climate Bill for federal agency approval of the MVP pipeline permits on the grounds of "national security." To wit, Manchin voted to cut carbon emissions as long as he could revive a carbon-emitting pipeline project that many of his constituents opposed. By October 2022, the project was shelved again, as Manchin withdrew his demands under ongoing pressure from environmental groups, political rivals, and local citizens.[11]

There are ninety-one think tanks, advocacy organizations, and trade associations who are paid approximately $1 billion annually to misreport facts, mislead the public, and manipulate public opinion concerning climate change. Additionally, the fossil fuel industry has dominated the legislative agenda in the United States, spending ten times the money as environmental activists to influence laws relevant to climate change. The top four oil companies—BP, Shell, Exxon Mobile, and Chevron—spend approximately $200 million per year to prevent or delay the implementation of policies intended to slow climate change, including $13 million spent by BP to stop the implementation of a carbon tax in Washington State. Government agencies that are charged with regulating industry to protect the environment, occupational safety, and public health are run by industry insiders and for the benefit of corporate interests. They use their financial influence to sway legislators; they use their money to confuse the public about the reality of climate change.[12]

Against these formidable odds, we follow Ostrom and the IPCC in advocating for new institutions and laws that respect local control over their means of subsistence. We are creating spaces and institutions—community trusts, land conservatories, cooperatives, community gardens, social movements, and nonprofits—where we collaborate to seek change, protest injustice, protect the environment, produce livelihoods, and build meaningful lives in the region. Young people are building more inclusive, welcoming, regenerative, and just communities. We know that climate change threatens our very existence; the longer we wait to make transformative change, the harder it will be for future generations to survive. Our need for just transitions is an urgent one. The following chapters share experiences, principles, and ideas for policies and practices that will foster a just transition (or many just transitions) in Appalachia and provide ideas for those working toward similar change around the world.

The Path Ahead

This volume is divided into sections. The first section focuses on democratization and equity: the importance of including everyone in democratic participation and decision-making in social, political, and economic governance. We lead with Billings's chapter, "What Would Make a 'Just Transition' Just? Democracy, Class Justice, and a Green New Deal," a theoretically driven chapter of particular interest to scholars and students. His chapter, like the introduction that precedes it, emphasizes the importance of deepening democracy beyond simply voting in elections to include actual participation and deliberation in governance decisions and, also, democratizing institutions beyond government to include, especially, workplaces and businesses through the institution of employee-owned enterprises and cooperatives. If we want a truly democratically governed society and commons, we must include stakeholders in decisions that pertain to them, such as the adoption of technologies, land uses, and the allocation of profit and resources.

The remaining chapters in this section highlight the importance of dismantling white supremacy, patriarchy, heteronormativity, and oligarchy to advance democracy and social justice. From the perspective of critical race theory, Frances B. Henderson examines how power and race intersect within discussions of post-coal futures in Central Appalachia, often omitting Black voices and needs. Taysha DeVaughan outlines principles from the Indigenous Environmental Network and discusses how organizations such as Southern Appalachian Mountain Stewards (SAMS) can integrate Indigenous knowledge structures and principles into transition work in the region. Next, Lora Smith-Tovar shares ideas for community-directed reinvestment in Appalachia, which, she argues, would produce more equitable outcomes than traditional philanthropy directed by wealthy nonlocals. This section ends with the mission statement of "Stay Together Appalachian Youth" (STAY), illustrating the strength of youth-led visions of a more equitable and just region.

Many of this book's recommendations resonate with Appalachian cultural values, such as local community independence from outside dominance, social solidarity, and reciprocal relations between family and neighbors. Furthermore, even though they do not draw directly from Ostrom, most chapter recommendations conform to her principles, especially those highlighting the importance of democratic, local decision-making that is respected by outsider authorities and free from corporate domination. It is encouraging that Appalachian youth, like young people around the world, are at the forefront of just transition work, calling for diversity, inclusion, justice, and climate action. Organizations such as STAY and Young Appalachian Leaders and Learners (Y'ALL), a group within the Appalachian Studies Association, and events like "It's Good to Be Young in the Mountains" and the "Appalachian Big Ideas Festival" give us hope for the future. Much work is needed to dismantle colonialism, imperialism, white supremacy, patriarchy, heterosexism, and homophobia in the region, our nation, and the world. And, finally, more scholarship is required focusing on how a just transition would involve and empower women, LGBTQIA+ folks, people of differing abilities, and other marginalized groups, particularly from an intersectional perspective centered on how different multiple structures of inequality—class, race, gender, sexuality, ability, age, and so on—interact to create different forms of oppression.[13]

The next section of the book focuses on regenerating the region's health and ecological vitality through changing landownership and utilizing practices to allow for more local communal control and monitoring, just as Ostrom's principles suggest. For too long, land has been ravaged by harmful deforestation and mining practices at the behest of absentee owners or lessors who regard land as a mere factor in the production, to be exhausted and then discarded. Communities who live there cannot access this land for things they need, like food and housing; in fact, the disturbed and exhausted soil threatens survival with landslides and flooding. A chapter by Tom Hansell and Julie Shepherd-Powell interrogates questions of land use and control, examining specific proposals and strategies to increase local land ownership, promote economic diversification, and support sustainable development in the coalfields. They show how land-related policies fit into the broader work of Appalachian transition. Kathryn Engle, Elyzabeth W. Engle, Candace Mullins, Martin Richards, and Maggie Smith Mosley consider local food systems initiatives and organizations in the region, showing how these organizations build capacity at the local level and pursue long-term strategies to promote more just and regenerative local food economies. The local food movements aspire to improve human health and well-being, a topic that is the focus on Rachel E. Dixon's and S. Douglas Scutchfield's chapter on the importance of emphasizing human health as a goal of the just transitions movement. While it is obvious that a move away from fossil fuel use will have many public health benefits, a just transition demands that we protect the health and welfare of those who have already been harmed by fossil fuel production and consumption and recognize the health risks associated with a major economic transition such as this.

The final section of this book focuses on strategies to decentralize economic and political power in the hopes of nurturing a just and progressive localism rather than a nativistic, racist, exclusionary, right-wing "populism." As a reminder of the importance of "nesting" localities in mutually regulating and collaborative social structures, Ivy Brashear, Peter Hille, and Betsy Whaley advocate networking and collaboration among different regional nonprofits and philanthropies to work more effectively. Next, Sylvia Ryerson and Judah Schept document local resistance to the US Bureau of Prisons' plan to construct a prison in Letcher County, Kentucky, one of many such projects that have been presented as a "post-coal" economic development project providing jobs to a desperate, poor region. While many communities in Appalachia and throughout the nation have welcomed such projects, scholarship raises serious doubts about whether prisons bring lasting social and economic benefits to local communities. Furthermore, local opponents in Letcher County, Kentucky, view prisons as socially, racially, and environmentally unjust institutions that do more harm than good for Appalachian communities, a stance that state and federal authorities do not respect. Again, outside authorities disregard the preferences of local communities. This section closes with a youth-centered initiative: the Highlander Center's Appalachian Transition Fellowship Program. This program has provided paid internships for young adults to work for change in the region, thus jump-starting communities' transition to a more equitable future and also providing skills, training, and networks of support to youth in the region. Finally, the book concludes with a brief summary of its common themes and further exploration into whether a just transition, democracy, and justice are compatible with capitalism (as we know it).[14]

Notes

1. The term "regeneration" extends earlier terms, such as sustainability (limiting our impact on ecosystems so that we humans return as much as we use) and restoration (returning ecosystems to health); see Maria Beatrice Andreucci et al., eds., *Rethinking Sustainability towards a Regenerative Economy* (Cham: Springer, 2021); on just transition, see Quinton Sankofa, Movement Generation Justice and Ecology Project, "Transition Is Inevitable, Justice Is Not: A Critical Framework for Just Recovery," https://movementgeneration.org/transition-is-inevitable-justice-is-not-a-critical-framework-for-just-recovery, accessed June 5, 2019.

2. David M. Kotz, *The Rise and Fall of Capitalism* (Cambridge: Harvard University Press, 2015); see also Thomas Piketty, *Capital in the Twenty-First Century*, trans. Arthur Goldhammer (Boston: The Belknap Press of Harvard University Press, 2014); Larry Bartels, *Unequal Democracy: The Political Economy of the New Gilded Age* (Princeton, NJ: Princeton University Press, 2009); David Harvey, *The Enigma of Capital and the Crises of Capitalism* (New York: Oxford University Press, 2010); Wendy Brown, *Undoing the Demos: Neoliberalism's Stealth Revolution* (Boston: MIT Press, 2015); Naomi Klein, *The Shock Doctrine: The Rise of Disaster Capitalism* (London: Picador, 2008).

3. Julia Fox, "Mountaintop Removal in West Virginia: An Environmental Sacrifice Zone," *Organization and Environment* 12, no. 2 (1999): 163–83; Richard M. Auty, *Sustaining Development in Mineral Economies: The Resource Curse Thesis* (New York: Routledge, 1993); Shannon M. Pendergast, Judith A. Clarke, and G. Cornelius Van Kooten, "Corruption, Development and the Curse of Natural Resources," *Canadian Journal of Political Science* 44, no. 2 (2011): 411–37; Michele Marrone and Geoffrey L. Buckley, *Mountains of Injustice: Social and Environmental Justice in Appalachia* (Athens: Ohio University Press, 2011); Mark D. Partridge, Michael R. Betz, and Linda Lobao, "Natural Resource Curse and Poverty in Appalachian America," *American Journal of Agricultural Economics* 95, no. 2 (2013):

449–56; Helen Matthews Lewis, Linda Johnson, and Donald Askins, eds., *Colonialism in Modern America: The Appalachian Case* (Boone, NC: Appalachian State University, 1978); Eric Bowen, Christiadi, John Deskins, and Brian Lego, *An Overview of the Coal Economy of Appalachia*, a report commissioned by the Appalachian Regional Commission, 2018, https://www.arc.gov/wp-content/uploads/2018/01/CIE1-OverviewofCoalEconomyin Appalachia-2.pdf.

4. Theda Perdue and Michael D. Green, *The Cherokee Nation and the Trail of Tears* (New York: Viking, 2007).

5. "Mother forest" is a term coined by folklorist Mary Hufford to remind us that, long before coal was mined commercially in Appalachia, humans and other species depended on the forest for food, medicine, and life (see https://www.loc.gov/collections/folklife-and-landscape-in-southern-west-virginia/articles-and-essays/stalking-the-mother-forest-voices-beneath-the-canopy); Kathryn Newfont, *Blue Ridge Commons: Environmental Activism and Forest History in Western North Carolina* (Athens: University of Georgia Press, 2012); on Appalachian history, see Ronald D. Eller, *Miners, Millhands, and Mountaineers: Industrialization of the Appalachian South, 1880–1930* (Knoxville: University of Tennessee, 1982); David Corbin, *Life, Work, and Rebellion in the Coal Fields: The Southern West Virginia Miners, 1880–1922* (Urbana: University of Illinois Press, 1981); Mary Beth Pudup, Dwight B. Billings, and Altina L. Waller, eds., *Appalachia in the Making: The Mountain South in the Nineteenth Century* (Chapel Hill: University of North Carolina Press, 1995); Dwight B. Billings and Kathleen Blee, *The Road to Poverty: The Making of Hardship and Wealth in Appalachia* (London: Cambridge University Press, 2000); Steven Stoll, *Ramp Hollow: The Ordeal of Appalachia* (New York: Hill and Wang, 2017); on social trust, see Shannon Elizabeth Bell, "'There Ain't No Bond Like There Used to Be': The Destruction of Social Capital in the West Virginia Coalfields," *Sociological Forum* 24, no. 3 (September 2009): 631–57; Carson Mencken, Christopher Bader, and Edward Clay Polson, "Integrating Civic Society and Economic Growth in Appalachia," *Growth and Change: A Journal of Urban and Rural Policy* 37, no. 1 (March 2006): 107–27.

6. UN Environmental Programme, "Emissions Gap Report 2022," October 27, 2022, https://www.unep.org/resources/emissions-gap-report-2022.

7. Steven L. Fisher, ed., *Fighting Back in Appalachia: Traditions of Resistance and Change* (Philadelphia: Temple University Press, 1993); Mary K. Anglin, "Lessons from Appalachia in the Twentieth Century: Poverty, Power and the 'Grassroots,'" *American Anthropologist* 104, no. 2 (June 2002): 565–82; Shaunna L. Scott, "Discovering What the People Knew: The 1979 Appalachian Land Ownership Study," *Action Research* 7, no. 2 (2009); 185–205, https://doi.org/10.1177%2F1476750309103257; Herbert Reid and Betsy Taylor, *Recovering the Commons: Democracy, Place, and Global Justice* (Urbana: University of Illinois Press, 2010); Steven L. Fisher and Barbara Ellen Smith, eds., *Transforming Places: Lessons from Appalachia* (Urbana: University of Illinois Press, 2012); Stephanie M. McSpirit, Lynn Faltraco, and Conner Bailey, eds., *Confronting Ecological Crisis in Appalachia and the South: University and Community Partnerships* (Lexington: University Press of Kentucky, 2012); Elizabeth Catte, *What You Are Getting Wrong about Appalachia* (Cleveland: Belt Press, 2018).

8. Elinor Ostrom, *Governing the Commons: The Evolution of Institutions of Collective Action* (London: Cambridge University Press, 1990).

9. Altina Waller's account of the preindustrial use of courts and local juries to adjudicate conflicting claims over land and timber rights in the Tug River valley of Central

Appalachia indicates that the courts at one time did perform a conflict-resolution function similar to that advocated by Ostrom; see Altina Waller, *Feud: Hatfields, McCoys, and Social Change in Appalachia, 1860–1900* (Chapel Hill: University of North Carolina Press, 1988).

10. Mason Adams, "'They Care about Corporations': Landowners Demonstrate Pipeline Project's Toll," *Virginia Mercury*, June 12, 2019, https://www.virginiamercury.com/2019/06/12/they-care-about-corporations-landowners-demonstrate-pipeline-projects-toll.

11. Rebecca Hersher, "Key Moments in the Dakota Access Pipeline Fight," NPR, February 22, 2017, https://www.npr.org/sections/thetwo-way/2017/02/22/514988040/key-moments-in-the-dakota-access-pipeline-fight; American Civil Liberties Union, "Stand with Standing Rock: Protect Protesters' Rights," https://www.aclu.org/issues/free-speech/rights-protesters/stand-standing-rock, accessed January 25, 2023; Gregory Schneider, "Women Sitting in Trees to Protest Pipeline after Judge Threatens Fines," *Washington Post*, May 5, 2018, https://www.washingtonpost.com/local/virginia-politics/federal-judge-rules-against-tree-sitters-protesting-gas-pipeline/2018/05/05/000b14b8-5016-11e8-af46-b1d6dc0d9bfe_story.html; Mike Ludwig, "Appalachian Pipeline Blockade Ends with Arrests after 932 Days," *Truthout*, April 2, 2021; Lindsey Kennett, "Second, Final Mountain Valley Pipeline Tree-Sitter Arrested in Montgomery County," 10News, https://www.wsls.com/news/local/2021/03/23/authorities-extracting-mountain-valley-pipeline-tree-sitters-in-montgomery-county, accessed March 31, 2021; Jennifer A. Dlouhy, "Oil Companies Persuade States to Make Pipeline Protests a Felony," Bloomberg, August 19, 2019, https://www.bloomberg.com/news/articles/2019-08-19/oil-companies-persuade-states-to-make-pipeline-protests-a-felony; Emily Cochrane and Lisa Friedman, "Manchin's Gas Pipeline Deal Irks Both Parties, Snarling Spending Bill," *New York Times*, September 21, 2022, https://www.nytimes.com/2022/09/21/us/politics/manchin-pipeline-spending-bill.html; Ari Natter and Erik Wasson, "Gas Pipeline Dealt a Blow as Manchin Withdraws Energy Permitting Bill," Bloomberg, September 27, 2022, https://www.bloomberg.com/news/articles/2022-09-27/gas-pipeline-dealt-a-blow-as-manchin-withdraws-permitting-bill.

12. Jane Mayer, *Dark Money: The Hidden History of the Billionaires behind the Radical Right* (New York: Doubleday, 2016); Steven Livitsky and Daniel Ziblatt, *How Democracies Die* (New York: Crown, 2018); Colin Schultz, "Meet the Money behind the Climate Denial Movement," *Smithsonian Magazine*, December 23, 2013, https://www.smithsonianmag.com/smart-news/meet-the-money-behind-the-climate-denial-movement-180948204, accessed June 1, 2019; Yale Environment 360, "Fossil Fuel Interests Have Outspent Environmental Advocates 10:1 on Climate Lobbying," *E360 Digest*, July 19, 2018, https://e360.yale.edu/digest/fossil-fuel-interests-have-outspent-environmental-advocates-101-on-climate-lobbying; Sandra Laville, "Top Oil Firms Spending Millions Lobbying to Block Climate Change Policy, Says Report," *Guardian*, March 21, 2019.

13. Marat Moore, *Women in the Mines: Stories of Life and Work* (New York: Twayne, 1996); Sally Ward Maggard, "From Farm to Coal Camp to Back Office and McDonald's: Living in the Midst of Appalachia's Latest Transformation," *Journal of the Appalachian Studies Association* 6 (1994): 14–38; Sally Ward Maggard, "Coalfield Women Making History," in *Back Talk from Appalachia: Confronting Stereotypes*, ed. Dwight Billings, Gurney Norman, and Katherine Ledford (Lexington: University Press of Kentucky, 1999), 228–50; bell hooks, *Belonging: A Culture of Place* (New York: Routledge, 2009); Rebecca R. Scott, *Removing Mountains: Extracting Nature and Identity in the Appalachian Coalfields* (Minneapolis: University of Minnesota Press, 2010); Hillery Glasby, Sherrie Gradin, and Rachael Ryerson, eds., *Storytelling in Queer Appalachia: Imagining and Writing the Unspeakable Other*

(Morgantown: West Virginia University Press, 2020). See also Z. Zane McNeill, ed., *Y'All Means All: The Emerging Voices Queering Appalachia* (Oakland, CA: PM Press, 2022), and "Speculative Fabulation: Queering Appalachian Futurisms," special issue, *Journal of Appalachian Studies* 28, no. 1 (Spring 2022); Zane McNeill and Rebecca Scott, *Queering Appalachian Ecologies for a Sustainable Future* (Lexington: University Press of Kentucky, 2024.

14. J. K. Gibson-Graham, *The End of Capitalism (as We Knew It)* (Minneapolis: University of Minnesota Press, 1996).

Democratization and Equity
Meaningful Participation for All

1

What Would Make a "Just Transition" Just?

Democracy, Class Justice, and a Green New Deal

DWIGHT B. BILLINGS

The question "What is justice?" takes on particular salience as citizens in Appalachia begin to imagine and fight for climate justice and a "just transition" from an exploitative capitalist economy based on fossil fuels. Here, democratic political reform and reform in labor and employment must go hand in hand, as do questions about how to imagine what political justice and economic justice in the future might look like. In this chapter, I argue that climate justice and a just economic transition cannot be achieved without political reform, since historically, major portions of Appalachia have been dominated by political clientelism and corruption where right-wing and centrist officials promote the interests of fossil fuel industries at the expense of human and planetary well-being, and market fundamentalists, nationally and in the region, seek to shrink the public sector, privatize the commons, and oppose citizen action and public investments that would strengthen infrastructures of democratization, economic diversification, and decarbonization. But political reform alone, obviously essential in its own right, is not enough. Democracy must not only be defended in the public sphere and public policymaking but also be extended to the workplace: a place where, historically, it has been vigorously and violently excluded.[1]

In a speech while he was running for president in 2020, Joe Biden said, "When Donald Trump thinks about climate change, the only word he can muster is 'hoax.' When I think about climate change, the word I think of is 'jobs.'" That may well be an effective sound bite, but—alone—it does not help us think about what a truly "just transition" from fossil fuels would entail. After all, the coal industry historically created lots of jobs in Appalachia, but along with jobs came the usurpation of land and natural resources, economic exploitation, workplace death and injuries, environmental ruin, and political domination. Obviously, we need much more than simply "jobs, jobs, jobs"—which too often is the mantra in some corners of Appalachia. We need "just jobs" and new, noncapitalist political and economic structures that will support them.[2]

In contrast to other chapters in this volume, which are closer to the ground about what *is* and *should be* happening concretely in Appalachia, I hope to offer some thoughts about two social theories that might complement our practical thinking about what we should be struggling for, in order to thus avoid the disappointment that too often happens when we are urged to sign on too quickly to schemes that promise short-run fixes to long-run problems. My hope is that insights from social theory might help us think more precisely about struggles for justice and the conditions that will sustain them.

In what follows, I first discuss how Jürgen Habermas's theory of law and democracy provides a conception of political justice and a robust normative defense of participatory democracy that is highly relevant as citizens struggle to rebuild and redirect Appalachian economies. Unfortunately, however, Habermas fails to extend his guiding concepts of "communicative action" and "discourse ethics" into the economic realm and the labor process. To remedy this deficit, I draw on a nonreductionist Marxist approach to class analysis and class justice to suggest one possible way to think about economic justice. Finally, I examine recent national proposals for a Green New Deal in light of these theories about justice and their implications for Appalachia.

Political Justice and Democracy

Many people in Appalachia get their ethical and moral bearings from religious traditions. For some, religious beliefs support commitments to social, economic, political, and environmental justice, including a deep concern for planetary life in the context of the current climate emergency. In the Roman Catholic tradition, for instance, *The Telling Takes Us Home: Taking Our Place in the Stories that Shape Us: A People's Pastoral from the Catholic Committee of Appalachia* (2015) expresses all of these concerns for justice profoundly and passionately. Like Roman Catholics, mainline and Evangelical Protestants and members of other faiths in the region have made significant contributions to the struggles against labor exploitation, mountaintop removal mining, and now the fight for climate justice, at the same time that other coreligionists take their cues from the religious right and oppose progressive change. But what ethical groundings might guide the actions of those not aligned with religious traditions? How might their ethical and moral commitments be secured more firmly in secular terms? Further, if as some commentators, such as Naomi Klein, believe that the "climate movement has yet to find its full moral voice," how might the climate movement's moral claims be bolstered? Habermas's theory of discourse ethics, when augmented by a theory of class justice, provides one possible answer.[3]

Like John Rawls, Amartya Sen, Joseph Stiglitz, Brian Berry, and many others, Habermas is a "liberal egalitarian." Adherents to liberal egalitarianism, as Tony Smith characterizes them, are morally committed to the principle that "all persons are equally worthy of concern and respect as *ends* in themselves." This commitment entails demands for global human flourishing and well-being, autonomous agency, ample resources and capabilities to achieve reasonable life plans, and opportunities to engage effectively in democratic public life. Intuitively, these demands are all worthy of assent. Habermas, in particular, justifies these moral imperatives in terms of what he believes to be the inherent telos of human communication: the achievement of *mutual understanding*.[4]

Habermas's wide-ranging sociological and philosophical theories are far too complex to be summarized here. I can only highlight a few relevant features. One is the distinction between "instrumental rationality" and "communicative rationality or action." Instrumental rationality is the use of reason to find the most effective or efficient means for achieving ends, whether those ends happen to be rational and just—like preventing the impending climate disaster—or irrational and unjust—such as pouring CO_2 into the atmosphere to generate electricity for profit when it is known to cause devastating planetary harm. But how can what's morally right be discerned from what's wrong—what's just from unjust—in a multicultural world where the processes of modernization have shattered the authority of past dogmatic traditions and religious worldviews for many people who thus must then decide what should be done with nothing more than their own shared powers of reasoning? Those for whom the old gods are dead, according to Habermas, are forced to rely on nothing more than "communicative action" to reach consensus regarding the proper ends of their collective social life through rational argumentation ("discourse") and thus coordinate their interpersonal actions in accordance with those rationally agreed-upon ends and means.

Grammarians study how an infinite variety of sentences can be generated by a small set of underlying language rules. Semanticists study what words and sentences denote. In contrast, Habermas's theory of communicative action refers to *speech pragmatics*, that is, what people *do* when they speak. Some speech acts, of course, are simply instrumental attempts to induce or manipulate the behavior of others by deception, threat, force, or the promise of rewards. But Habermas sees such strategic utterances as "parasitic" perversions of the more fundamental purpose of speech, which is to reach understanding through dialogue. (A cry of "Help!" from a dark alley might in fact be a trick to entrap a Good Samaritan, but the utterance "Help!" itself has an original meaning that is not deceptive.) Successful strategic demands may thus have their intended empirical effects on hearers because of the speaker's power to deceive, reward, or punish, but—as such—they are not rationally motivating as they would be if hearers were to respond to requests or demands solely on the basis of *valid* reasons for doing so. The rational motivating force of communicative action is thus found in the offering, discussion, acceptance, or rejection of *claims to validity*, as I show below.[5]

According to Habermas, reaching understanding takes place within the context of intersubjectively shared "lifeworlds" that consist of (1) shared *cultural* knowledges, (2) solidary *social* relationships, and (3) *personal* capacities and identities. Since modern multicultural lifeworlds are less and less bolstered by holistic and dogmatic worldviews, they are increasingly given, tested, replenished, and transformed by communicative action.

Anita Puckett's brilliant ethnographic study of Appalachian speech pragmatics in Harlan County, Kentucky, provides many empirical examples of speech utterances that can be redescribed in terms of Habermas's more abstract theory of communicative action. In one instance, an outside visitor to a workplace kitchen tells a worker named Debbie, "You ought to clean off that table." Debbie ignores her and later says to a coworker, "Who does she think she is? I oughta do this and I oughta do that. Ain't nobody telling me what to do." Persons in positions of formal authority such as bosses, doctors, and government officials (including police) do, of course, give orders but, according to Puckett, in informal situations, Appalachian folks try to achieve cooperation only in polite, indirect, and normatively appropriate patterns of speech that respect individual autonomy, integrity, and equality and then only in appropriate role situations. As the title of Puckett's book suggests, they "seldom ask, never tell." Certainly, they never order each other around.[6]

But now let's look more closely at this particular utterance. It is not yet a discourse, but, if necessary, it could become one. Rather, let's call it a metacommunication. From the standpoint of Habermas's theory, Debbie is making three *validity claims* to her coworker. Her claims *to moral validity* are central. She implicitly claims the valid right to say this to her coworker and to expect an appropriate response while simultaneously she claims to be correct about her normative understanding that the visitor's demand was indeed inappropriate—that is, "seldom ask, never tell." At the same time, Debbie is implicitly making a *truth claim* about the state of the world (the visitor did in fact say such and such), and she is making an *expressive claim* (that she is sincerely indignant about being ordered around). Her three claims to validity—truthfulness, rightfulness, and sincerity—attest to and, she hopes, will reaffirm her understandings that correspond to the cultural, social, and personal components of her particular Appalachian lifeworld.

Puckett's sociolinguistic study of how Appalachians request help and use normatively appropriate speech patterns to gain cooperation from community members (especially in matters of collective labor) is an example of empirical pragmatics in a distinct sociocultural setting. In contrast, Habermas's highly abstract analyses seek to determine the meanings of linguistic expressions only in terms of the *formal properties* of speech situations in general, not particular language uses such as those Puckett describes in Harlan County. He refers to his approach as "universal pragmatics." By reconstructing theoretically what speakers and hearers must necessarily *presume* and *take for granted* when they engage in communicative action to determine what they can agree to accept as factually true, morally right, and sincere, Habermas aims to show that participants in ideal speech act situations must presuppose a number of factors: that agreements will be reached solely on the basis of good (valid) reasons, and hence the use of power and force to influence decisions is ruled out; that all potentially interested participants are free to participate in deliberation (none are excluded); and that all participants have equal rights to attempt to make the case for why their claims should be accepted. In the case of deciding what is just, Habermas suggests the following *discourse principle*: "Only those action norms are valid to which all possibly affected persons could [in principle] agree as participants in rational discourse." Habermas's discourse principle of morality is thus procedural rather than substantive. It does not legislate specifically what to do in a given situation but rather how to decide what should be done based on the principles of participatory fairness. Two important implications follow that will return us to the politics of climate change.[7]

On the micro level of interpersonal interaction, Habermas attempts to show that the liberal egalitarian principle—as Smith articulated above, that "all persons are equally worthy of concern and respect as ends in themselves"—rather than being arbitrary, is grounded in the actual demands for freedom, equality, and respect that are inherent in the rational core of human communication, that is, the pragmatic presuppositions that reaching interpersonal understanding requires. At the macro level of society, this *discourse principle* can be translated into what Habermas terms the *"democratic principle"* that "only those laws count as legitimate to which all members of the legal community can assent in a discursive process of legislation [and judicial decision-making] that has in turn been legally constituted." In short, the subjects of law must also be able to see themselves as the authors of law. Space does not permit a discussion of the many rich insights (and limitations) of Habermas's *Between Fact and Norm: Contributions to a Discourse Theory of Law and Democracy*. For me its bottom line is this: for democracy to work and for laws to be accepted as legitimate, the communicative processes that make rational agreement possible among individuals must be translated at the macro level into sources of "communicative power" that are formulated through deliberation in vibrant public spheres and then effectively channeled into the official organs of lawmaking, court actions, administration, regulation, and enforcement.[8]

Writing two decades or more ago, Habermas's hopes for the potential power of progressive public opinion to shape policy rested on his belief in the efficacy of protests and demonstrations, social movements, political parties, and, when necessary, civil disobedience to make its demands realizable. Tragically, however, in dire times such as ours when climate disaster is looming, the prospects for participatory democracy are weakening. As Seyla Benhabib writes, "Equality"—(and I would add freedom and solidarity)—"has been undermined by privatization and monetization . . . [by] the impacts on livelihoods and communities [that have been] destroyed by outsourcing, capital flight, and global competition" . . . and by the failure of "the institutions of liberal democracy [that are] not showing themselves to be strong enough to withstand the destructive effects of financial globalization, increasing inequality, climate change, and the crises of political representation." While Habermas might agree with this disheartening assessment, he would nonetheless contend that discursively achieved and broadly popular moral understandings still have at least some empirical force, especially when enforced by the authority of democratically enacted law.

Communicative action alone, however, is not enough to overcome the impasse we face in the politics of climate change. Describing a telling experiment in well-meaning interpersonal communication efforts between Appalachian environmentalists and fossil fuel exponents, Susan Hirsch and E. Franklin Dukes report that almost no agreement could be reached. Nor is communicative action alone enough to ensure social cooperation and coordination at the societal level. How many of us, after all, have time to engage in rational discourse over the just price of gasoline or join a movement to fight the oil industry when we simply are in a rush for a fill-up? What besieged college admissions officers have time for extended deliberations with individual applicants and their parents when they can simply routinize decisions with standard test scores and grade point averages? According to Habermas, the "delinguistified media" of money and bureaucratic power save us from such communicative overloads, that is, they "speak" to and for us—as in the expression "Money talks." Law does the same thing by substituting rules and sanctions for endless discussions, yet monetization, bureaucratization, and illegitimately imposed laws also threaten to displace the communicative processes that are necessary to secure and reproduce the lifeworld. The result is what Habermas ominously terms the "colonization" of the lifeworld by capitalist markets and government bureaucracy. Despite all this, Habermas—like fellow liberal egalitarians—believes that the just treatment of all persons as ends rather than means can somehow be achieved in capitalist society with adequate regulation. Marxists do not.[9]

In capitalist enterprises, laboring subjects are typically treated as commodities to be bought and then disposed of once their use as means for the production of profits has been fulfilled. Workers are not typically treated as having value in and of themselves but rather as means for the economic values they create. The capitalist organization of work and society thus stands inexorably in the way of, and contradicts, the meaningful economic and political changes that climate justice and a just transition for its displaced workers will require.[10]

Labor and Class Justice

Tony Smith, as I have noted, does an excellent job of showing that the moral imperative of liberal egalitarianism, that is, the treatment of all persons as ends rather than means, is entirely compatible with the moral aims of Marxism but incompatible with the Marxist position that these imperatives can only be achieved in a postcapitalist economy and society. For Marxists, the regulation of capitalism does not eliminate labor exploitation. We know all too well in Appalachia just how inadequate the protection of labor and the environment against capitalist firms has been.

The best approach to conceptualizing class justice that I have found is one by George DeMartino, who builds on Stephen Resnick and Richard Wolff's nonessentialist approach to class analysis. Resnick and Wolff's intervention in Marxian theory is premised on at least three central ideas. The first is "overdetermination," which stresses that all social processes can be understood or theorized as mutually constitutive so that no one of them, including class, can be singled out as *the* overriding or essential cause of social inequality and change. Class, in this reckoning, is not *the* essential motor of history (as in deterministic versions of Marxism) but, rather, an important *discursive entry point* for analysis and criticism, a story or accounting device, if you will, that highlights issues of justice that other approaches necessarily miss by not focusing on the economic exploitation brought about by certain forms of the production of goods and services. The achievement of class justice does not, for instance, ensure the achievement of racial, gender, or sexual justice. Class, race, gender, and sexuality are conceptually distinct but intersecting processes that must each be addressed together.[11]

Second is the rejection of capital-centric discourses that overestimate the ubiquity, omnipresence, and unity of capitalism. Many of the noncapitalist economic activities of Appalachians and how they make their livings—including self-provisioning and self-employment, obtaining welfare benefits, flea-marketing, gifting, coops, NGOs, public sector employment, and the like—would be overlooked by capital-centric thinking, as would how these activities might be built on in the future.[12]

Third is the idea that class is best thought of as a *process* rather than a *group*, and this is where class justice can best be identified. Marxian class analysis begins with the idea that a central goal of economic effort is to produce a "surplus," that is, the "residual that arises from the fact that those who perform the labor necessary to provision society produce more than they by themselves can consume." Without an economic surplus, there would be no support for the wider community of nonproducers, including profits for capitalists; no funds for public needs such as health care, housing, education, defense, care of children and the elderly, and so on; and no funds to finance further surplus production. Class analysis probes how economic surpluses are (1) *produced*, (2) *appropriated*, and (3) *distributed* in various sites. These three class processes of production, appropriation, and distribution can be illustrated by contrasting capitalist coal-mining firms and noncapitalist worker self-directed enterprises (WSDEs).[13]

Typically, capitalist coal firms are legally headed by their boards of directors, which are selected by top shareholders (or their proxies), who hire CEOs and managers to direct the firm's many operations. In turn, firms hire direct producers (miners) to extract coal from the ground as well as other workers—as either internal or subcontracted employees—to provide the necessary conditions for this fundamental class process to take place, including an array of essential but "nonproductive" managers, lawyers, accountants, sales representatives, personnel officers, advertising agents, lobbyists, and so on. When miners produce coal of more economic value than they can themselves consume or for which they are rewarded, they are engaged in "surplus labor." That surplus labor is converted into "surplus value"—a principal source of the firm's profits—when the coal is sold at more than its costs of production, including wages. Marxists label this discrepancy as "exploitation."[14]

A nonessentialist view of capitalist firms recognizes that mining firms may seek profits for a variety of reasons including creating conditions for future gains such as by investing in new technologies, leasing new coal lands, outdistancing competitors, funding politicians sympathetic to their interests, paying so-called experts to deny the science of climate change, or currying favor with the public through legitimation efforts like the "Friends of Coal" campaign. The creation of a surplus, however, remains a central objective.

When asked what coal was worth in the 1968 documentary film *Appalachia: Rich Land, Poor People*, a prominent eastern Kentucky coal operator (David Zegeer) replied as follows: "Nothing, unless you can get it out and make a profit on it. If you can't make a profit of a penny or more, you'd just as well leave it in the ground. It's not worth anything to you." He went on to add, "If we are wrong in mining coal in eastern Kentucky . . . then this whole country is based on the wrong philosophy. You do it any other way, you're just talking about socialism. So, if what we are doing is wrong, then this whole country is wrong." Marxists define the extraction of surplus value from productive workers as "exploitation," both an economic fact and a moral wrong.[15]

Besides directing production, capitalists also dominate two other class processes: *appropriation* and *distribution*. Since boards of directors legally own the products or services their workers produce, they are entitled to appropriate the surplus produced by their exploited workers and then to distribute it to a variety of recipients. Appropriators must meet a variety of obligations including distributing cuts of the surplus to lenders, landlords, mineral holders, government tax collectors, and so on, and they may choose to distribute portions to various others (such as themselves, industry associations, lobbyists, politicians, and political parties, etc.). From the ability to appropriate and distribute economic surpluses follows the power to shape society, to determine whether the surplus is directed toward only a few favored recipients, such as corporate CEOs, top managers, and shareholders as is typical in the United States, or more broadly to workers and the needs of a broader public. For workers to be excluded from the appropriation and distribution of the surpluses they produce is manifestly unfair. As DeMartino argues, to be "cut off" from appropriation is to be disenfranchised, that is, to be denied the rights of participation in how one's community is shaped and defined. While one can see that it is morally unfair to exclude direct producers from this process, it could also be argued that the vast "supporting cast" of workers who also provide the conditions that make the production of a surplus possible, including both those inside the firm and those outside it in the broader community of teachers, care workers, homemakers, and others, should not be excluded. Since in many ways this cast includes the whole community that makes economic life possible, a broadened understanding of class justice as fairness in appropriation and distribution as well as production demands the political democratization of these processes in the workplace *and* in the wider society. To paraphrase our eastern Kentucky operator, "You do it any other way, you're just talking about capitalism."[16]

Noncapitalist WSDEs function entirely differently from capitalist firms. As the labor economist Bruce Pietrykowski writes, "The principles that govern worker cooperatives—democratic decision-making, one member one vote, collective ownership, employment maintenance prioritized over layoffs, equitable sharing of the surplus revenue produced, managers who are hired by members and who are cooperative members—are markedly different than the practices used by capitalist firms."

In these firms, direct producers and their associates democratically choose—based on the principle of one worker, one vote—what to produce and how to produce it, thus extending the principles of communicative action and participatory democracy beyond the demos (to which Habermas arbitrarily confines them) and into the workplace. In response to market opportunities, government policy initiatives, or other signals, members could choose to make their living by meeting the needs of their local communities and of the planet by environmental reclamation, for instance, rather than by the destructive practices of mining and hydraulic fracturing ("fracking") that are currently offered by capitalist firms as the only important game in Appalachia. Significantly, these co-op members would be far less likely to choose to implement unsafe working conditions for themselves or to pollute their communities, as capitalist coal mining companies have been doing for more than a century in Appalachia (by one estimate, capitalist corporations in the United States externalize production costs of $2.6 trillion annually onto the public).[17]

Since in this form of economic organization, producers legally own the surpluses they produce, WSDE members are its rightful appropriators and distributors as well. Again democratically—based on the WSDE principle of one worker, one vote—they can choose among various options. Besides meeting necessary obligations, like paying taxes or interest on loans, they might, for instance, choose how much of the surplus they have produced to keep for themselves as income versus how much to reinvest in expanding the workforce, purchasing new technology, diversifying production, or perhaps distributing cuts of the surplus to meet members' needs for education and training, health care, or other needs of their families and communities.

WSDEs are not only more democratic than capitalist firms but also more egalitarian. When these enterprises need managers, for instance, they can rotate management roles among members or choose to select professional managers with salaries only marginally greater than the members. Although capitalist ideology legitimates itself in terms of freedom of choice, these choices are not available to workers in capitalist firms. Nor generally is the choice to treat workers as ends rather than means an option. Instead, authoritarianism and brutality often prevail. As a former Amazon senior operations warehouse manager has said recently, Amazon "incentivizes you to be a heartless son of a bitch."[18]

Millions of Americans participate in thousands of cooperative endeavors, especially consumer and credit co-ops, but WSDEs in the sphere of production are less common, perhaps numbering only in the hundreds in the United States. Nonetheless, numerous studies have shown that WSDEs often surpass capitalist firms in productivity, efficiency, employment stability, and wealth retention in their local communities. They work best when linked into networks that permit the sharing of resources, including funding, job sharing, training, management, insurance, and marketing. Two of the best-known network examples globally are the Mondragon cooperatives in the Basque region of Spain and Italy's cooperative economy in Emilia Romagna.[19]

The Mondragon's cooperative enterprises consist of roughly one hundred worker-directed cooperatives and 147 subsidiary companies (many in manufacturing) that have employed as many as eighty thousand workers worldwide and that, in 2013, owned total assets of €35.8 billion. Mondragon members also work in finance, retail, and education, with subsidiary jobs in banking, health care, insurance, retirement, and other services. Mondragon member-to-manager earnings ratios are typically in the range of 1:5 or slightly higher, in contrast to the average ratio of workers' wages to corporate CEOs of nearly 1:300 in the United States. A mandatory "solidarity fund" enabled the Mondragon enterprises to maintain employment without losing income by shifting workers across allied firms after the global 2008 economic crash.[20]

Examples closer to home include successful cooperative networks of service providers in Cincinnati and Cleveland, Ohio, while Cooperation Jackson, an ambitious effort to build a democratic political economy with Black self-determination and worker-directed enterprises at its center in the majority-Black capital of Mississippi, also bears watching. Within Appalachia, Ohio's Appalachian Community Economic Network has been highly successful in spawning and sustaining a large cooperative network around food production and services. Historical lessons can be learned from the successes and failures of worker-owned co-ops initiated in the 1970s by the Glenmary Sisters in Appalachian Virginia. Finally, the remarkable success of Kentucky's Community Farm Alliance in capturing and utilizing massive funding from the national tobacco settlement to support local agricultural initiatives and the transition from tobacco farming shows what can be achieved at a statewide level based on political opportunity, effective organizing, and widespread citizen support. I stress the value of WSDEs because of how they might contribute to struggles for democracy and class justice in Appalachia and the potential role they might play in a Green New Deal.[21]

A Green New Deal for Appalachia

Year after year, average temperatures in the United States and throughout the world have grown hotter and hotter, and we are experiencing worldwide climatic disasters on an unprecedented scale, including floods; droughts; famines; hurricanes; forest fires; rising oceanic temperatures and sea levels; the melting of glaciers, polar ice caps, and the permafrost; species declines and extinctions, and on and on. A majority of people in the United States now believe that climate change is the most immediate threat to planetary life as we know it and that global temperature rise must be stopped—and soon. The reality of climate change is registering in Appalachia by rising temperatures and drastic increases in rainfall and flooding, including the devastating floods in eastern Kentucky in 2022 and Hurricane Helene in North Carolina in 2024. Corporate-owned politicians in the region, however, have staunchly resisted this conclusion. Nonetheless, a number of progressive political leaders in the United States and abroad have begun trying to put combating climate change on the forefront of the political agenda. Some members of the US Congress and Senate have proposed a Green New Deal for the United States, including a just transition for workers displaced in the fossil fuels industries. A significant number of their congressional colleagues have endorsed the concept, as did many of the Democratic candidates who ran in the 2020 presidential primary elections.[22]

Plans for a Green New Deal purposively evoke memories of the wide-ranging, progressive political and economic transformations that were achieved during the Great Depression—policies that have been steadily reversed under the rubric of neoliberalism. Among onetime presidential candidates, Bernie Sanders's 2020 plan for climate action was the boldest and most detailed. It identified the climate crisis as "the single greatest challenge facing our country" and proposed "to achieve 100 percent sustainable energy for electricity and transportation by no later than 2030 and to fully decarbonize the economy by at least 2050" while creating twenty million new jobs, many of them in the public sector, at a cost of \$16.3 trillion over the next ten years—a cost the plan claimed was 50 percent less than doing nothing and allowing climate change to go unchecked. In theory, a Green New Deal could be paid for by increasing taxes on wealthy individuals and corporations, eliminating fossil fuel subsidies, making the fossil fuel industries pay for the legacy costs of their pollution, scaling back expenditures for the military—the nation's single greatest contributor to atmospheric CO_2—and many other measures.

Importantly for Appalachia, Sanders's plan promised a "fair transition for [fossil fuel] workers," including "five years of unemployment insurance, a wage guarantee, housing assistance, job training, health care, pension support and priority job placement for displaced workers, as well as early retirement support for those who choose it or can no longer work." It also proposed a nationwide ban on fracking, and major funding increases for the Appalachian Regional Commission. Significantly—in light of my emphasis in this chapter on class justice and how WSDEs operate more justly than do capitalist firms—the Sanders plan also prioritized cooperatives and employee-owned firms in federal procurement.[23]

Even though Sanders did not win the Democratic nomination for president, his comprehensive plan remains the gold standard for what it will take to combat climate change and, at the same time, protect and compensate workers and their communities, which are at the center of these far-reaching processes. While congressional allies of fossil fuels have thus far succeeded in blocking such comprehensive legislation, President Biden had at least begun to tackle climate change. His 2022 "Inflation Reduction Act" allocates billions of dollars to advance solar and wind power and electronic vehicles. While not yet showing results, his Interagency Working Group on Coal and Power Plant Communities at least promised "a new commitment to a better future for coal production communities."[24] These advances are set to be reversed by Trump.

While talk of a Green New Deal is beginning to influence national political discourse and policy, local communities, grassroots organizations, and multistate coalitions such as the Reclaiming Appalachia Coalition and the Alliance for Appalachia (to name but two) have not been sitting idly by, waiting for action from the federal government. As a reporter for *The Nation* put it in 2018, "Appalachia Already Has a Plan to Get Past Coal." Groups and organizations in the mountains have been promoting post-coal opportunities in heritage-, eco-, adventure-, and cultural-tourism; environmental reclamation; sustainable forestry and wood products; agriculture and food services; health care; and jobs in wind and solar industries, ranging from retrofitting houses to manufacturing and installing solar systems, along with many other ventures. Important initiatives in this direction are emerging across the region, but scaling up these initiatives to ensure a just transition for displaced workers, and for those already out of work because of coal's decline, will ultimately require massive funding. Obviously, the adoption of an extensive Green New Deal—were it to include genuine participation from local workers and communities—would represent a major step forward for both combating climate disaster and protecting workers and their communities from abandonment.[25]

The current success in securing a just transition for coal miners in Germany and Spain shows that this can, in fact, be done with adequate political will. The economic and social devastation that occurred in the anthracite coalfields of Pennsylvania in the early twentieth century, when its coal industry collapsed, on the other hand, shows what would undoubtedly happen without proper government intervention.[26]

Discussion

We can, of course, expect—and have seen—massive opposition to a Green New Deal from the coal, oil, and gas industries; their global corporate allies; and wealthy investors. Each of these actors has indisputable records of contributing to climate change, exploiting labor, destroying the environment, and creating health crises, externalizing costs, capturing and controlling significant elements of the state, and misleading and manipulating the public. Many observers, such as Roger Hallam, Britain's cofounder of Extinction Rebellion, believe that only unprecedented levels of nonviolent civil disobedience can challenge their power. The chances for such, at least in Appalachia, are diminished to the extent to which workers in the region fear job loss, mistrust government, and succumb to corporate propaganda. Given the region's history of elite domination, many grassroots activists are understandably skeptical that federal dollars will go to the right places. Additionally, UMWA president Cecil Roberts adds to these fears when he says, "I ask anybody who has been hearing those two words [just transition] over the past thirty years to point to one, just one just transition, in this country . . . and you can't."[27]

Despite such skepticism about climate policy, as wind and solar power become cheaper than their alternatives for electrical generation, market forces will likely continue to decrease the extent of coal mining and coal burning. The same is likely to be true for fracking. So much gas has been produced recently that the market for it is currently glutted, and many firms in this overextended industry are going out of business. More workers in West Virginia and Pennsylvania are currently employed in fracking than in mining coal; further declines in fracking—though good for the environment—will only increase unemployment in the region.

Nonetheless, dangerous gas pipelines are still being dug across Appalachia and threaten to release significant quantities of methane into the atmosphere that are even more threatening to the climate than CO_2. When gas production soared in Appalachia during the Obama administration, it was legitimated as a boost to national energy independence and as a bridge fuel toward non-fossil-fuel renewable energy sources. But natural gas poses perhaps even greater threats to public health, the environment, and climate than does coal. It is, as one commentator put it, a "bridge to nowhere." Additional threats connected to fracking include the plans of international capitalist investors to build on natural gas resources to construct megacomplexes in Appalachia to dramatically expand the production of petrochemicals and the manufacture of plastics. Opposing fracking, pipelines, and their related industries will be just as essential to achieving climate justice as fighting Big Coal will be.[28]

Fighting Big Coal and its carboniferous cousins will be made difficult in Appalachia not only by the exercise of corporate power and the resistance of workers who fear further job losses but also by the strong emotional attachments that many people in the region have to coal and coal mining. In response to seeing the omnipresent Friends of Coal automobile tags throughout Kentucky, I've heard people ask, "How can you be a friend of a rock?" You can be. It's encouraged by the industry. Even as coal production and mining jobs diminish, public relations campaigns like Friends of Coal encourage coalfield residents to believe that the coal industry remains an essential component of employment, patriotism and citizenship, masculinity, community well-being, and regional identity—not just in the past but in the present as well.
Similar messages are conveyed by many of the coal mining heritage museums that dot the coalfields and by advertising campaigns that support fracking.[29]

Adam Malle, an organizer for the Southern Appalachian Mountain Stewards, has reportedly said that "[coal miners] are watching their whole livelihood and proud culture disappearing and somebody comes and says 'I can bring that back for you' is a powerful message for some, and has a lot to do with holding on to that hope that they can keep what they have." In his 2016 campaign for the presidency, Donald Trump clearly benefited from making false promises to put coal miners back to work. The affect theorist and culture critic Lauren Berlant reminds us that we often remain emotionally attached to, and desire, objects and ideas that—while perhaps having satisfied (or not) our needs in the past—obstruct our flourishing in the present. Brilliantly, Berlant calls such hopes "cruel optimism." Potentially, the very thought of a Green New Deal promotes a utopian alternative to the cruel optimism of continued reliance on fossil fuels and what the great Kentucky singer-songwriter Merle Travis called the "lure of the mines" in his powerful song "Dark as a Dungeon."[30]

Jürgen Habermas has lamented that "in the present period we manifestly suffer from an apparent retreat of utopian energies, from a closure of horizons." When House Speaker Nancy Pelosi initially dismissed the resolution for a Green New Deal in the Congress as a "green dream or whatever," she perhaps misspoke an important truth. The idea of a Green New Deal is, in the best sense of that phrase, a new and potentially reinvigorating utopian imaginary. One of its most salient aspects is that it connects the dots linking climate disaster; capitalism and corporate power; politics and the state; inequality; and social, racial, and labor injustice to an emancipatory program that is well rooted in progressive American traditions such as the first New Deal. A commentator in Great Britain succinctly identifies the utopian dimension of the Green New Deal when he writes, "The purpose is not just to decarbonize today's economy but to build the democratic economy of tomorrow, one based on new and purposeful goals that center . . . 'life-making over profit-making.'"[31]

Radical political change in Appalachia requires that efforts to democratize governance and strengthen the communicative processes that are vital to a robust regional civil society and public sphere must be combined with economic struggles for class justice. Struggles for class justice, political justice, and climate justice together point toward a new and better Appalachia. Habermas's insights into what makes for fairness in communication point to the appropriate communicative *processes* to reach this goal, while Marxian class analysis identifies the *content* for these struggles. While the achievement of a Green New Deal might seem daunting, and even out of reach for many of us right now, the personal motto of the great Italian Marxist Antonio Gramsci might give us the fortitude to struggle courageously for it if we combine "pessimism of the mind"—a stereotypic trait so often attributed to us in Appalachia—with undaunting "optimism of the will."[32]

Notes

My thinking about the positive dimensions of utopianism has been influenced by numerous commentaries on this topic by the Marxist economist David Ruccio, in his highly informative online blog series *Occasional Links and Commentaries*. I am grateful to David for his helpful comments and encouragement on this chapter as well as to Robert Goldman, Stephen Fisher, and the editors of this volume.

1. Dwight Billings and Kathleen Blee, *The Road to Poverty: The Making of Wealth and Hardship in Appalachia* (New York: Cambridge University Press, 2000); Phillip Lewin, "'It's Not about Policy, It's about Personality': Legitimating Rural Political Regimes" (paper presentation, the annual meeting of the American Sociological Association, Montréal, 2017); Herbert Reid and Betsy Taylor, *Recovering the Commons: Democracy, Place, and Global Justice* (Urbana: University of Illinois Press, 2010).

2. Nives Dolsak and Aseem Prakash, "Biden's Climate Plan Needs to Do Better on the Concepts of 'Just Transition' and 'Critical Minerals,'" *Forbes*, July 16, 2020, https://www.forbes.com/sites/prakashdolsak/2020/07/16/bidens-climate-plan-needs-to-do-better-on-the-just-transition-and-critical-minerals/#3e03fdff309b. For a brief discussion of policy precedents in the United States for a "just transition" and what that would entail, see Ann Eisenberg, "The Coal Industry Is Shrinking—Here's What Miners Need for a Just Transition," Trellis, December 5, 2019, 3, https://greenbiz.com/article/coal

-industry-shrinking-heres-what-miners-need-just-transition. She writes, "A just transition should focus on sustainably rebuilding regional economies, and should be informed by input from people who are affected." On the fear that striving for a just transition in the Global North may tip off a new wave of imperialism to obtain necessary raw materials (especially minerals) in the Global South, see Rufus Jordana, "False Hopes for a Green New Deal," *Open Democracy*, August 29, 2019.

3. So, too, did two earlier Appalachian bishops' pastoral letters, *This Land Is Home to Me* (1975) and *At Home in the Web of Life* (1995). Significantly though, the authors of this latest call for justice issued it as a "people's pastoral" without authorization by the church hierarchy, suggesting that a new assertiveness is rising at least among some Appalachian Catholic clergy and laity. See Michael Iafrate, "Responding to the Appalachian 'People's Pastoral'" (paper presentation, the Appalachian Studies Conference, Blacksburg, VA, 2018).

4. Tony Smith, *Beyond Liberal Egalitarianism: Marx and Normative Social Theory in the Twenty-First Century* (Chicago: Haymarket Books, 2018). The most accessible and brief introduction to Habermas's vast body of writing that I have found is James Gordan Finlayson's *Habermas: A Very Short Introduction* (New York: Oxford University Press, 2005). For Habermas's view of the role of religious discourse in contemporary society, see his *An Awareness of What Is Missing: Faith and Reason in a Post-Secular Age* (Malden, MA: Polity, 2010). Traditionally, philosophical justifications of morality, such as that of Immanuel Kant, are monological; they are carried out as debates with one's self, that is, within individual consciousness. In contrast, Habermas understands the justification of moral assertions to be dialogical, that is, based on uncoerced interpersonal argumentation and agreement.

5. Phenomenologists such as Alfred Schutz typically described lifeworlds from the standpoint of individual consciousness. Habermas, on the other hand—wisely—conceives of our lifeworlds as being structured and reproduced by interpersonal communication.

6. Anita Puckett, *Seldom Ask, Never Tell: Labor and Discourse in Appalachia* (New York: Oxford University Press, 2000), 141.

7. Jürgen Habermas, "Universal Pragmatics"; Jürgen Habermas, *Between Facts and Norms: Contributions to a Discourse Theory of Law and Democracy* (Cambridge, MA: MIT Press, 1996), 107.

8. Habermas, *Between Facts and Norms*, 110; Habermas's concept of "communicative power" is derived in part from the political thought of Hannah Arendt. See Jürgen Habermas, *Philosophical-Political Profiles* (Cambridge, MA: MIT Press, 1985).

9. Habermas, *Between Facts and Norms*, chap. 8. Seyla Benhabib, "High Liberalism: John Rawls and the Crisis of Liberal Democracy," *Nation*, November 11/18, 2019, 30–33. On the current political scene, also see Wendy Brown, *Undoing the Demos: Neoliberalism's Stealth Revolution* (Brooklyn, NY: Zone Books, 2015).

10. Susan Hirsch and E. Franklin Dukes, *Mountaintop Mining in Appalachia: Understanding Stakeholders and Change in Environmental Conflict* (Athens: Ohio University Press, 2014); Habermas's theory of the colonization of the lifeworld by money and power is argued in his *The Theory of Communicative Action (Volume 2): Lifeworld and System* (Boston: Beacon Press, 1987); Smith, *Beyond Liberal Egalitarianism*.

11. A nonessentialist approach to class analysis, as I discuss below, recognizes that in particular situations, a capitalist employer may sometimes make decisions based on other considerations as well.

12. George DeMartino, "Realizing Class Justice," *Rethinking Marxism* 15, no. 1 (January 2003): 1–31; Stephen Resnick and Richard Wolff, *Knowledge and Class: A Marxian*

Critique of Political Economy (Chicago: University of Chicago Press, 1987), esp. 38–108. For a comprehensive introduction to the wide-ranging debates concerning Karl Marx's approach to justice, see Norman Geras, "The Controversy about Marx and Justice," *New Left Review* 150 (March–April 1985): 47–85, and his "Bringing Marx to Justice: An Addendum and Rejoinder," *New Left Review* 195 (September–October 1992): 37–69.

13. For a theoretical discussion of "capitalocentrism," see J. K. Gibson-Graham, *The End of Capitalism (as We Knew It): A Feminist Critique of Political Economy* (Cambridge, MA: Blackwell, 1996); for the implications of this critique for building noncapitalist local economies, see J. K. Gibson-Graham, Jenny Cameron, and Stephen Healy, *Take Back the Economy: An Ethical Guide for Transforming Our Communities* (Minneapolis: University of Minnesota Press, 2013). On diverse livelihoods in Appalachia, including noncapitalist forms, see Rhoda Halperin, *The Livelihood of Kin: Making Ends Meet "The Kentucky Way"* (Austin: University of Texas Press, 1990); DeMartino, "Realizing Class Justice," 17; When unions are strong, as UMWA was at one time, workers may receive a cut of the surplus beyond their wages as well, such as when the Mineworkers Health and Retirement Fund was wrested from coal operators. Resnick and Wolff refer to these cuts as "subsumed" class payments that are made possible by the power dynamics in the "fundamental" class process of surplus value production. On the importance and decline of the once life-giving UMWA health and retirement fund, see Richard Mulcahy, *A Social Contract for the Coal Fields: The Rise and Fall of the United Miner Workers of America Welfare and Retirement Fund* (Knoxville: University of Tennessee Press, 2000). Finally, for a discussion of the relationships between WSDEs and their communities, see Richard Wolff, *Democracy at Work: A Cure for Capitalism* (Chicago: Haymarket Books, 2012).

14. DeMartino, "Realizing Class Justice," 8. For an illustration of diverse class processes within a single hypothetical household in Appalachia, see Dwight Billings, "Rethinking Class beyond Colonialism," *Journal of Appalachian Studies* 22, no. 1 (Spring 2016): 57–64.

15. "Nonproductive" workers such as these do not themselves directly produce goods or services, but they help create and maintain the conditions that make production possible.

16. This film can be found at https://archive.org/details/appalachiarichlandpoorpeople. The coal operator's words exemplify the Marxist distinction between the creation of "use values" and "exchange values." Coal may be useful (or harmful, as we have learned), but it is mined by capitalist firms for its exchange value, that is, its potential profitability. There is perhaps no better example of this distinction than Big Pharma's knowing production of addictive painkillers, which have plagued Appalachia and elsewhere. On the Friends of Coal campaign, see Shannon Bell and Richard York, "Community Economic Identity: The Coal Industry and Identity Construction in West Virginia," *Rural Sociology* 75, no. 1 (March 2010): 111–43.

17. Bruce Pietrykowski, *Work* (Medford, MA: Polity, 2019), 101. On externalization costs, see Anthony Flaccavento, *Building a Healthy Economy from the Bottom Up* (Lexington: University Press of Kentucky, 2016), 89. Richard Wolff provides an important discussion of WSDEs that is written from the approach to Marxian class processes that I am utilizing throughout this chapter, in his *Democracy at Work: A Cure for Capitalism* (Chicago: Haymarket Books, 2012).

18. Quoted in Will Evans, "Behind the Smiles: Amazon's Internal Injury Records Expose the True Toll of Its Relentless Drive for Speed," November 25, 2019, https://revealnews.org/article/behind-the-smiles.

19. Flaccavento, *Building a Healthy Economy*, chap. 3; W. F. Whyte and K. K. Whyte, *Making Mondragon* (Ithaca, NY: ILR Press, 1998); Vera Negri Zamagni and John Duda,

"Learning from Emilia Romagna's Cooperative Economy," February 18, 2016, https://thenextsystem.org/learning-from-emilia-romagna.

20. Gar Alperovitz and Thomas Hanna, "Mondragon and the System Problem," *Truthout*, November 1, 2013; Pietrykowski, *Work*.

21. Kali Akumo and Ajamu Nangwaya, *Jackson Rising: The Struggle for Economic Democracy and Black Self-Determination in Jackson, Mississippi* (Ottawa: Deraja Press, 2017). For information on ACEnet, see https://acenetworks.org; Helen M. Lewis and Monica Appleby, *Mountain Sisters: From Convent to Community in Appalachia* (Lexington: University Press of Kentucky, 2003); Jenrose Fitzgerald, Dwight Billings, and Lisa Markowitz, "Not Your Grandmother's Agrarianism: The [Kentucky] Community Farm Alliance's Agrifood Activism," in *Transforming Places: Lessons from Appalachia*, ed. Stephen Fisher and Barbara Ellen Smith (Urbana: University of Illinois Press, 2012), 210–25.

22. Nadja Popovich, John Schwarz, and Tatiana Schlossberg, "How Americans Think about Climate Change," *New York Times*, March 21, 2017; see also Richard Wike, "What the World Thinks about Climate Change in Seven Charts," Pew Research Center, April 18, 2016, https://www.pewresearch.org/short-reads/2016/04/18/what-the-world-thinks-about-climate-change-in-7-charts. On changing attitudes in Appalachia and the Southeast, see James Bruggers, "Caught Off Guard: The American Southeast Struggles with Climate Change," *Inside Climate News*, WFAE, January 27, 2020, https://insideclimatenews.org/news/27012020/southeast-climate-change-action-flooding-hurricanes.

23. Bernie Sanders, *The Green New Deal*, 2020, https://berniesanders.com/issues/green-new-deal.

24. See, for example, Julian Brave NoiseCat, "Joe Biden Has Endorsed the Green New Deal in All but Name," *Guardian*, July 20, 2020. For a more critical view, see Dolsak and Prakash, "Biden's Climate Plan Needs," 2020. For the direction of the Trump 2025 administration, see Claire Zhang, "Trump Reverses Climate Policies on First Day in Office," *American Physical Society, Advancing Physics News*, February 18, 2025, https://www.aps.org/apsnews/2025/02/trump-reverses-climate-policies.

25. Michelle Chen, "Appalachia Already Has a Plan to Get Past Coal," *Nation*, November 27, 2018; Betsy Taylor, Mary Hufford, and Kendall Bilbrey, "A Green New Deal for Appalachia (Part One)," *Journal of Appalachian Studies* 23, no. 1 (Spring 2017): 8–28.

26. Nick O'Malley, "How Germany Closed Its Coal Industry without Sacking a Single Miner," *Sydney Morning Herald*, July 14, 2019; Arthur Neslen, "Spain to Close Most Coalmines in 250M Euro Transition Deal," *Guardian*, October 26, 2018; Thomas Dublin, *When the Mines Closed: Stories of Struggles in Hard Times* (Ithaca, NY: Cornell University Press, 1998). Lessons from Welsh mine closures also offer important lessons for Appalachia; see Tom Hansell, *After Coal: Stories of Survival in Appalachia and Wales* (Morgantown: West Virginia University Press, 2018).

27. On Extinction Rebellion, see Roger Hallam, *Common Sense for the 21st Century: Only Nonviolent Rebellion Can Now Stop Climate Breakdown and Social Collapse* (White River Junction, VT: Chelsea Green Publishing, 2019). On skepticism among activists in Kentucky, see Mason Adams, "Biden Vows to Support Struggling Appalachian Counties, but Residents Are Weary of Failed Promises," Energy News Network Canary Media, June 2, 2021, https://energynews.us/2021/06/02/biden-vows-to-support-struggling-appalachian-counties-but-residents-are-weary-of-failed-promises; Ohio Valley Resource, "Mine Workers Leader Wants to Save Last Coal Jobs as Biden Tackles Climate," United Mine Workers of America, April 20, 2021, https://umwa.org/news-media/news/savingcoaljobs.

28. Ryan Cooper, "America Needs to Stop Its Natural Gas Pipeline Mania," *Week*, February 10, 2020; Michael Sainato, "Fighting the Fossil Fuel Economy in Appalachia," *American Prospect*, January 17, 2020.

29. Bell and York, "Community Economic Identity"; Rebecca R. Scott, *Removing Mountains: Extracting Nature and Identity in the Appalachian Coalfields* (Minneapolis: University of Minnesota Press, 2010). In contrast to ads that attach hypermasculine images to coal mining, pro-fracking ads focus on women employed in the gas industry and mothers who are reassured about their children's health and well-being; Shannon E. Bell, Jenrose Fitzgerald, and Richard York, "Protecting the Power to Pollute," *Environmental Sociology* 5, no. 3 (2015): 285–313.

30. Quoted in Michael Sainato, "'Coal Is Over': The Miners Rooting for the Green New Deal," *Guardian*, August 12, 2019, https://systemchangenotclimatechange.org/article/coal-over-miners-rooting-green-new-deal; Lauren Berlant, *Cruel Optimism* (Durham, NC: Duke University Press, 2011). For an important discussion of gender differences in hopes and expectations for the future, as well as a stress more generally on the role of emotions in the current Appalachian conjuncture, see Barbara Ellen Smith, "Another World Is Possible? Labor Geography, Spatial Dispossession, and Gendered Resistance in Central Appalachia," *Annals of the Association of American Geographers* 105, no. 3 (2015): 567–82.

31. Quoted in Peter Dews, ed., *Habermas, Autonomy & Solidarity: Interviews* (London: Verso, 1986), 212; Pelosi is quoted in Matthew Rosza, "'Green New Dream or Whatever': Nancy Pelosi Dismisses Alexandria Ocasio-Cortez's 'New Deal' Climate Plan," *Salon*, February 7, 2019; Matthew Lawrence, "Road Map to a Green New Deal from Extraction to Stewardship," Common Wealth, May 7, 2019, https://www.common-wealth.co.uk/reports/road-map-to-a-green-new-deal-from-extraction-to-stewardship.

32. Francesca Antonini, "Pessimism of the Intellect, Optimism of the Will: Gramsci's Political Thought in the Last Miscellaneous Notebooks," *Rethinking Marxism* 31, no. 1 (2019): 42–57, https://doi.org/10.1080/08935696.2019.1577616.

2
There Are No Black People in Coal Country
Race Formation and Just Transitions in Central Appalachia

Frances B. Henderson

During his 2016 presidential campaign, Donald Trump donned a coal miner's hat in a rally in West Virginia and declared himself a friend of coal. Since then, coal and coal miners have come to be shorthand for a general Appalachian community left "disenfranchised" by "progressives, the environmental movement," and Democrats, generally. When asked how Trump could capture the votes of Appalachia so easily, a resident explained, "We're a forgotten people. He mentions West Virginia, he mentions the coal workers, and that was pretty much all he had to do to seal this deal." Erased from this Trump's consideration are the Black coal miners who have lived and worked in Appalachia for decades but nonetheless have remained invisible in the scholarship of the region. Seeking to understand why Black Appalachians are so often ignored, this chapter discusses the racialization (the process of giving a racial character to something) of Appalachian communities as white and what this means for the Black communities in the shadow of the "Friends of Coal" discussion. Drawing on existing narratives of Black Appalachian communities, this chapter uses critical race theory (CRT) as a lens through which to examine and make further visible the lived experiences of Black communities in coal country. Finally, the chapter seeks to understand how current discussions of post-coal narratives continue to conceptualize coal and coal miners, and the possible implications for the region and African American communities in the region in particular. I argue that in order to have "just" transitions, we have to deal overtly with racism, legacies of racialization and invisibility, and how racism is reproduced in just transitions movement work.[1]

Critical Race Theory in the Context of Appalachian Transitions, or, Are All the Appalachians White?

What is the role of CRT in the study of Appalachia? Simply put, CRT is a broad social scientific approach to the study of race, racism, and society at large.

CRT emerged in the 1970s as a movement of activists and scholars engaging in study and transformation in the relationship between race, racism, and power. Note here the activist dimension, as CRT seeks to understand *and transform* the ways in which society organizes itself around racial hierarchies. Scholars Derrick Bell, Allan Freedman, and Richard Delgado were among the first to articulate the theory as a way to frame the subtle and insidious ways that racism shaped everyday life of people of color even after or beyond the civil rights gains of the 1960s. Later, CRT would inform writings on intersectionality by legal scholars Kimberle Crenshaw, Angela Harris, and Marie Matsuda, among others.[2]

Broadly speaking, critical race theorists hold that race is a social construct that is embedded in the way that society is structured and that racism is a common part of the everyday experience of most people of color in the United States. In service of a racial hierarchy that privileges white people over all other groups, racism serves both psychic and material purposes for the dominant white group. The fact that race and racism remain embedded in and invisible to most in everyday life, especially those whom it serves, makes them difficult to address and remedy.

CRT posits that while race is a social construct, it has very real and concrete material manifestations. Theorists argue that racism is a means by which society allocates privilege, status, and access and that racial hierarchies are used to justify the distribution of these resources in society. By advancing the interests of white elites (who benefit in material terms) and working-class white people (who benefit psychically from being part of the dominant racial group), large segments of society "have little incentive to eradicate it." These justifications take the form of the reproduction of racial hierarchies, racial separation, and ideologically driven historical records that seek to erase the presence and centrality of people of color to the formation of the nation. To this end, CRT seeks to replace "comforting majoritarian interpretations of events" with those that better reflect the experiences of minorities. This is not for the sake of correcting the historical record as much as for the purpose of correctly addressing what these majoritarian interpretations mean for the manifestation of power within racial hierarchies. This is to say that CRT argues that, in order to correct the imbalance in the ways in which resources are distributed and accessed based on racial hierarchy, the reality of the presence of people of color must be addressed first. For the purposes of this chapter, I use a CRT lens to examine the ways in which the racialized and gendered formulation of Appalachian coal country as white male, and the erasure of Black people from Appalachian coal country narratives, has distorted the history of the region and has major implications for just transitions toward sustainable development.³

"There Are No Black People in Coal Country"

The 2016 release of J. D. Vance's *Hillbilly Elegy* marked the extension of the poor, white Appalachian narrative into twenty-first-century politics. Vance's book has been roundly criticized by Appalachian scholars for its problematic reassertion and dependence on well-worn tropes that situate Appalachians as poor, white, degenerate, and Other. However, the reassertion of this trope by a media darling served as an affirmation of then-candidate Donald Trump's assertion that there exists a group of "forgotten men and women of America" who had been left behind in Appalachia. It uses a phrase made popular by Franklin Roosevelt's early twentieth-century radio address that positions "the forgotten man" as the man in the lower rungs of society who needed economic help and protection from big business. This "forgotten man" would become the focus of federal policy at various points throughout the twentieth century. Trump argued that there was a group of forgotten Americas who for too long had been the silent majority. Unlike Roosevelt, Trump's use of the phrase "forgotten men and women" of America was not meant to represent "the man at the bottom of the economic ladder," necessarily. Trump's use of the phrase more closely resembled Nixon's and was instead a nod to the white middle- and working-class Americans who had felt left out and left behind by the rapidly changing racial demographics of the country and the creep of multiculturalism into what were once solidly white, middle-class, heteronormative, patriarchal spaces. Those who surrounded Trump and worked for the presidential campaign were apparently well versed in at least the Nixon version of the forgotten man as it became a campaign slogan and could be seen on the placards held by Trump supporters who flanked the candidate during his 2016 campaign rallies. By 2024, Vance's contribution to Trump's "forgotten man" discourse was recognized when Trump chose Vance as his vice presidential candidate in the 2024 campaign.⁴

Trump's 2016 campaign rallies in "coal country" (mostly Central Appalachia) were marked by his requisite donning of a coal miner's hat and being flanked by mostly white male coal miners baring "Coal Country for Trump" or "Trump's a Friend of Coal" signs for photo ops. Buoyed by resentment toward what was perceived in the region as the Obama administration's intentional neglect or dismantling of the coal mining industry through clean energy policies and incentives, the identity politics employed by Trump proved to be an effective rallying cry. The decades-long process of extraction and "accumulation through dispossession" on the part of coal companies had preceded Obama's clean energy polices in the decimation of the region and had produced a type of generational poverty in Appalachian communities that was accompanied by "cultural responses impacted by neglect and violent repression of coal communities." Campaigning on a promise to bring back coal and tapping into a reserve of anger and frustration over cultural and political alienation, Trump's brash and abrasive talk struck a nerve as white working-class miners who had struggled to maintain coal mining jobs in the region faced the inability to rely on coal as their parents may have. This structural economic reality coupled with the cultural narrative that centered around the idea that those elites and nonelites outside of the region looked down on Appalachians as dumb, ignorant hillbillies made the gendered racialized trope of the forgotten Appalachian man ripe for exploitation. However, both white and Black coal miners were experiencing the same economic crush as brought on by the turn away from coal, but Black people were not visible at the campaign rallies, nor were they even implicit in Trump's appeal to the "friends of coal."[5] Trump was successfully reworking a well-worn trope about Appalachia that had successfully racialized the region as poorer, white, and disenfranchised.[6]

This should sound familiar. In an act of identity entrepreneurism, Trump deftly reinvigorated the forgotten man and woman trope and successfully connected it to not only the coal miners' perceived "negative" consequences of liberal economic and environmental policies but also a sense of cultural and political isolation. This cultural and political isolation started well before the Obama administration but was heightened by the hypervisibility of an African American president who was willing to discuss and address, albeit in a limited and measured fashion, some forms of racial inequity both in rhetoric and policy. I suggest that reliance on this conceptualization of Appalachian coal country as "white" and void of people of color does a great disservice to the history of the region and the path forward toward just transitions. In many ways, the racialization of Appalachia as white has been a process seemingly dominated by others, those outside of the region, but has been adopted by people inside and outside of the region when it is politically expedient. One might argue that Donald Trump's success with voters in Appalachia in 2016 represented a reflection of the dissatisfaction among the white people of Appalachian coal country, who do not have access to the benefits of whiteness that are afforded to those white people who are solidly middle class and living outside of the region. But instead, the true forgotten people of Central Appalachian coal country are the Black people who live(d) and work(ed) in the region. Their continual erasure has real material implications for the formulation of just transitions in coal country.[7]

How Did Appalachia Come to Be Synonymous with Whiteness?

The processes of the racialization of the poor Appalachians as white began in the mid- to late 1800s and would continue to be reworked throughout much of the twentieth and into the twenty-first centuries. The growing demand for land as European immigrants (mainly Scots-Irish and German) pushed their way into the region in the late 1700s led to a series of wars and conflicts with Native Americans, who had occupied the region for centuries and claimed it for their own. Through the processes of dispossession and genocide, white people displaced and destroyed the social and economic organization of the Native Americans who resided in Appalachia, resulting in the forced migration that would come to be known as the Trail of Tears. The wilderness of Appalachia became a frontier for explorers and a home for Scots-Irish immigrants who settled in the rural backcountry, and tensions between coastal elites and backcountry rural white people began to grow prior to the Civil War. The Civil War exacerbated the growing differences as white coastal elites, scholars, and missionaries began to denigrate the peoples of Appalachia. Defining the population that they served as white people, missionaries and scholars of the region reinforced the idea that the Appalachian region was "unaffected" by the influx of immigrants from Southern and Eastern Europe and that it had been unaffected by the Southern slavocracy due to its location and isolation.[8]

This perceived isolation suggested a type of racial and cultural purity that made these mountain people descendants of Anglo-Saxons, even though poor and backward, deserving of help despite their ways. Thus, as Werner notes, the seclusion of white Appalachians (especially those who came to be known as mountaineers of the central region), and their preserved racial identity acted as a counter to the threat to America's racial and cultural composition posed by immigration at the turn of the century. Subsequently, within the context of "the national panic and concern about inferiority of Southern and Eastern European immigrants between 1880–1920, and the dilution of the national Anglo-Saxon stock of American white people, Appalachian whites were held up as a bulwark against this miscegenation." This was frequently invoked outside and inside of the region in service of economic and cultural endeavors. For example, in 1904, then Berea College president William Frost referred to the image of a sacred and pristine Appalachia as a fount of pure Anglo-Saxon stock that needed to be preserved and uplifted, in his attempt to shift the college's mission from educating former enslaved people to educating white mountain people. Thus, Frost's articulation of Berea's mission became one of uplift and was used to recruit white Southerners to the college and preserve racial and social linguistic purity while simultaneously uplifting the poor white people of the region. This is another early example of the strategic use of the "Appalachian as white" ideal. This ideal would emerge again nearly seventy years later, during the War on Poverty.[9]

Notably, in service of capital, industrialists painted Appalachians as a degenerate, lawless people who lived a degraded life, who would be better served by their removal from the land and into industrial labor. Thus we see these two narratives dovetail: missionaries perceived them as pure white folk in need of and deserving uplift; industrialists, adopting scientific racism, saw an isolated, backward, and inferior people. Conflicts over land, timber, and labor rights were manipulated to fit both narratives, constructing mountain white people as "hillbillies" who were simultaneously victims of or obstacles to progress.[10]

By the 1950s, Appalachians participated in mass migrations from the southern United States to urban centers in the Northeast and Midwest in search of work. Their presence in urban areas outside of the South and Appalachia challenged white notions of poor urban Black people and confounded issues of class and racial identity. This perplexity was most visible in the 1960s War on Poverty. In his 1960 presidential campaign, John F. Kennedy made white Appalachians the moral face of poverty. By campaigning extensively in West Virginia, Kennedy brought attention to the "forgotten class" that had been left behind due to "isolation" and industrialization. While the mythology of Appalachian isolation and "backwardness" would later be proven a myth by historical sociologists, at that time, Kennedy's moral plea to Americans to see white Appalachians as the face of poverty was powerful. His appeal highlighted the fact that in the midst of prosperity experienced by white middle-class America in the 1950s and 1960s, there still remained a significant portion of the population that was in poverty because of technological advances and mechanization of industrial processes that marked progress. And those suffering poverty in that moment were given a distinctly white face. And as such, buoyed by the myth of racial innocence of the region, the plight of white Appalachians became symbolic of the national unease around the potential negative consequences of progress for the American (white) working class.[11]

Absent from this depiction of Appalachia was the African American population living in the mountains. Despite the fact that Black people made up the second-largest racial group in Central Appalachia, their numbers were dwarfed in comparison to the number of white people in the mountains and have been historically concentrated in small towns. Due to the relatively small number of Black people living and working in the region in the 1960s, it was easy to elide the fact that they existed next to white Appalachians. Put another way, the invisibility of Black people in Appalachia allowed for the region to be classified as raceless and operate under the assumption that race was a nonfactor in the region, thus hindering the development of a conceptualization of race, whiteness, and white supremacy in Appalachia (and Appalachian studies). Barbara Ellen Smith suggests that there are three reasons for this. First, the myth of the racial innocence and purity of the Appalachian people has been perpetuated and is stubbornly persistent. Second, the out-migration of Black people since World War II led to relatively low levels of civil rights activism in the region, allowing white people there to avoid confrontation with institutional white supremacy and distance themselves from the prejudice in their own communities and lives. Finally, when civil rights activism did challenge this institutionalized white supremacy, the problems were attributed to outsiders and not to the people of Appalachia, where white and Black communities enjoyed good "race relations." Thus, in light of the smaller number of people of color, whiteness in Appalachia has remained "unmarked and unremarkable-to whites."[12]

The preponderance of white people in Appalachia and the failure to challenge the process of racial oppression and exclusion that led to that particular demographic outcome affirm the assertion that Appalachian coal country is raceless. This is to suggest that race and discourses around race only become important when Black people are physically present and when issues, challenges, and histories perceived to be Black are brought into sharp relief. Smith argues that "in contexts where the population is all white, race is also absent, or at least far less relevant. This erasure of whiteness perpetuates it as normative (only People of Color are racially marked)." If white people are the only ones left in Appalachian coal country, there is no race, racism, or white supremacy, so the logic goes. However, like much of the rest of the United States of America, Central Appalachia is undergirded by segregation, exclusion, and other norms of white supremacy. And as is the case in much of the rest of the nation, there are and have been Black people in the region. At this point, I turn to a brief examination of their history in the coal region of Central Appalachia.[13]

Black People in Appalachian Coal Country— A Rich but Invisibilized Legacy

The demographic reality of Appalachia is that Black people have consistently made up about 7–13 percent of the population regionally but were often spatially segregated and clustered in certain areas of the region. For many African Americans of the region, Appalachia became a landing place or a layover on the way out of the American South even before the Civil War. Wagner and Obermiller note that railway construction and mine openings drew newly emancipated Black laborers and their families from the plantation South into the mountains.

By 1890, the African American population of Central Appalachia was 30,226, a number that doubled by 1910. During the decade of World War I, the African American population in the region continued to increase, reaching 108,872 by the time immigration ended in 1930. Sharecropping, bonded labor, and Jim Crow laws in the post–Reconstruction South induced economic, social, and political precarity for African Americans living in the shadow of white supremacy. These conditions led some Black farmers to migrate during the first half of the twentieth century in search of better opportunities. In addition, by the turn of the twentieth century, industrialization and its concomitant demand for labor and coal led Appalachian mining companies to the South in search of laborers. Ronald Lewis notes that "by the end of the second decade of the 20th century, 96 percent of the blacks living in central Appalachia resided in sixteen coal counties. By far the greatest increases in the black population came in southern West Virginia, where 69 percent of the region's African Americans (totaling 60,488) and 62 percent of the state's black miners (totaling 17,799) resided by 1920. Here the scope of industrial transformation was greatest and, correspondingly, the demand for labor was strongest as well."[14]

Having been sought after by coal companies for their experience and expertise in extraction in states such as Alabama and for their work ethic, tens of thousands of African Americans migrated to coal country in search of work and a better life. Life for African Americans in the post–Reconstruction South was marred by the racial terror of white supremacist groups, state-sanctioned racial violence at the hands of the police, and sharecropping conditions, which kept Black farmers in a perpetual state of debt and servitude. Drawing coal miners and Black farmers alike, few of these new laborers saw themselves as much more than temporary migrant workers in search of a way to provide for family and send money home. However, while developing the skill and temperament necessary for coal mining, many of those migrants put down roots in Appalachia around those coal towns. These communities became part of an expansive network of friend and familial relations that would later facilitate the great migration to midwestern cities like Detroit and Chicago, as well as to Central and northern Appalachian urban areas like Cincinnati and Pittsburgh. However, missing from much of the scholarship about Central Appalachia until recently were the experiences of these Black coal miners and their families. The process of racialization of white people in the region obscured the complex and rich diversity of the region, that is, to say that some presences were ignored in process of constructing Appalachia to meet various political economic and social agendas. In the introduction to the influential work *Blacks in Appalachia*, William Turner observed that the common narrative around Appalachia and hillbillyness obscures the long-standing presence of

Black people in the region. He notes that Black people had been in the Appalachian region in moderate numbers and various capacities (as explorers, trappers, landowners, guides, enslaved labor, and spouses to Native Americans) for several decades when the major influx of white immigrants arrived, and that African Americans in Appalachia faced notable political and economic disenfranchisement *after* the Civil War. Much like their kin in other parts of the country, Black people in Appalachia suffered from poverty. However, Black Appalachians experienced parochial constraints and problems different from those of the majority of Black people in America.[15]

Post–Civil War dreams and promises of political and social equality withered on the vine and were quickly squelched as white people reasserted their dominance over African Americans through economic strangulation, racial segregation, and political disenfranchisement. For those Black people who migrated, work in the coal mines of Central Appalachia represented at least an opportunity to make better money and free themselves from the stranglehold of poverty and Jim Crowism that shrouded life in the South in the late nineteenth to early twentieth centuries.

While the prospect of work and a better life drew Black miners, farmers, and their families to the region, once there, Black people in Appalachia endured the problems and constraints that characterized the Appalachian region while simultaneously suffering from the racism and discrimination that marked the country. Notably, coal companies did not operate in a vacuum and were subsequently imbued with some of the same ideas about racial hierarchy that permeated the rest of the United States. Perhaps nowhere was this more visible than in the coal towns of the Appalachian region, where many African Americans lived and worked. In her influential recent work, *Gone Home: Race and Roots through Appalachia*, Karida Brown provides a fuller description of the coal company town as follows: "The company-owned town was a socially engineered space, and no facet of private or social life was beyond its purview. . . . They surveilled everything, from community members' actions and bodies to their ideas, notions, and discourse. . . . In the company-owned coal town, there was little separation between the private, the public, and the industrial. Coal was the raison d'etre."[16]

Given the deep and broad reach of coal companies into daily life and their role in structuring social relations within camp towns, quotidian existence in coal towns was defined by racial and class hierarchy. Life for African Americans in coal-company towns of Lynch and Bentham, Kentucky, coal towns where Black coal miners made up a large part of the industry, reflected the de jure segregation and white supremacy of the day as well. Incorporated by US Steel Corporation in 1917, by the middle of the twentieth century, Lynch was a company town with all of the attendant economic and feudal relationships. Like other coal towns in the region, and especially in the Jim Crow South, Lynch's schools were racially segregated, and neighborhoods were stratified along racial lines. This meant that despite any isolation or insulation from broader cultural norms in the United States that Appalachia offered, racialization and racial hierarchy continued to shape the interactions and visibility of Black people in coal towns well into the latter part of the twentieth century. Nonetheless, Black residents of Lynch and other coal-company towns created a beautiful and complex tapestry of life in the mid-twentieth century.[17]

Noting the sense of normalcy, the centrality of family life, daily routines and rhythms, and the camps as an extension of family, those voices highlighted by Brown recall a lived experience marked by community as well as struggle and difficulties. The children of Black coal miners in Lynch and Benham recall a type of solidarity among Black people that came from living in a small rural company town where everyone—parents, neighbors, children, mine bosses, teachers—had a role to play and knew their place. But the narratives also reflect a racialization of those Black communities consistent with the experience of living in the Jim Crow South. Coal companies outwardly reflected a type of benign racial tolerance for all workers, but it was well known that management held similar stereotypical views around race that most white Americans held. Subsequently, coal-company policies structured the material conditions of life across racial dimensions, and they also regulated a racial subjectivity of a particular kind. This racial subjectivity served to reinforce the national racial hierarchy, in Appalachian coal towns and mines, while simultaneously seeking to prevent miners from organizing across racial lines over labor conditions. Thus they sought to put *everyone* in their place.

What Does It Mean to Know Your Place?

It means that as they emerged from the mines after a full day of work, Black and white coal miners both were covered in the same soot but had to use segregated showers. It meant that schools remained segregated and that Black children understood very early on the extent and limits of their friendships with white children and knew both the geographical boundaries and the invisible cultural boundaries that they could not traverse. Knowing one's place meant ongoing Black invisibility and lack of access to resources. For example, in the 1960s, during the War on Poverty, the distribution of resources and services to those in Appalachia skewed unevenly toward the poor white people of the region while paying little attention to the needs of African Americans in the region. Positioning herself as an Appalachian, a Black Appalachian, regional activist Mary Rice Farris described the impact that the "Appalachian as white" narrative had on her community, in her testimony to Robert F. Kennedy during a historic War on Poverty tour. Explaining that the War on Poverty program resources were mostly distributed to white communities while African American communities were disproportionately poor and suffering, she articulated the impact that Black invisibility had on receiving this help within African American communities in Appalachia, noting "that white communities throughout Appalachia had begun to get food stamps, which allowed people access to a wider range of foods, while Black communities continued to have access only to commodities food programs, in which foodstuff was rotting or full of worms." Farris articulates a clear understanding of what Black invisibility in Appalachia means in material terms. Constructed as a white deserving poor, the Appalachian narrative left little to no room for discussion of whiteness or white supremacy as it occurred in the region, or for the inclusion of Black Appalachians in programs designed to help the region. Nonetheless, resistance to segregation and racism in Appalachian coal regions took the real and tangible form of organizing in churches, separate cultural/recreational activities, and social spaces. Spaces such as social clubs and churches fortified both the social and political needs of Black people in the coal towns. Subsequently, knowing your place also meant a rich legacy and history of pride, ownership, and activism that is reflected in the established networks of connectivity in Black Appalachian coal communities.[18]

The mechanization of coal extraction in the middle of the twentieth century led to the change in demographics, most notably the out-migration of many young Black people in search of well-paying industrial jobs. Having been the beneficiaries of a segregated company-town education, Black youths moved to nearby midwestern industrial cities like Cincinnati, Chicago, and Detroit in search of work, but they carried their connections, norms, foodways, dialect, and traditions with them. Many return annually to visit those places that they left behind and the family and people who still populate them. But when they left, so did the imperative to paint the region as anything other than white. Much of the Black population left the coalfields at the beginning of the decline of the coal industry, which meant that over the past couple of decades, mostly white coal miners would face the loss of jobs and fights around Obama's shift to clean energy policies, thus making white people the public face of coal miners' distress. This face overshadows the presence of those Black people who remain part of the communities, whose forebears came to coal communities and whose exploited labor helped fuel the industrialization and modernization of the country, potentially rendering them invisible and voiceless in the effort to move toward just transitions.

A Tale of Two Appalachias and One Way Forward

The invisibility of Black people in the scholarship and history of Appalachia is mainly mapped on their segregated lives and opportunities. While Black Appalachians worked in mines and went to schools, movies, and community centers, for many years they did it separately in segregated spaces. Thus their centrality to the region and its economic, political, and social life was obfuscated by their marginalized physical location. This erasure continues in the twenty-first century, as the Appalachian identity is still widely characterized as white working class, poor, and culturally insular, even as census data as far back as 2000 reflects a rapid shift in demographics in parts of the region. Like much of the rest of the country in 2000, the Appalachian region reported an increase in "minority" population in northern, southern, and Central Appalachia. The region saw a 50 percent increase in nonwhite population between 1990 and 2000 (outpacing the overall 43% increase in nonwhite population in the rest of the United States). Black people made up the majority of the "minority" (nonwhite) population. The 2000 census data shows that while in the rest of the United States, population growth among Hispanics outnumbered non-Hispanic Black people for the first time, non-Hispanic African Americans continued to make up the bulk of Appalachia's nonwhite population, accounting for two-thirds (1.9 million) of the 2.8 million nonwhite Appalachians. Recent Appalachian Regional Commission reports affirm these demographic trends, noting that between July 2010 and July 2019, the share of population that identifies as minority has increased 2.9 percent. While the increase in those who identify as Hispanic nonwhite continues to outstrip the rate of increase in the number of African Americans in the region, in 2019, African Americans still constitute the largest minority group in Appalachia. Data shows an average increase of about 0.5 percentage points in the number of African Americans in Central Appalachia over the last ten years. As is consistent with historical spatial patterns, most Black people who live in Central Appalachia continue to live in the urban/metro areas and small towns of the region, with about 15 percent of the Black population found in rural areas. And as mentioned previously, many of the Black residents (and white residents) who lived in coal-company towns have since left. This spatial distribution of Black people leaves open the possibility of subverting attempts to pigeonhole the region as anything other than a white space.[19]

What does the ongoing erasure of African Americans mean for the just transition from coal to sustainability in the region? As noted previously, despite the fact that Black populations have not been large, Black people in Appalachian coal country formulated deep roots and connections to the region through work, love, and community activism. These roots still saturate much of the activism in the region today. The summer of racial reckoning in 2020 demonstrated the depth and the extent to which activism around race permeates the region. Protests against police brutality marked the summer in cities and towns in Central Appalachia. Places such as Harlan, Corbin, Lynch (Kentucky), and Charleston and Wheeling (West Virginia)—not heretofore known as hotbeds of antiracist activism—came alive with protests initiated by cross-generational and interracial activists. As evidenced in the rich history of organizing in Lynch and other communities, Black Appalachians possess ways of interacting within their own communities and with those outside of their community. They are grounded not only in the history of community but also in their marginalization in the region.

The efficacy of just transitions will depend on how the contours of Appalachian transformations are geographically and racially defined; and without a CRT lens that makes visible Central Appalachia as a place where African Americans have historically played important roles in development of the region, transition activism will fall short of justice. If coal country continues to be geographically and culturally defined as white, this "regional discursive formation" will limit the histories and potentials of the region. What is important to note is that white supremacy not only forms the framework for the historical legacy of extraction and exploitation in the region but also still undergirds, in overt and subtle ways, the development policies and organizations working in the region today. As such, in the absence of an overtly antiracist framework, just transitions in Appalachia policy will be a site where racial inequities and injustices are not only reproduced but also embedded. In efforts to facilitate transformation of a mostly rural and white Appalachia, policy and funding decisions are bound to prioritize these people as most in need, overlooking the needs of BIPOC residents of small towns (some of which were coal towns) that are part of Appalachia and that boast larger numbers of Black residents. For example, seemingly high-profile transitions organizations working in Central Appalachia lack the intersectional lens necessary to facilitate just transitions. Despite cursory nods to diversity via slight descriptive representation on webpages (in other words, one or two BIPOC people are featured in photos on the website), a deeper dive into the programs, donors, and coalitions suggests very little engagement with BIPOC communities. Similarly, some organizations seem to lack a collective vision in terms of transition, opting to fill the economic gaps left by decline of coal as opposed to taking the opportunity to transform the region into a place that is sustainable, where this transformation is distributed evenly.[20]

If Appalachia and just transition organizations take a color-blind approach to development, then the continued racialization of Appalachian identity as white will render invisible communities like Lynch—where there remains a notable Black population—foreclosing the opportunity for innovation from within them and alliance with others around them. Put differently, the continued characterization of coal country as white makes invisible racial narratives that undergird the economic, social, and political relationships in the region. As Osborne notes, "The function of racism and white supremacy is to strengthen hierarchies that oppress working class and poor people of all races and ethnicities including *whites*" and divide potential allies in their efforts to build a more just society.[21]

The long-standing characterization of coal regions as white perpetuates the myth of racial innocence and leaves the task of reckoning with the legacy and reality of racial hierarchy as the work of those who are visibly marked as nonwhite. The work of making all histories and peoples of the region visible and deconstructing historical and current patterns of racial inequity must be a central part of the work of envisioning a better future and just transitions. As a fuller, accurate, and more complex experience, identity, and history of Central Appalachia are considered, what do just transitions look like? In its 2021 report on transition in the region, the Highlander Center suggests that just transition must honor the work of the people who came before those doing the work now; it must "address and dismantle systemic racism and the harms of capitalism" while not repeating and reproducing the same unjust exploitative practices of the past, and it must "center collective care for land and living beings" while being led by those who live in the region and who are familiar with the wants and needs there.[22]

The identity entrepreneurism employed by Trump and others provide limited opportunities for inclusion and activism of marginalized groups in the Appalachia. Buy-in from Black communities will be shaped by perceptions of broader "white" society and the opportunities therein. Put differently, the perceived whiteness of transition frameworks, solutions, activism, and activist organizations remains a mechanism of exclusion for communities of color in the region. This is not peculiar to Central Appalachia; the landscape of transition activism is replete with examples. One such is a closely related advocacy movement: the movement for environmental justice (EJ). People of color were pioneers of EJ movements and have a long-standing activist history around environmental racism and environmental justice. As early as the 1970s, Black environmental activists in North Carolina made connections between toxic dumping and housing and food insecurity, air quality and economic development. Native Americans and Indigenous peoples have historically been at the forefront of movements against land appropriation, desecration of sacred sites, and loss of traditional fishing and hunting access. Chicano and Latinx communities have founded hundreds of local EJ organizations.[23] However, as Agyeman et al. note, these "early EJ activists (mostly people of color and low-income people) were not members of the so-called mainstream environmental organizations (whose membership is dominated by middle- and upper-class whites)."[24]

The fact that EJ movements took place outside of the context of mainstream environmental organizations suggests several things. First, mainstream environmental and transition organizations historically have not taken an antiracist approach, one that understands the relationship between race, environmental injustice, and ways of living and knowing. Second, the work of EJ activism among people of color took place outside of the mainstream EJ movement, which suggests that the widely held belief around and experience of people of color in environmental and transition activist spaces has been one that leads to a type of movement and activism that fails to engage with the challenges of transition in an intersectional manner. Dominant economic development plans in Central Appalachia fail to engage with the gendered and raced nature of coal extraction and its legacy, relegating the role of racial justice as an afterthought, at best, to the grander transition plan. If one of the goals of just transition in Appalachia is justice and societal change by way of distributive and recognition justice, then acknowledging Black people as residents, salient cultural identities, and stakeholders in Appalachia must be central to the transition process. Literature on just transitions highlights the centrality of coalition politics, civil society organizations, and transition advocacy actors in the quest for just transitions, but it does not necessarily trouble the assumptions and power relations around race, class, and gender that undergird these coalitions.[25]

This perception of opportunities, in addition to the historical context of a community itself, makes recognition and inclusion important aspects of any just transition. Furthermore, the unwillingness to appropriately *see*, engage, and deconstruct the hidden racial structures that scaffold the inequality and inequity in the region will reproduce similar systems of oppression and foreclose the opportunity to envision change beyond existing ideals and norms. The effect will be the continued invisibilization of Black people's ways of being and knowing in Appalachia, muzzling potential healing and progress in the region beyond the dominant coal country experience. Within the context of just transitions in Appalachia, CRT has the important role of not only rendering Black coal families visible but also providing a historical understanding of the ways in which racialized bodies and relations have led to specific economic and development outcomes. An understanding of the ways in which racial hierarchy framed the industry provides an opportunity to unpack the hiring, firing, and educational practices that impacted opportunity for out-migration in the region and the implications that this has on conceptualizing paths forward. In this instance, the invisibility of Black people in the region obscures the centrality of their labor in the coal extraction process but also obfuscates the importance of BIPOC ways of living and knowing to the process of societal change through just transitions.²⁶

Notes

For the purposes of this chapter, I use the Appalachian Regional Commission's designation to identify and demarcate Central Appalachia. Here, Central Appalachia is geographically defined as the central and eastern counties of Kentucky along with the southwestern counties of West Virginia, the westernmost counties of Virginia, and the central northern counties of Tennessee, all of which border Kentucky to the east, southeast, and south, respectively. For more on subregional geographical designations, see Kelvin Pollard and Linda A. Jacobson, "The Appalachian Region: A Data Overview from the 2015–2019 American Community Survey," Appalachian Regional Commission, June 10, 2021, 180, https://www.arc.gov/report/the-appalachian-region-a-data-overview-from-the-2015-2019-american-community-survey.

1. Sheryl Gay Stolberg, "Trump's Promises Will Be Hard to Keep, but Coal Country Has Faith," *New York Times*, November 28, 2016, https://www.nytimes.com/2016/11/28/us/donald-trump-coal-country.html; Edward J. Cabbell, "Black Invisibility and Racism in Appalachia: An Informal Survey," in *Blacks in Appalachia*, ed. William H. Turner and Edward J. Cabbell (Lexington: University Press of Kentucky, 1986), 3. The phrase "Friends of Coal" is actually the name of an elaborate movement to counter the environmental justice movement in coal country. Initiated in the early 2000s, Friends of Coal was an organization founded by the West Virginia Coal Association to frame and amplify the centrality of coal to the economy of West Virginia. It has since become a regional catchphrase loosely used to signify the support for the coal industry in Appalachian coal region. For more on Friends of Coal, see Shannon Elizabeth Bell and Richard York, "Community Economic Identity: The Coal Industry and Ideology Construction in West Virginia," *Rural Sociology* 75, no. 1 (2010): 111–43. Finally, thanks goes to Kathryn Engle for language about decentering whiteness in transitions.

2. Richard Delgado and Jean Stefancic, *Critical Race Theory: An Introduction*, 3rd ed. (New York: New York University Press, 2011), 6–8.

3. Delgado and Stefancic, *Critical Race Theory*, 9–11. While this is not a central focus of this chapter, it is worth noting that recent moves by the right wing of the GOP to "ban CRT" from US elementary schools (where it is *not* taught as part of the curriculum) demonstrate that recognition of the existence of Black people, nationally and regionally, is perceived as a threat to the status quo.

4. J. D. Vance, *Hillbilly Elegy* (New York: HarperCollins, 2016). While Vance's *Hillbilly Elegy* was in large part well received by mainstream media, it was met with criticism from Appalachian studies scholars. For their powerful responses see Anthony Harkins and Meredith McCarroll, *Appalachian Reckoning: A Region Responds to* Hillbilly Elegy (Morgantown: West Virginia University Press, 2019); see also David Davenport and Gordon Lloyd, "Donald Trump Rediscovers Franklin Roosevelt's Forgotten Man—Or Is It

Someone Else?," History News Network, https://historynewsnetwork.org/article/165143, accessed August 8, 2020.

5. And so we return to the idea that "there are no Black people in coal country." Obviously, Black people have lived in Appalachia for centuries and have built families and lives there. This phrase is a play on the erasure of African Americans from the popular media narrative and representation of the region as white.

6. Emilie Peine, Amy Price Azano, and Kai A Schafft, "Beyond Cultural and Structural Explanations of Regional Underdevelopment: Identity and Dispossession in Appalachia," *Journal of Appalachian Studies* 26, no. 1 (2020): 40–56. For more on the connection between structural and cultural narratives in the formation of Appalachian communities, see Steven Stoll, *Ramp Hollow: The Ordeal of Appalachia* (New York: Hill and Wang, 2017). Political pundits disagree as to whether Trump had dropped his emphasis on reviving coal mining in 2024, but he does continue his attacks on climate change science and renewable energy while advocating for more production of fossil fuels generally.

7. Nancy Leong defines identity entrepreneurs as "out-group participants who leverage their out-group status to derive social and economic value for themselves" (1351). For more, see Nancy Leong, "Identity Entrepreneurs," *California Law Review* 104, no. 6 (2016): 1333–99, and Lisa R. Pruitt, "Acting White? Or Acting Affluent? A Book Review of Carbado & Gulati's *Acting White? Rethinking Race in 'Post-Racial' America*," *Journal of Gender, Race, and Justice* 18, no. 1 (2015): 159–84. Interestingly and perhaps not coincidentally, Trump identifies himself as an "outsider" to government and politics, which is another way that he allies himself with white, working-class males—from Appalachia and elsewhere—in spite of his wealth and class privilege.

8. Phillip J. Obermiller and Thomas E. Wagner, *African American Miners and Migrants: The Eastern Kentucky Social Club* (Urbana: University of Illinois Press, 2004); Tammy L. Werner, "The War on Poverty and the Racialization of 'Hillbilly' Poverty: Implications for Poverty Research," *Journal of Poverty* 19, no. 3 (2015): 308; see also David E. Whisnant, *Modernizing the Mountaineer: People, Power, and Planning in Appalachia*, rev. ed. (Knoxville: University of Tennessee Press, 1994).

9. Werner, "War on Poverty and the Racialization of 'Hillbilly' Poverty," 308–309.

10. For more on feuds in the region toward the turn of the nineteenth century, see Altina L. Waller, *Feud: Hatfields, McCoys, and Social Change in Appalachia, 1860–1900*, Fred W. Morrison Series in Southern Studies (Chapel Hill: University of North Carolina Press, 1988).

11. The myth of the "isolated" Appalachians has been challenged by many historians who have demonstrated that Appalachia has been integrated into global capitalist markets at least since European colonization. See, for instance, Wilma Dunaway, *The First American Frontier: Transition to Capitalism in Southern Appalachia 1700–1860* (Chapel Hill: University of North Carolina Press, 1996); Werner, "War on Poverty and Racialization of 'Hillbilly' Poverty," 315.

12. Barbara Ellen Smith, "De-Gradations of Whiteness: Appalachia and the Complexities of Race," *Journal of Appalachian Studies* 10, no. 1/2 (2004): 38–57.

13. Smith, "De-Gradations of Whiteness," 42–43.

14. Obermiller and Wagner, *African American Miners and Migrants*; Ronald L. Lewis, "Beyond Isolation and Homogeneity: Diversity and the History of Appalachia," in *Back Talk from Appalachia: Confronting Stereotypes*, ed. Dwight B. Billings, Gurney Norman, and Katherine Ledford (Lexington: University Press of Kentucky, 2000), 35.

15. William Turner, "Introduction," in *Blacks in Appalachia*, ed. William Hobart Turner and Edward J. Cabbell (Lexington: University Press of Kentucky, 1985), xix.

16. Karida L. Brown, *Gone Home: Race and Roots through Appalachia* (Chapel Hill: University of North Carolina Press, 2018), 68.

17. Brown, *Gone Home*, 57.

18. Brown, *Gone Home*, 67–78; J. Wilkerson, "Unraveling the Hidden Black History of Appalachian Activism," *Salon*, August 1, 2018, https://www.salon.com/2018/08/03/unraveling-the-hidden-black-history-of-appalachian-activism_partner.

19. Pollard and Jacobson, "Appalachian Region," 28; Pollard and Jacobson, "Appalachian Region," 27; Kelvin M. Pollard, "A 'New Diversity': Race and Ethnicity in the Appalachian Region," Appalachian Regional Commission, November 18, 2020, 9, https://www.arc.gov/report/a-new-diversity-race-and-ethnicity-in-the-appalachian-region.

20. For more on the ways in which whiteness impacts the regional discursive formations in Appalachia, see Robert Todd Perdue, "Trashing Appalachia: Coal, Prisons and Whiteness in a Region of Refuse," *Punishment & Society* 25, no. 1 (January 2023): 1–21; Hayden Wilburn, "In Search of Justice: White Privilege in Appalachia," *Journal of Appalachian Studies* 8, no. 1 (2002): 126.

21. Emma Ockerman, "African Americans in Appalachia Fight to Be Seen as a Part of Coal Country," *Washington Post*, August 10, 2017, https://www.washingtonpost.com/news/post-nation/wp/2017/08/10/african-americans-in-appalachia-fight-to-be-seen-as-a-part-of-coal-country; Brown, *Gone Home*; Obermiller and Wagner, *African American Miners and Migrants*; Guy Larry Osborne, "Fighting Racism in Appalachia: A Progress Report from the Grassroots," *Journal of Appalachian Studies* 10, no. 1–2 (2004): 144 (emphasis mine).

22. The Highlander Center, "Beyond Transition: Appalachia's Pathway to Justice and Transformation," March 2021, 7.

23. Julian Agyeman et al., "Trends and Directions in Environmental Justice: From Inequity to Everyday Life, Community, and Just Sustainabilities," *Annual Review of Environment and Resources* 41, no. 1 (2016): 321–40.

24. Despite the rich history of Black Appalachian activism around civil rights and economic rights (see, especially, the Highland Education and Research Center), environmental justice and transition have historically been dominated by white environmental activists. A cursory Google search of just energy organizations in Appalachia provides a plethora of websites featuring information about groups engaged in work around just transitions in the region. First glance at some of these organizational websites feature white people and families on organization webpages and literature, with a few BIPOC activists woven into photos to seemingly represent diversity. While this is not a scientific survey of the field of organizations, for the casual observer, the absence of BIPOC in organizational literature reinforces the idea that just transitions organizations are dominated by and centered around white people in Appalachia; Agyeman et al., "Trends and Directions in Environmental Justice," 321–340, esp. 337.

25. David J. Hess, Rachel G. McKane, and Kaelee Belletto, "Advocating a Just Transition in Appalachia: Civil Society and Industrial Change in a Carbon-Intensive Region," *Energy Research & Social Science* 75 (2021): 4.

26. W. H. Gibson and S. Wakefield, "'Participation' White Privilege and Environmental Justice: Understanding Environmentalism among Hispanics in Toronto," *Antipode* 45, no. 3 (2013): 646–62.

3

Stopping the Bad, Building the New, and Telling Our Story

An Indigenous Perspective on Rematriation as Just Transition

Taysha DeVaughan

I am an Indigenous environmental activist living in southwest Virginia. I see many similarities in Appalachian culture and my own Indigenous culture, which inspires me to fight for the conservation, liberation, and justice of these mountains. I am an enrolled member of the Comanche Nation of Oklahoma and a descendant of the Hasinia band within the Caddo Nation of Oklahoma. In both my cultures, our beliefs are centered on our responsibility to serve, protect, and honor Mother Earth or the environment in which we live. An example of how we carried out this responsibility can be found in our precolonial methods of hunting and housing. As a plains people, the Comanche utilized the buffalo, we hunted only what was needed to feed the camp, and we used the bones for making utensils and the hide to make the teepee and clothing. The Caddo utilized land management practices through strategic brush burning, similar to what forestry departments do today. Although everyday life has changed for my people, our principles still thrive today through our programs such as land management, environmental protection agencies, farming and grazing departments, water testing, and other conservation efforts of the tribal government. Similar to state regulatory agencies, tribal governments established these programs to address the harmful practices that pollute our environment.

In far southwest Virginia, these lands were once stewarded by Indigenous groups, including the Cherokee, Shawnee, and Yuchi. Due to forced removal and genocide, these nations are no longer present in the same way here and have survived in other parts of the country. Today the Eastern Band of Cherokee calls North Carolina home. The act of removal was traumatic not only to the people but also to the land from which the managers and stewards were forcibly removed. However, Appalachian Indigenous approaches to agriculture, irrigation, and hunting were similar to those of the plains because both had the spirit of relational environmentalism. These people sought to live in conjunction with the land rather than on it—to live with it rather than take from it. Some nations also have governments and programs geared toward preservation and should be contacted, consulted with, and included in the process of creating solutions around healing the land. Although these nations may not live on this land today, they have an enduring relationship with this area. Many residents claim Cherokee ancestry, and the story of the three sisters—corn, beans, and squash—is taught in school. The resilience of the Indigenous people who were here before lingers in the memories of many mountain folk. We must honor these relationships by healing the trauma of removal. Mountain folk who then and now occupy this space descend from various places around the world, including Ireland and Scotland. These groups have their own valued relationships with the natural world; they stewarded this land with traditional mountain knowledge that predated the industrial resource extraction era of our region's history.[1]

Oklahoma, where I am from, suffers from the impacts of oil and natural gas production, including pipeline spills and the impact of fracking on water. Appalachia, where I now live and work, suffers from the effects of coal mining, timber production, and, also in some parts, fracking. Appalachia's water supply, like that in Oklahoma, is under threat. Appalachia also suffers a great deal from respiratory illnesses and landslides. In Oklahoma and Appalachia, environmental activists and citizens have similar experiences and hold in common these truths: the land is a living, breathing organism; it becomes more valuable when you work and live on it respectfully, holistically, and regeneratively. It becomes less valuable when you take resources without repairing, healing, or giving back.

The communities living on these lands should not have to bear the entire burden of the harmful impacts of extraction while the benefits of that extraction flow to other places and people. In Appalachia's history, I see commonalities with my own Comanche and Caddo history. People value community, as it is key to the health and success of a people. I sense a fighting spirit in Appalachia when I learn about the struggles of labor unions. From these similarities, I have found a connection to the mountain folk of Appalachia and am dedicated to fighting for its beauty, health, and well-being.

Communities that have been targeted for extraction and pollution, including communities of color and those in Appalachia, all deal with their unique circumstances; however, they also share similar problems concerning ill health, poverty, and undiversified economies. Just transitions must provide an opportunity for us to address our shared historical trauma and heal our relationships with one another, the land, and our environment. Such a transition is needed sooner rather than later. To develop solutions that are of, by, and for the community, I follow a combination of frameworks. The work of the Indigenous Environmental Network (IEN) points to ways to use Indigenous knowledge to build more sustainable ways of life and promote just transition. The IEN is "an alliance of Indigenous Peoples whose Shared Mission is to Protect the Sacredness of Earth Mother from contamination & exploitation by Respecting and Adhering to Indigenous Knowledge and Natural Law."[2]

First, the IEN states:

> Just Transition is a new term, but to most of our Indigenous peoples, it is understood, first by our heart, and secondly by our mind. Just Transition is a framework, a set of principles, to shift from a "stopping the bad to building the new." In Indigenous thought, it is a healing process of understanding historical trauma, internalized oppression, and de-colonization leading to planting the seed and feeding and nurturing a Good Way of thinking. It is lifting up Original Instructions and Teachings of respecting ourselves, our clans, our family systems, and how we are all related with all living things and our relationship with the spirit, personality and consciousness of the sacredness of Mother Earth and Father Sky.[3]

Following this framework allows me as an activist in Appalachia to navigate through the environmental justice movement using my own culture as a reference point. The framework focuses on healing and nurturing and building on Indigenous knowledge and ways of life to build better relationships. By applying these principles, environmental solutions can be identified in most (if not all) impacted communities.

A second useful framework comes from the Climate Justice Alliance. The Alliance is a group of various organizations throughout the country and world working toward climate solutions. The organization focuses on "the social, racial, economic and environmental justice issues of climate change." They build "local living economies," models focused on clean community energy; regional food systems; zero waste; efficient, affordable, and durable housing; public transportation; ecosystem restoration; and stewardship within scientific planetary boundaries. I often refer to the just transition model that it has created, which states:

> Just transition is a framework for a vision-led, unifying, and place-based set of principles, processes, and practices that build economic and political power to shift from an extractive economy to a Regenerative Economy. This means approaching production and consumption cycles holistically and waste-free. The transition itself must be just and equitable,

redressing past harms and creating new relationships of power for the future through reparations. If the process of transition is not just, the outcome will never be. Just Transition describes both where we are going and how we get there. The Just Transition framework focuses on stopping the bad to build the new by divesting from the exploitation of labor and extraction of resources and investing in cooperative labor and regeneration. Just Transition challenges the dominant worldview of colonialism, consumerism, and the concentration of power governed through violent force and advances a worldview of sacredness and care, as well as ecological and social well-being governed through deep democracy.[4]

This passage refers to colonialism, which could be defined as centuries of global plunder, the profit-driven industrial economy rooted in patriarchy and white supremacy that severely undermines the life support systems of the planet. We need to be rooted in Indigenous practices to combat this worldview. Decolonization is an important part of the just transition conversation as Indigenous communities around the country and world are working to create healthy relationships between people and the planet. To achieve this, we need more Indigenous people in different leadership positions. Indigenous leadership provides a different worldview that adds diversity to our conversations and points of view that have been marginalized yet hold many solutions.

I am also a former president of the Southern Appalachian Mountain Stewards (SAMS). We are an organization of concerned citizens, and our mission is working to build just and equitable communities while addressing current and legacy costs of extraction in our region. SAMS has been in operation for the last ten years. The catalyst for this organization was the death of a young boy in Wise County, Virginia, who was crushed in his sleep by a dislodged boulder when a local coal company was building a new haul road without a permit. Since then, SAMS has been advocating against mountaintop removal and for various environmental justice solutions.[5]

SAMS has not yet adopted a framework of just transition principles. However, we address just transitions through programming such as promoting economic diversity, preserving traditional mountain knowledge, and calling for corporate accountability. Operating as a nonprofit, SAMS provides structure and opportunities to implement programs, actions, and conversations around these principles in our communities. We use multiple strategies to achieve our mission, including direct action, programs, and community involvement. We use direct action, such as a protest, when something needs to happen rapidly. We use community involvement to engage in routine decision-making processes such as public hearings or public comments. Armed with these frameworks and the community relationships that SAMS offers, I as an activist am now able to put in motion the actions needed to cause social change.

Like the IEN, SAMS works toward both stopping the bad and building the new at the same time as telling our story. One of our first goals is to stop the bad by ending the practice of mountaintop removal. We have evidence of the negative health and community impacts of mountaintop removal. Stopping the bad means that we hold coal companies accountable for the cleanup and reclamation of abandoned mine lands and the enforcement of permit standards. Mountaintop removal has caused historical trauma to our land and our communities through devastating blasting and poisoning of our waterways. Coal companies also created internalized oppression through various strategies of class and racial divisions—between the "boss" and the "miners" and between minority miners and white miners—to maintain their power and resist unionization. The phrases "I sold my soul to the company store" and the "wrong side of the tracks" demonstrate the internalized oppression of these mine town and camp residents.[6]

To heal from these past traumas, we have to first hold companies accountable for their harmful practices. This includes filing for public hearings when a new mining permit is submitted. It includes tracking the permit violations each coal company has accrued and the lack of enforcement or payment of fines. Citizens' organizations may also be able to sue coal companies for violations. SAMS also works to put pressure on state regulatory agencies, including the Department of Energy, and to advocate for more and better enforcement of existing standards.

Stopping the bad also includes testing local waterways for acid rain runoff. SAMS has conducted citizen mine-site inspections on Looney Ridge in Wise County. Our organization monitors places where reclamation is supposed to have occurred but has not. We also work to track the local ecotourism companies' practices for creating new hiking/biking/ATV trails. In this way, SAMS keeps track of what is happening on the ground in local communities and works to bring to light some of the problems with resource extraction and other land use in the mountains.

We must participate in the creation and implementation of policies that will promote ecological and public health in our region—for example, supporting the Black Lung Disability Trust Fund and the Reclaim Act. The Black Lung Disability Trust Fund is a tax system that requires coal companies to pay taxes on the amount of coal mined and applies those taxes to a trust fund for health benefits to our miners dealing with black lung. The Reclaim Act is another federal policy that ensures that abandoned mined lands are cleaned up and revitalized and that promotes economic development.[7]

To further advocate for policies that protect communities and restore the environment, we must also take a seat at the table. This means seeking appointments or board seats for positions at local, state, and federal levels; running for political office; and participating actively in political campaigns. I was appointed to and chaired Virginia's Council on Environmental Justice, where I act in my role as a grassroots community member to bring forth the healing perspective and regenerative practices I discussed earlier. Working within the government structure is different from my other work because, instead of advocating and agitating from the outside, I now have a voice that is counted where policies are being made. I receive and share information, resources, and networks that I might otherwise not have access to. Examples of this can be seen at all levels—federal, state, and local—where grassroots groups are calling for more intentional public engagement and access to public comment. Specifically in the Donald E. McEchain Act, formally the Environmental Justice for All Act, you can see the language in the bill and the actions the legislators took to include our frontline-impacted people at the front end of crafting this new piece of legislation. Imperative to building these complex pieces of legislation is not only our perspective but also our participation. I have seen calls for public comment and participation to be more accessible to the public at large at all levels of government when you see marginalized people at the table. Being intentional about the impacted people's involvement from the very beginning is the most successful way to build deep relationships with trust. This deep relationship building produces better policy proposals.

While we address and advocate for stopping the bad, we must also build the new by enacting programs that revive traditional mountain knowledge in agriculture, herbalism, artistry, music, storytelling, dancing, quilting, and woodworking. These are the seeds that will grow the "Good Way" of thinking, acting, and being. This is also the step where we heal the impact of extraction by rooting our solutions in Indigenous voices. Returning to this traditional knowledge of the relationship to the land and of each other will help create a regenerative economy, which means we are looking to experiment with different economic models. *A People's Orientation to a Regenerative Economy* provides some guidance for building a regenerative economy.

> A regenerative economy is based on ecological restoration, community protection, equitable partnerships, justice, and full and fair participatory processes. Rather than extract from the land and each other, this approach is consistent with the Rights of Nature, valuing the health and well-being of Mother Earth by producing, consuming, and redistributing resources in harmony with the planet. A Regenerative Economy values the dignity

of work and humanity and prioritizes community governance and ownership of work and resources, instead of oppressive systems that devalue people and their labor through violent hoarding by a few. Rather than limit people's ability to fully shape democracy and decisions that impact our communities, a Regenerative Economy supports collective and inclusive participatory governance. It requires re-localization and democratization of how we produce and consume goods, and ensures all have full access to healthy food, renewable energy, clean air and water, good jobs, and healthy living environments. A regenerative economy requires an explicit anti-racist, anti-poverty, feminist, and living approach that is intersectional and eschews top-down, patriarchal, classist, xenophobic, and racist ideology.[8]

In Appalachia, we can build a regenerative economy through a return to traditional practices, including barter, herbalism, and nurturing native plants for use as medicines, textiles, and other necessities. There are numerous local festivals whose origins are based around different merchants, farmers, and makers of all kinds coming together to trade their items with each other. Herbalism allows us to return to community health care. While we value Western medicine, we embrace a more holistic approach to the health of individuals, communities, and ecosystems.

Different economic models provide opportunities to provide more fulfilling, sustainable, and democratic work in the region. The barter system is a model that was used in the region for years before the capitalistic coal companies took over. The project we call AppalCEED stands for Appalachian Communities Encouraging Economic Diversity. AppalCEED is an umbrella program that houses SAMS's workshops, lectures, and events that relate to diversifying the local economy. AppalCEED projects are rooted in mountain knowledge and seek progress in our communities not just for the sake of progress but to build on our capacities. As part of this effort, in 2018 SAMS partnered with the University of Virginia at Wise to hold intergenerational and community workshops on hemp production and processing as part of our effort to promote a regenerative economy in Central Appalachia. This helps us involve the community, the youth, the university, and the key players in the hemp industry.

Equally important, we must tell our story—a story where we are not victims of extraction but survivors of an era where profit was valued over people. We are invested in telling our stories to people from outside, to decision-makers, and to people who tell a different story. The prevailing narrative paints Appalachia as a place co-opted for political reasons, used for political gain, and plundered for profit. If the story being told is from the side of extraction, it doesn't take into account the people who have family legacies and ties to the land and live and work in the region. We work to center people's lived experiences—highlighting stories that need to be told. Narratives about resource extraction, the environment, the economy, and transition should be told from the perspective of the most vulnerable, not from that of the people who are making a profit from them. SAMS's work challenges stereotypes of what this region looks like to the outside world and provides paths forward toward change.

SAMS has taken a comparative approach to resource extraction communities and has visited with groups from outside of southwest Virginia that are dealing with similar issues by hosting film screenings and other gatherings. We also hold membership meetings where we can discuss the issues we are facing, the opposition we face, and what we can do to enact change. We provide a safe and open space for people to get involved with difficult issues in their community, telling our stories among ourselves, and looking for points of commonality and collaboration.

These principles can be applied to the July 2022 flooding in eastern Kentucky and southwestern Virginia, a tragic event that left deep scars in the affected communities. In the immediate aftermath, the focus was on cleanup efforts, distributing essential resources like water and cleaning supplies and ensuring that aid reached those who needed it most. This period highlighted the resilience and solidarity of the community, as volunteers from all walks of life came together to support one another, forging long-lasting bonds in the face of adversity. However, the challenges extended beyond the initial response. The Federal Emergency Management Agency (FEMA) faced criticism for its delayed arrival, inadequate funding disbursement, and a cumbersome application process that was further complicated by limited internet access in the region. This experience underscored the need for more efficient and accessible disaster relief mechanisms, particularly in rural and underserved areas, a need that was felt again during Hurricane Helene's aftermath in September 2024. The 2022 flooding reignited discussions of the role of environmental factors, such as mountaintop removal and logging practices, in exacerbating the impact of such natural disasters; the 2024 hurricane reignited discussions of the impact of global warming on rainfall intensity. These conversations highlighted the importance of adopting sustainable land management practices and addressing the long-term consequences of resource extraction and carbon emissions on the ecosystem and local communities.

The aftermath of these disasters offer poignant examples of the challenges faced during a just transition—a transition that aims to create an equitable and sustainable future while addressing the socioeconomic impacts of shifting away from environmentally harmful industries. Key elements of just transitions include:

1. Building resilient and prepared communities: ensuring that communities have the resources and support systems in place to effectively respond to and recover from natural disasters, with a focus on marginalized and vulnerable populations.
2. Investing in sustainable infrastructure: prioritizing the development of infrastructure that can withstand the impacts of climate change and natural disasters while also promoting environmental conservation and responsible land management practices.
3. Economic diversification and job creation: providing alternative economic opportunities and retraining programs for workers in industries that contribute to environmental degradation, ensuring a just transition that supports both environmental sustainability and economic stability.
4. Inclusive decision-making: engaging local communities, Indigenous groups, and affected stakeholders in the decision-making processes surrounding land use, resource management, and economic development, ensuring that their voices and concerns are heard and addressed.
5. Environmental justice: recognizing and addressing the disproportionate impact of environmental degradation and climate change on marginalized communities and prioritizing their protection and empowerment.

The experience of the 2022 flooding and 2024 hurricane underscore the urgency of a just transition—one that acknowledges the interconnectedness of environmental, social, and economic issues—and seeks to address them holistically, fostering resilient and sustainable communities while ensuring that no one is left behind.

In conclusion, pairing the framework of a just transition provided by the IEN and the Climate Justice Alliance with the on-the-ground work of SAMS has allowed me to put regenerative, healing, and just principles in action in the Appalachian region, my adopted home. Most of all, I have found others rooted in the same values and principles as myself in Appalachia, which makes advocating for environmentalism a collective experience. Through stopping the bad, building the new, and sharing our stories, we can work together toward just transition. Just transition is not just an economic model—it is a principle that guides us to put the most vulnerable and impacted people at the forefront of our thoughts and solutions. It also acknowledges the continued impacts of colonialism and provides ways to combat the challenges we currently face. Ways such as rematriation, or the process of returning ancestral remains, sacred objects, and other culturally significant items to their rightful Indigenous communities, are crucial for the healing of the land for several reasons.

1. Spiritual and cultural significance. Many Indigenous cultures have deep spiritual connections to the land, and their ancestral remains and sacred objects are intrinsically tied to these lands. Rematriation allows these communities to reunite with their ancestors and restore the spiritual balance and harmony with the land that has been disrupted by colonization and the removal of these sacred items.
2. Reconnecting with traditional practices. Rematriation enables Indigenous communities to reconnect with their traditional practices, ceremonies, and teachings that are often associated with the land and the objects being returned. This revitalization of cultural practices can foster a deeper understanding and appreciation for the land, promoting sustainable land management practices and environmental stewardship.
3. Addressing historical injustices. The removal of ancestral remains, sacred objects, and cultural artifacts from Indigenous communities was a deliberate act of cultural erasure and oppression during colonization. Rematriation is an important step in acknowledging and addressing these historical injustices, promoting healing and reconciliation between Indigenous and non-Indigenous communities.
4. Empowering Indigenous sovereignty. Rematriation affirms the sovereignty and self-determination of Indigenous communities over their ancestral lands, remains, and cultural heritage. It recognizes their inherent rights to govern and protect these sacred elements, which are deeply intertwined with their identities and connections to the land.
5. Ecological knowledge and land stewardship. Many Indigenous communities possess invaluable traditional ecological knowledge and sustainable land management practices that have been passed down through generations. Rematriation can facilitate the revival and application of this knowledge, contributing to the preservation and restoration of ecosystems and promoting environmental sustainability.
6. Intergenerational healing. Rematriation allows Indigenous communities to reconnect with their ancestors and cultural heritage, fostering intergenerational healing and strengthening the bonds between past, present, and future generations. This continuity is essential for the holistic well-being of communities and their relationships with the land.

By acknowledging the spiritual and cultural significance of ancestral remains, sacred objects, and traditional lands, and facilitating their return to Indigenous communities, rematriation supports the healing of the land by restoring balance, promoting sustainable land management practices, and empowering Indigenous sovereignty and self-determination. Programs, such as the Appalachian Rekindling Project, are actively working on rematriation and Indigenous stewardship. This process is a crucial step toward reconciliation, environmental justice, and the preservation of cultural and ecological diversity, and just transitions. [9]

Notes

1. See Native Land Digital, https://native-land.ca, accessed September 1, 2024, for an interactive global map of Indigenous territories.

2. Indigenous Environmental Network, "Just Transition," Circles of Wisdom: Native Peoples, Native Homelands Climate Change Workshop, Albuquerque, New Mexico, November 1998, https://www.ienearth.org/justtransition.

3. Indigenous Environmental Network, "Just Transition."

4. See Grassroots Global Justice Alliance, "Just Transition," June 8, 2020, https://ggjalliance.org/program-activities/just-transition; see also Climate Justice Alliance, https://climatejusticealliance.org/about, accessed September 3, 2024.

5. See Southern Appalachian Mountain Stewards, https://www.samsva.org, accessed September 1, 2024.

6. For example, see Michael Hendryx et al., "Mountaintop Removal Mining and Multiple Illness Symptoms: A Latent Class Analysis," *Science of the Total Environment* 657 (2019): 764–69, htps://doi.org/10.1016/j.scitotenv.2018.12.083.

7. The Revitalizing the Economy of Coal Communities by Leveraging Local Activities and Investing More (RECLAIM) Act was originally introduced in 2017. See 117th US Congress, "H.R.1733—RECLAIM Act of 2021," https://www.congress.gov/bill/117th-congress/house-bill/1733, accessed September 1, 2024.

8. See United Frontline Table, "A People's Orientation to a Regenerative Economy: Protect, Repair, Invest, and Transform," June 2020, https://climatejusticealliance.org/wp-content/uploads/2020/06/ProtectRepairInvestTransformdoc22x.pdf.

9. See Appalachian Rekindling Project, https://www.appalachianrekindlingproject.org/, accessed March 11, 2025.

4

Community-Controlled Philanthropy

Toward a Just Reinvestment Strategy for Appalachia

Lora Smith-Tovar

Let me begin this chapter with a personal truth: I believe philanthropy is inherently dysfunctional and an incomplete pathway to bringing about lasting social and systems change in Appalachia. I say "dysfunctional" because philanthropy is precipitated by extreme income disparity and an economic system that allows a few people to hoard excess wealth while many others go without the basic means for survival. When rich individuals or corporations donate to a pooled fund, start a donor advised fund, or create and endow a family or private foundation, money is protected. Wealth stays guarded, philanthropic endowments are overwhelmingly invested in Wall Street and grow substantially year to year, and the rich avoid paying taxes that could go toward vital social safety-net programs. Most troubling, endowed private foundations resting on millions to billions of dollars are only required to give away 5 percent of their endowed assets annually to retain their tax-free charitable status. To give a sense of the uneven scale of this arrangement, in 2020, US-based philanthropies invested $1.2 trillion into global financial markets. Those same foundations gave out only $88.6 billion in grants during that same time period. This means US philanthropic institutions gave over thirteen times the amount of money to extractive global stock markets as they did to their philanthropic efforts for "social good."[1] For a place like Appalachia, it is unlikely that a land, people, and economy harmed by extractive capitalism will be saved by a tool of capitalism.

Beyond my issues with philanthropy's economic origins, power dynamics embedded in the practice of the majority of US foundations rely heavily on hierarchy and outdated organizational structures. There are those that host and have decision-making power over the money and those that ask for the money. Foundations are not governed by community accountability measures, nor are they required to be transparent about what they do and how they do it. Much of philanthropy is founded in relationships, meaning that in order to even get in the door for funding, you have to have access to a certain social network. And not surprisingly, most foundations are based in large coastal cities and are white led, with white-led nonprofits receiving the majority of funding in this country. Historically, the field has been reliant on 501(c)(3) structures and nonprofits, with federal tax exemptions that necessitate making grants to institutions as opposed to resourcing the individuals and decentralized movements it takes to shift culture and create deep systemic change.

Simply put, capitalism creates the problems, then some tiny portion of capital is set aside tax free for philanthropic and nonprofit institutions charged with addressing those problems. A civil society built on more just economic, social, and political systems would not require nonprofits and foundations to solve for basic human needs or even exist at all. But here we are. In spite of my misgivings, I believe that with thoughtful interventions, philanthropy can be used more creatively to push against the limits of our current financial systems and shift power dynamics within communities. There are serious challenges and barriers to philanthropy's effectiveness in facilitating change in Central Appalachia, but new models of participatory practice offer opportunities to reimagine what social change work looks and feels like for our communities. Most importantly, a practice that prioritizes local control over resources can help us shift who has power, what that power is, and how it is yielded.

The Big Black Hole: Appalachia's Lack of Philanthropic Resources and Infrastructure

Inside national philanthropy, there is a narrative that places like Central Appalachia are "big black holes" where you can throw a lot of dollars but see little to no change. Those of us who work here know that this is not true; the problem lies not with Appalachia but with the funder who has little to no knowledge of the region. Grassroots power is not generated by wealthy foundations but, rather, by people.

The National Committee for Responsive Philanthropy published a series of reports in 2017 called "As the South Grows." Their research found that grant making by national foundations between 2010 and 2014 totaled $43 per person in eastern Kentucky as opposed to $4,095 per person in a coastal city like San Francisco. When further broken down, of that $43 per person spent in eastern Kentucky, only 2 percent went to economic development, and another 2 percent went to movement-building work to organize people and shift public policy. On average, national foundations are spending a mere 86¢ per person in a place like eastern Kentucky for economic development and civic engagement and policy change efforts while still asking us, What's wrong with Appalachia?[2]

Those of us who live and work here know that when we start to tug on our most pressing national policy issues, like racial justice, poverty and income inequity, climate change, voter disenfranchisement, immigration, reproductive justice, prison abolition, and beyond, we find their roots buried deep in rural soil. We also know that while our places are critical for moving progressive policies forward, they remain some of the poorest places in the nation and receive the least amount of philanthropic investment. There are many reasons for these funding inequities, including the fact that philanthropic headquarters are located in large urban areas. A lack of proximity creates urban bias and an unrealistic expectation concerning metrics of success.

Private and Public Philanthropy Gets Organized for an Appalachian Transition

Recognizing the long-standing disinvestment and ongoing ebb and flow of interest in the region, the Appalachia Funders Network (AFN) was founded in 2010 by a group of funders including staff from the Mary Reynolds Babcock Foundation, the Claude Worthington Benedum Foundation, the Greater Kanawha Valley Foundation, the Appalachian Regional Commission (ARC), and the Ford Foundation as a place philanthropy could organize and attract more partners to the region. The network now hosts over sixty dues-paying members that represent national, regional, and local foundations all working together to accelerate an equitable "Appalachian Transition" by convening funders for learning, analysis, and collaboration.[3] The work of AFN has centered around the framework of "Appalachian Transition" borrowing language from the international framework of "Just Transition" birthed by labor unions; Black, Indigenous, and People of Color (BIPOC)-led movements; and environmental justice organizations working to shift extractive economies and the enclosure of political and financial power to regenerative economies and deep democratic governance based in solidarity. This grassroots history and framework of just transition can be explored through resources developed by Movement Generation and Climate Justice Alliance.[4]

In our region, however, the framework for just transition was shaped predominantly by white male-led nonprofit leadership, many of whom were embedded in organizations located on the peripheral boundaries of Central Appalachia. Their analysis, which focused heavily on economic-development demonstration projects and workforce development, became a watered-down template strategy for AFN and many foundations making grants in the region. AFN articulates the Appalachian Transition framework as follows:

> The Central Appalachian region is experiencing an economic transition that presents unprecedented opportunities to set a new course for our economy and communities. The growing Appalachian Transition

movement is a response to several challenges, including the decline of the coal industry as a source of employment and economic growth, a pervasive public health crisis, the undervaluing of natural resources, and prolonged under-investment in our region's organizations, businesses, community capacity, and youth. Appalachian Transition is about overcoming these challenges by capitalizing on the current vision and leadership across the region. The Transition movement is gaining traction as it pulls in a diverse and growing coalition of actors who share a common vision: a region of healthy communities and locally-rooted economies that promote sustainable and broadly-shared prosperity. While the momentum towards a new path forward is strong, we recognize that the change we envision will take long-term partnerships, shared leadership, and sustained investments to be fully realized. We are excited to use the Appalachia Funders Network as a vehicle to help funders deepen their analysis, build constructive relationships, and make strategic investments that strengthen our communities and economy for a lasting transition.[5]

That strategy to engage funders has been working, drawing in national partners like the Marguerite Casey Foundation, the Gates Foundation, Margaret A. Cargill Philanthropies, the Chorus Foundation, and the Educational Foundation of America, among others, who could find new nonprofit and philanthropic partners to collaborate with on shared goals. Having a shared narrative and goal of Appalachian Transition helped make the region more legible and fundable to national foundations that can now find their place within a place-based just transition framework, whether they are focused on issue areas like arts and culture, sustainable agriculture, renewable energy, or health. Foundations within the network are continuing to learn, through gatherings and shared projects, how they can best work together by understanding what national foundations need in order to invest in Appalachia while providing outside funders a ready analysis about the region.

Government Funding

The just transition movement within Appalachia provided funders with a shared language that could move between nonprofits, politicians and policymakers, foundation board rooms, and government agencies at the state and federal level. It built a frame to hang strategies on that connected to global movements, including funding for civic engagement, policy change, and new approaches to economic development. Still, the levers of power within government agencies, private foundations, and the nonprofits doing this work were made up almost entirely of executive leadership that was white, male, professional, and in some cases representative of the status quo. Not surprisingly, the movement for larger federal investment grew to look like those in leadership with government funding focused almost entirely on traditional economic growth.

Jobs were prioritized as the primary outcome for this work in messaging and proposed funding strategies by government agencies—not just any jobs, but rather those in male-dominated trades. The POWER (Partnerships for Opportunity and Workforce and Economic Revitalization) program launched by ARC under the Obama administration offers a good illustration of this. During its formation, foundation and nonprofit leaders from outside and inside the region advised ARC staff and Obama's senior staff members on regional priorities for economic development. To date, the program has invested over $368 million in funding to 449 projects located across 360 coal-impacted counties. While this may be seen as a boon for the region, it arguably increased social inequities by disproportionately investing in male-centric workforce training opportunities, allocating resources to large intermediary organizations and projects that included some not located in the region, and largely ignoring grassroots input.

A similar government funding program run through the Abandoned Mine Lands (AML) fund may be an applicable bellwether for what impacts we will see from this type of public funding in the coming years. In a report by the Kentucky Center for Investigative Reporting, journalist R. G. Dunlop evaluated the success of several large AML-funded projects like the Appalachian Wildlife Center in Bell County, Kentucky.[6] The Center, an elk-viewing tourist attraction that promises to deliver a "Disney like experience," received a $12.5 million AML grant in 2016 and over $1.3 million in funding from ARC's POWER program in 2022. As of 2025, the proposed project, now rebranded as Boone's Ridge, has yet to be realized. Leaders of the project are still projecting a center that will draw over one million tourists annually, support two thousand jobs, and have an economic impact of over $113 million for the region. A critique of this and similar projects that have not yet come to fruition after making large promises and capturing massive amounts of capital is that they do not come from the community; nor were there diverse community voices consulted or much local buy-in for the projects.[7]

Over the life cycle of these federal funding programs, we have seen piecemeal solutions that promised to transform former miners into any number of different avatars: coders, ag-tech greenhouse operators, solar installation techs, traditional craftsmen. Male labor was prioritized over the enabling factors and systems that underpin our current Appalachian economy, including the unpaid labor of women. Organizations and private businesses from outside the region rushed to take advantage of government funding even though they had no local relationships or experience working in the region. Meanwhile, local and small grassroots organizations often lacked the capacity to access or manage larger government grants and were left out. Some were also deemed "too radical" for funding or were not considered by public agencies after angering political leaders.

As a result, I learned we cannot depend on outside private philanthropic and public dollars to fund community solutions. Instead, we need community control over those assets and reinvestment strategies for places that have had exorbitant wealth extracted. I believe we can better realize that promise with new approaches to grant making and emerging place-based funds.

An Experiment in Shifting Power and Control: The Foundation for Appalachian Kentucky

The Foundation for Appalachian Kentucky started as an idea among a small group of people in Perry County, Kentucky, in 2010. Through a series of community meetings, local residents articulated that they must start keeping and attracting their own resources in order to make their homeplace better. As Gerry Roll, one of the Foundation's founders, explains it, "We knew that if we were reliant on outside funders whose interest in us comes and goes and government grants only, we'd continue to just be pulling people out of the river and never get to the source of why people were drowning in the first place." To date, the Foundation is the only nationally accredited community foundation located in and serving eastern Kentucky; it has grown to have over $36 million under management and in the same amount of time has distributed over $44 million directly to eastern Kentucky people, nonprofits, small businesses, family farmers, artists, rural day cares, affordable housing projects, and other community-controlled initiatives.[8]

While it is a nationally accredited community foundation, CEO Kristin Walker Collins likes to say, "We're more than a traditional community foundation." That's because the Foundation for Appalachian Kentucky was patterned from a rural development philanthropy model that has been used across the world in underserved rural places from Kentucky to Kenya. As opposed to traditional community foundations that are focused on building endowments and assets under management that are directed by individual donors, rural development philanthropy focuses on the capacity and development needs of an area to address major issues and prioritizes regular people invested in their place over wealthy donors. Collins says, "We meet communities and organizations where they are—we don't tell them where they need to be. Instead, we bring the tools and resources they need to make their own plans and shape their own futures. We build communities, build capacity, and then build assets—because real change happens when the people who call a place home have the power to decide what's best for their future." The Aspen Institute hosts the Rural Development Philanthropy Network and outlines the unique role that rural community foundations play in rural development.

> Rural community foundations are unique in their ability to see and influence a wide and interconnected array of rural community and economic development challenges and opportunities. Why are they extra-special rural actors?
>
> The whole picture: Unlike nonprofits that focus exclusively on one issue area of community and economic development (CED)—for example, on attracting new business, on conserving natural resources, on providing social services, on improving job skills, or on organizing arts and cultural events—community foundations can support the entire range of CED activities.
>
> Strategic flexibility: Along with this vision, community foundations can offer the exceptional flexibility to respond at the right time in the right way to a community challenge.
>
> Inclusive and nonpartisan: Community foundations are one of the few institutions whose job it is to bring diverse and sometimes divergent members of the community together in a nonpartisan manner. Rural community foundations have a long-standing tradition of bringing bankers together with shopkeepers, teachers with millionaires, artists with truck drivers, pastors with drain commissioners, lobstermen with school children. The boards of community foundations typically are widely reflective of communities they serve.
>
> The regional resource: Even more so than their metro counterparts, in rural areas, community foundations are often the *only* institution that spans the many jurisdictions in a natural economic and cultural region. Indeed, in many rural places, community foundations have become the key player to pull the region together. And because they match charitable resources with community opportunities, they can handle all the sides of a program transaction, from convening to study a problem, to donor services that establish funding streams to address it, to leveraging in resource partners (outside foundations, government, business), to identifying and building the capacity of organizations to carry out the work, to offering fiscal agency to rural nonprofits—in some cases, they even operate programs themselves.

Permanence: Community foundations, because they build permanent endowed funds from local donors dedicated to the geographic area they serve, are in a rural region *to stay*. Rural communities can trust that their community foundations will neither fly by night nor fade away.[9]

The Foundation for Appalachian Kentucky mirrors this vision of rural community foundations as rural development hubs. Of the over 170 separate funds the Foundation holds, less than 3 percent are donor-advised funds. The others are endowments for regional nonprofits, fiscal sponsorships for grassroots organizations, county-level affiliate funds, some endowed and some still building toward endowments, component funds focused on an issue area or specific initiative, and pass-through funds and grant making for larger foundations wishing to work with a local partner. This means the Foundation plays a role in everything from administering funds for large foundations focused on regional civic engagement and policy change efforts to fiscally sponsoring and fundraising for a local African American cultural center. While this may not sound groundbreaking, the fact that the Leslie County Community Foundation, one of their county-level affiliate funds, is raising money from people in and outside of Leslie County that is controlled by people in Leslie County who direct how those funds are spent is not insignificant. Who controls the money controls decision-making power. Having agency and self-determination is crucial to Appalachian people's self-autonomy and future. My experience has taught me that eastern Kentuckians know what their biggest challenges are and, with the right kinds of investment, can scale solutions that hold important lessons for the rest of the country.

The Appalachian Impact Fund (AIF), which I cofounded in 2017 with a donor, is a place-based, social impact investment fund housed at the Foundation for Appalachian Kentucky. It makes grants and "impact investments," which look like 0–2 percent interest, recoverable grants from a community-controlled, revolving loan fund that provides patient capital—that is, capital that can be held for a long time rather than demanding a rapid financial return on investment in favor of social and ecological returns. Maybe most importantly, the board that has decision-making power over the dollars AIF has to allocate is majority controlled by community members living in eastern Kentucky. The fund makes grants and investments to support affordable childcare, affordable and energy-efficient housing, promising sectors like arts and culture, protection of natural resources, small businesses, and local and sustainable food and agriculture.

During my five-year tenure at AIF as cofounder and executive director, we distributed over $4.6 million in grants to individuals and nonprofits, deployed over $1.5 million in impact investments, leveraged an additional $7.5 million in new funding for the region from partners, supported over 1,430 jobs, and helped over 660 small businesses and family farmers grow. We accomplished this with one staff person, the back-office support of the Foundation, our many community partners, and a dedicated volunteer board. Yes, AIF board members were concerned about jobs and the economy, but during my time of service, they were more concerned with listening to what communities wanted, learning, adapting, and making sure the needs of working families and young people were centered in our funding priorities. In fact, two of the first grants AIF made were to the STAY (Stay Together Appalachian Youth) Project, a youth and queer-led regional organization, and the Black Appalachian Young and Rising initiative, a Black youth caucus. During my time as AIF's director, we learned that when we resourced the strategies of community members who received the least amount of funding in an already marginalized and underresourced place, we produced better results for everyone.

Disaster Philanthropy and Mutual Aid

Beginning in 2021, parts of eastern Kentucky, southwestern Virginia, western North Carolina, and West Virginia experienced increased flooding brought on by a combination of climate change and the legacy of extractive industries. The July 2022 flood in eastern Kentucky left forty-four people dead, nearly nine thousand homes damaged or destroyed, and thousands of adults and children displaced. While the destruction on the ground was shocking, the failure of the federal government to provide adequate financial and material assistance to flood survivors was one of the biggest failures those of us working on relief efforts at the time saw. In the absence of government assistance, local people and local nonprofits stepped up to provide the philanthropic support needed to help people survive. EKY Mutual Aid, started in 2020 amid the COVID-19 pandemic, played a pivotal and lifesaving role during this time, helping to distribute over $100,000 directly to flood survivors, facilitating direct person-to-person cash payments by members and donations of supplies facilitated online through social media pages, and coordinating volunteers. Small rural community centers, like the Hemphill Community Center in Letcher County, became vital hubs for people in need of basic supplies, hot meals, drinking water, and mental health support. The CANE Kitchen in downtown Whitesburg served three free meals a day and fed thousands of people while providing a safe space to gather, learn about other available resources, and process collective grief through art and therapeutic activities. Housing organizations in the region, including the Housing Development Alliance and

H.O.M.E.S. Inc., mucked out houses that had been partially destroyed and began the tremendous effort of building 2,300 new homes.

I was serving as the chief strategy officer at the Foundation for Appalachian Kentucky during the 2022 flood. That year, we received a crash course in disaster philanthropy and became a conduit for national foundations that trusted us to handle large sums of money and distribute those dollars where they were needed most. Between August and December, the Foundation raised and distributed over $10.6 million in funding for flood victims. Over $5 million of that went out in the form of cash directly to individuals and families. The rest was cash that went to small family farms, local nonprofits, family resource centers, and a pooled initiative for rebuilding houses in Letcher, Knott, Perry, and Breathitt counties. Having a local community foundation that was responsive and knowledgeable about the communities impacted, networked across the region, and able to take in large sums of money was integral to many eastern Kentuckians receiving aid. In some cases, we were told by individuals that we were the only cash aid they received after being denied support by the Federal Emergency Management Agency (FEMA) and other government agencies. PODER Emma, Cooperate WNC, and Beloved Asheville, among many other grassroots and mutual aid efforts, played similar roles in the aftermath of Hurricane Helene in 2024.[10]

The local disaster philanthropy infrastructure and strong mutual aid networks that have risen from increased climate events have changed and will continue to innovate and challenge how philanthropy is practiced in Appalachia. These networks further demonstrate that local people have the skills to own, control, and distribute money and other resources in effective ways, both within and outside nonprofit structures.

The Waymakers Collective: A New Model for Wealth Redistribution

While the call for a just transition gave nonprofits and funders a shared vision for an economy that could nurture and sustain Appalachian people, I rarely hear people in Appalachian communities use the term. Instead, they describe a need for meaningful work; affordable housing; safe, quality, and affordable childcare; better educational opportunities; and basic infrastructure like sewers and clean drinking water. Communities are also struggling with the opioid epidemic and having tough conversations about harm reduction and needle exchanges. Community members express a desire for more recreational activities, especially for local youth; more support for arts and cultural work; they want solutions to food insecurity; and they ask for access to better health care and health outcomes. None of this is contrary to the principles of just transition. However, these issues have not taken center stage in regional just transition narratives, nor are they funded at the same scale as traditional economic development strategies, such as industrial recruitment, workforce training, and entrepreneurship development.

In light of this, I often found myself asking, What would a transition built around caretaking and place-keeping look like? What could a philanthropic practice look like that transferred the ownership of money and decision-making power to people living in Appalachia? And what would happen if philanthropy seriously supported individuals and movements beyond a 501(c)(3) structure?

One example of shifting to a different funding strategy is the Central Appalachian ArtPlace America project that birthed the Waymakers Collective.[11] ArtPlace America was a pooled fund made up of larger foundations and individual major donors started in 2010 to accelerate the field of "creative placemaking."[12] From the beginning, ArtPlace announced it would sunset, meaning it would spend down all of its assets by 2020. In 2019, ArtPlace brought together a group of thirty community leaders from Central Appalachia, including grassroots community activists and artists, to be responsible for allocating a gift from an anonymous donor of $4.5 million to support arts and culture work in Central Appalachia.

I was honored to have been invited to be one of those original thirty community leaders, and over the next several years, I served on the transition team that (1) shifted the money from ArtPlace America's control to a new fiscal home at the Appalachian Community Fund in Knoxville, Tennessee, (2) helped as we built a democratically controlled collective that governs our funds, and (3) helped design our initial strategy and grant-making programs.

We began our journey to forming a collective by acknowledging the harm philanthropy has done to our region and people through creating models of scarcity and competition and funding predominantly white-led work that many times upheld oppressive systems and structures. Today, we are a Black-led fund, guided by our executive director, Joseph Tolbert, Jr., and prioritize granting money to Black, Indigenous, queer, rural, Latinx, and other underrepresented artists that typically do not receive funding in our region. In doing so, the Waymakers Collective is changing the story of who lives and creates in Central Appalachia. We function as a democratically controlled assembly, with each new grantee becoming a member of the assembly. All members have voting rights on major decisions concerning the collective. Each year the assembly elects new representatives to a governing body, called the Appalcore, from the assembly's membership. Members of the Appalcore oversee the day-to-day operations of the fund and are paid equitably for their time. The collective has only one full-time dedicated staff, keeping leadership dispersed. Instead of a traditional staffing hierarchy, the collective engages in consensus-based decision-making facilitated by the executive director. This nonhierarchical way of self-governance reflects our desire to live into our values and new ways of relating to and sharing power. As the authors of a Movement Generation–produced zine titled *From Banks and Tanks to Caring and Cooperation: A Strategic Framework for a Just Transition* assert, "If we are not prepared to govern, we are not prepared to win."[13]

The Waymakers Collective decided early on to not limit funding to nonprofit organizations. As a result, worker-owned cooperatives, individual artists, small businesses, and unincorporated entities have received money. We employ simplified grant applications, require no reporting, and oftentimes use an internal nominations process to ensure we reach individual artists, cultural bearers, and grassroots groups that may have never received a grant before. In a recent round of funding, everyone that applied for a grant received a check for their time and labor in filling out an application regardless of whether their grant application was funded. In 2023 and 2024, the collective chose to forgo an application process altogether and gave money directly to members of the assembly with no expectations attached. To go even deeper with our resources, we invest the money not being used for grant making in ways that are mission aligned. In 2022, we made our first impact investment with Oweesta, a nonprofit bank supporting Native American communities, as part of our commitment to reparations and land rematriation.

What is being built is not a community of grantees but a self-governing and loving community representing authentic and deep relationships, shared learning and support, healing, and mutual aid. These activities and the types of work being supported fit into a just transition framework but expand far beyond a narrow economic regional focus on jobs and the economy. The Waymakers Collective is helping to define that it is not only who has the power to control money but also how they go about governing themselves, making decisions, and centering powerful people targeted for oppression who have historically been overlooked by traditional philanthropy and much of our region's nonprofit infrastructure. We strongly believe this experiment in participatory and community-controlled resource allocation is a model for how philanthropy can be practiced in the region when large funders and donors relinquish all control.

Beyond Just Transition

It has been over fifteen years since the just transition movement launched in the region. I believe it is time to move away from the region's just transition framework as defined by philanthropy that has historically prioritized jobs and a "new" economy that too often looks like the "old" economy to one that prioritizes equitable processes and the self-determination of people, with a focus on transitioning control of money to rural, queer, youth, and BIPOC-led organizations, entities, movements, and, ultimately, individual people and families. One powerful pathway for foundations interested in funding in Central Appalachia involves seeking out local partners that have community members in democratically governed decision-making roles, as suggested by Edgar Villanueva. Villanueva, a member of the Lumbee Tribe of North Carolina, introduced the field of philanthropy to the goal of "decolonizing wealth," asking foundations to recognize that the institutions that control wealth are inherently broken in that they benefit the wealthy elite and those working for them. He suggests that we focus on healing by allowing those harmed to control funding and investments. In the words of Edgar Villanueva, "Money is like water; it's a precious, life-giving resource. Money should be a tool of love that facilitates relationships and helps us thrive, rather than something that hurts and divides us. If we use it for sacred, life-giving, restorative purposes, it can be medicine."[14]

When funders are intentional about equity and when they trust community, we can foster meaningful relationships in service to change. The grandmother of Appalachian studies, Helen Lewis, reminded us again and again that "it comes from the people." If philanthropy and capital are directed to the people most proximate to injustice, with commitments to social, class, gender, geographic and racial equity in place, it can create models for direct reinvestments that are restorative and regenerative. Among other things, a true just transition would mean a philanthropic reinvestment strategy that gives control over capital to working-class Appalachians dedicated to building collective well-being and power. This could be accomplished by large state, regional, and national foundations actively moving all or significant portions of their endowments to local, place-based funds in the region or other organizations committed to equitably stewarding them. It could also be accomplished by more foundations sunsetting, as ArtPlace America did, and putting themselves out of business through investing in existing participatory grant-making funds or, more radically, by giving money directly to individuals. While this may not be a simple ask, at least imagining these possibilities is a first step toward what an equitable redistribution of philanthropic wealth in this country could be.[15]

In Appalachia, we have innovative and brilliant leadership, as evidenced by the work we see happening within groups like the STAY Project, Beloved Asheville, PODER Emma, Black by God West Virginia, Black in Appalachia, The Appalachian Rekindling Project, Higher Ground, and the Waymakers Collective, as well as decentralized, independent groups of people working together like the EKY Mutual Aid network. The many ideas and possible futures these creative leaders are planting in fertile mountain soil need cash resources they control. They need resources that do not come with philanthropic barriers to admittance, nonprofit status, and outdated professional credentialing of the people doing the work, or cumbersome grant reporting on metrics that don't matter or translate to their communities. And they need resources now. If philanthropy is serious about making progress on poverty, climate change, racial injustice, and other issues threatening the stability of life as we know it, foundations must go "all in" and let go of money and control. We must trust Appalachian people to own and resource the futures of their own design.

Notes

1. Justice Funders, "The Just Transition Investment Framework," accessed March 17, 2025, https://justicefunders.org/jti-framework.

2. Ryan Schlegel, "As the South Grows – The Series" National Committee for Responsive Philanthropy, April 17, 2018, https://ncrp.org/resources/as-the-south-grows-the-series.

3. Appalachian Funders Network, "A Note on Appalachian Transition," accessed March 17, 2025, https://www.appalachiafunders.org/about.

4. Movement Generation, "Just Transition," accessed March 17, 2025, https://movementgeneration.org/justtransition.

5. Appalachian Funders Network, "A Note on Appalachian Transition," accessed March 17, 2025, https://www.appalachiafunders.org/about.

6. R. G. Dunlop, "The Elk, the Tourists, and the Missing Coal Country Jobs," Kentucky Center for Investigative Reporting, October 22, 2020, https://kycir.org/2020/10/22/the-elk-the-tourists-and-the-missing-coal-country-jobs.

7. Eric Dixon and Kendall Bilbray, "Abandoned Mined Land Program: A Policy Analysis for Central Appalachia and the Nation," AML Public Priorities Group, July 8, 2015, https://aclc.org/wp-content/uploads/2020/08/aml-policy-paper.pdf.

8. Borrowing from the definition provided by the Aspen Institute's Rural Development Philanthropy Network, "Community foundations are autonomous, nonprofit, nonpartisan, philanthropic organizations that raise and manage a variety of permanent endowment and non-endowed funds from a wide range of donors who care about or live in a specific geographic area. In turn, the foundation uses the stream of revenue produced by these funds to support community building and charitable activities within the geographic area served by the foundation. In recent years, community foundations have been among the fastest growing source of charitable dollars in the U.S. Community foundations are governed by a board of directors, typically a set of local leaders whose concerns, roles and demographic mix broadly represent the population of the place the foundation serves. A community foundation offers three primary services to its designated geographic area: A community foundation is a one-stop shop for local (and nonlocal) donors who wish to contribute their cash, trusts, bequest or real property to create permanent endowments that will benefit the community in perpetuity; Likewise, a community foundation is a one-stop shop for local (and nonlocal) individuals, foundations and public resource providers that seek to channel their current

non-endowed giving ('pass-through' resources) toward purposes that will benefit the community; Using the investment earnings on each endowed fund, any available pass-through dollars, and its ability to partner and leverage other resources into the effort, a community foundation makes grants, sponsors initiatives and builds capacity within the community to address local needs and opportunities." See https://www.aspeninstitute.org/publications/rural-development-hubs-strengthening-americas-rural-innovation-infrastructure/.

9. For the full report, see *Building Engines for Rural Endowment: An RDP Thinking and Action Framework*, http://aspencsg.org/rdp/rdp/overview.php.

10. See https://cooperatewnc.org/, https://www.belovedasheville.com/, and https://www.poderemma.org.

11. See https://www.waymakerscollective.org.

12. ArtPlace America defined "creative placemaking" as "the intentional integration of arts, culture, and community-engaged design strategies into the process of equitable community planning and development. It's when artists, culture-bearers, and designers acting as allies to creatively address challenges and opportunities. It's about these artists and all of the allies together contributing to community-defined social, physical, and economic outcomes and honoring a sense of place." In response to the work of ArtPlace America, there has been pushback to the idea of "creative placemaking" and a critique that the practice often offers soft power to developers and landlords and furthers gentrification in communities, especially low-income communities of color. Critics have instead argued for a practice of "creative placekeeping" that offers strategies to protect existing cultural practices, longtime residents being able to stay and live in place, and ownership of local assets by local people. See https://www.artplaceamerica.org/areas-of-work/introduction.

13. For more on this concept of self-governance and access to a free download of the zine, see https://movementgeneration.org/justtransition.

14. Edgar Villanueva, "Money as Medicine," *Stanford Social Innovation Review*, May 21, 2018, https://ssir.org/articles/entry/money_as_medicine.

15. Justice Funders, a national QTBIPOC-led organization reimagining philanthropic practice, offers a much deeper analysis on what these types of strategies could look like. In 2023, it released a framework for just transition investing targeted at endowed foundations. You can read its guide to shifting capital and power here: https://justicefunders.org/jti-framework.

5
Stay Statements

STAY TOGETHER APPALACHIAN YOUTH

Our Vision

We envision an economically and environmentally sustainable Central Appalachia where young people have the power to build and participate in diverse, inclusive, and healthy communities.

Our Mission

As young people from Central Appalachia, we are connecting across our region to make our home communities the places we can and want to STAY.

Young people living in Appalachia are struggling to thrive under the economic and social legacy of extractive industries like coal, gas, logging, and tourism, among others. Those jobs broke people's bodies or forced them to leave; and pharmaceutical companies flooded our region with opioids. Our local, state, and federal governments are trying to sell us prisons, small business, more tourism, and downtown revitalization as the solution. We've got high rent and low wages because opportunities for youth are few and often look like low-paid positions like AmeriCorps/VISTA, which exploits the labor of young people. We know that these are false solutions that rely on able-bodied workforces to work long/seasonal hours with low pay and few to no benefits and that they will only replicate our current conditions and cause suffering while lining the pockets of politicians and corporations.

The economic and environmental issues we face are compounded by acts of homophobia, transphobia, sexism, and white supremacy from members of our own communities. Trying to survive and just be young under compounding oppressions, while living with the legacy of extraction, takes a toll on our mental and physical health—not to mention that our access to health care is disappearing with the closing of rural hospitals and absurd medical costs. Instead of real transformative solutions, we get policing by cops and ICE in our schools, our hills, our hoods, and our hollers.

Young people in Appalachia are in crisis; we have been in crisis and we want to know, Why just transition? Why not liberation? We know that no one industry or government body is going to save us and that it will in fact take many people using a diversity of tactics in coordination across the region operating under shared principles to realize our vision of safe, sustainable, engaging, and inclusive Appalachian communities. We know that our liberation in Appalachia is tied up in the global struggle against capitalism and white supremacist colonial powers: Appalachia isn't free until Palestine is free. Freedom is closer than we think, but we know that culture does not shift in a day or an election cycle. Arriving at and sustaining liberation is a long-haul process. The STAY (Stay Together Appalachian Youth) Project is in this for the long haul, guided by a core set of beliefs:

We Believe That . . .

As mountain people, we are experts of our own lives. We have the ability to shape and share our own narrative about the past, present, and future of the region.

The land called "Appalachia" is the unceded territory of the Osage, Cherokee, Shawnee, Catawba, Muscogee/Creek, Moneton, Chickasaw, and Tsoyaha peoples.

Everyone deserves basic human rights no matter where they live, their economic background, race, ability, language, religion, sexual orientation, gender identity, presentation, or cultural background.

We are stronger when we bring together and support diverse voices in our region.

Our communities have a responsibility to support our Black youth, Indigenous youth, youth of color, and LGBTQIA+ youth living in the region.

Young people have the right to stay in the region and deserve viable opportunities and pathways to success.

When we young people are connected to resources, skills, and each other, we can realize our vision for change in the region.

We believe in intergenerational space and collaboration that prioritize youth leadership/power and values shared learning.

Despite having few avenues for community participation, leadership, and decision-making, young people in our region are already creating revolutionary change and working toward making Appalachia a place in which we can and want to STAY.

The STAY Project is a diverse network of young people between the ages of fourteen and thirty who are working together to create, advocate for, and participate in safe, sustainable, engaging, and inclusive communities throughout Appalachia and beyond. Formed in 2008, the STAY Project has made it possible for young people in Appalachia to create opportunities to gather, connect, play, share skills, and challenge each other so that together we can challenge systems of oppression and envision the world we want to build.

Regeneration
Land, Food, and Health

6

The Land and Us

Possibilities for Building Equitable Land Ownership in Post-Coal Appalachia

Tom Hansell and Julie Shepherd-Powell

Eastern Kentucky, 1988

A helicopter flies over a lush Appalachian mountainscape. A camera swoops over the mixed hardwood forest, filling our eyes with countless shades of green. Just over the next ridge, the scene changes. Suddenly, tan highwalls and brown rubble fill the screen. Mammoth mining equipment scrapes away the hillside to expose black coal seams. Then the voice of Everett Akers, a local entrepreneur who lost his cable television business to strip mining, exclaims, "When you own and control land, you are a free man. When you own land and can't control it, you can't control yourself. You are a slave!"[1]

Local control of land is an essential, yet often overlooked, element of just transition in the Appalachian coalfields. Akers's comments from the iconic Appalshop film, *On Our Own Land*, still resonate over thirty years later. Residents of the coalfields have been left with abandoned mine lands, fewer jobs, and lack of financial capital to invest in a just and equitable future for the region. Further, as the historic flooding of July 2022 demonstrates, absentee corporations own most of the high ground required to build safe and resilient residential communities. A just transition increases opportunity for historically disenfranchised people, and control of land is an essential element to provide coalfield residents the means to realize their visions for a sustainable future.

In this chapter, we offer a critical analysis of current strategies to increase local control of land and other natural resources in the region. We ground this analysis in historical context, including a brief overview of landownership in Central Appalachia. Additionally, we describe and critique three different approaches to addressing the problem of absentee ownership. These include collective land ownership, policies to encourage homesteading, and the Commons Communities Act proposed by historian Steven Stoll. We provide the national context of recent legislation that aims to address regional issues of joblessness and environmental degradation. We further draw on scholarship focused on the Global South to consider how patterns of land ownership, power, and resource extraction connect Appalachia to communities across the globe.

As Scott and Engle note in the introduction to this volume, "The just transition movement emphasizes the importance of locally based solutions and democratic decision-making." Accordingly, we use the term "communal" as shorthand to signify the potential for Appalachian coalfield communities to utilize participatory democracy to address land and resource ownership. By participatory democracy, we mean a structure to encourage maximum participation of community members affected by a loss of land and natural resources, especially those who live in areas where resource extraction has devastated the natural environment and where human labor has been exploited. We use "communal ownership" instead of "local ownership" as we note that in some cases, "local" can serve to reinforce power inequities and existing hierarchies *within* communities. Both "local" and "communal" may signal an existing space for collective action, such as a town or a county; however, "communal" is meant to indicate that all residents in these spaces are given an equal say in decision-making processes rather than allowing "local" elected officials and other power holders to dictate the use of land and other natural resources. Although some may argue that communal land ownership is not viable in the current legal and economic system, we believe that three models we propose herein can provide a new lens through which to imagine more equitable land ownership and a shift toward just transition. While no system is perfect, we hope that the concepts of participatory democracy and communal ownership as outlined in this chapter will provide ways to learn from the past while transitioning to a just, equitable, and inclusive future.[2]

A Brief History of Land Ownership in Central Appalachia

The Shawnee and other Indigenous people who lived in the Appalachian coalfields before European settlement had very different notions of land ownership than modern society has. Most Native American cultures treated land as commons for collective use. Although conflicts between tribes arose over hunting grounds, in general, there was more land than people, and collective ownership generally worked smoothly.[3]

In contrast to the Indigenous notion of collective ownership, some of the first people of European descent to travel through the Appalachian coalfields were hired by real estate speculators. For example, the journal of Dr. Thomas Walker is one of the earliest documents of the natural wealth of the Appalachians. Walker's expedition was sponsored by the Loyal Land Company to establish boundaries for land they had been granted. The Loyal Land Company was the predecessor of the landholding companies that currently own a larger percentage of the region. They brought the concept of private property to the region and a system of ownership that wrested land from Indigenous control. The mapping and other documentation by Walker and his successors helped establish a pattern of absentee corporate ownership that remains a major obstacle to a just transition.[4]

In Appalachia in the late 1800s, land agents traveled through the mountains, purchasing thousands of acres. Some buyers would only acquire the mineral rights underneath the land, separating the surface from the minerals and leaving the farmer with the responsibility of any taxes. Later in the twentieth century in Kentucky, the courts would rule that through these "broad form deeds," mining companies had the right to extract these minerals by whatever means necessary, including surface mining. It was not until 1988 that the Broad Form Deed Law was finally overturned in Kentucky, yet many eastern Kentuckians still deal with conflicts between the rights of surface owners and mineral holders.[5]

For the purposes of this chapter, we define absentee ownership as land owned by corporations with headquarters outside of the Appalachian region. Absentee ownership has been broadly criticized for its role in increasing inequality, as the land owners do not reside on or cultivate the land but still benefit from income extracted from the land. This continues to be a crucial economic issue in places like the Global South as well as Appalachia.

The first attempt to document patterns of land ownership in the Appalachian coalfields was a 1974 newspaper series by *Huntington Herald-Dispatch* reporter Tom Miller titled "Who Owns West Virginia?" Miller's study concluded that "absentee landlords own or control at least two-thirds of the privately held land in West Virginia." In 1978, the Appalachian Land Ownership Task Force was formed to document land ownership throughout the entire Appalachian region. The task force released the groundbreaking Appalachian Land Ownership Study in 1981. The study concluded that "absentee individuals and corporations own 43 percent of the total land area."[6]

In 2013, the West Virginia Center on Budget and Policy published a new study titled "Who Owns West Virginia in the 21st Century?" This report updated the 1974 study and confirmed that 50–75 percent of land in the state's southern coalfield counties was owned by out-of-state corporations. Not one of the state's top ten private landowners had headquarters in the state of West

Virginia. In recent years, the Appalachian Land Study Collective has been working on a more comprehensive regional study of absentee land ownership. Their goal is to update the 1981 Appalachian Land Ownership Survey using many of the participatory techniques that were employed during the original study. Their work has the potential to provide important data that will support a just transition for coalfield communities.[7]

Strategies to Increase Communal Land Ownership

The topic of land ownership is often overlooked in favor of trendier topics such as teaching miners computer coding or developing ecotourism attractions in the coalfields. However, local control of land may be the most important element required to build a foundation for a diverse and sustainable postindustrial economy. It may also be the most difficult element to address. Redistribution of land has caused violent conflict throughout history, and it is difficult to reconcile armed conflict with a just transition. Even though land redistribution is challenging, it may be a necessary step to achieve an equitable future in the coalfields. Three proposed strategies to increase local control of land and support sustainable development in the coalfields are collectives, homesteading, and the Commons Communities Act.

Collectives

Communal living and shared land ownership started with Indigenous people in what came to be known as "Appalachia." Additionally, land trusts, collectives, and other arrangements to share land and resources have existed on the fringes of Appalachian culture for centuries. For example, the Kingdom of the Happy Land, a nineteenth-century African American collective near Hendersonville, North Carolina, has received recent attention. During the twentieth century, religious groups, settlement schools, Mennonites, and back-to-the-landers all experimented with communal living or shared land ownership arrangements. While these examples increased cultural understanding and acceptance of shared land ownership, this chapter focuses on the role public policy can play in returning absentee land to communal control.[8]

The village of Arthurdale, West Virginia, was founded in 1933 as part of President Franklin D. Roosevelt's New Deal programs. The site was chosen for its proximity to Scotts Run, a coal-mining camp that had endured bloody labor battles. The idea was to resettle unemployed miners, who government officials believed might lead an armed uprising. Federal funds to purchase the land and build the town were approved as part of the National Industrial Recovery Act of 1933. Miners and other potential homesteaders had to be approved by a board before they moved into Arthurdale. In a move that was highly controversial, only native-born white Americans were selected; Black people and foreign-born people were excluded from this communal living situation. Homesteaders were expected to maintain their homes, participate in democratic decision-making, and work in some kind of business such as furniture manufacturing, garment making, or agricultural enterprises.[9]

This experiment in communal ownership only lasted seven years. In 1940, the federal government sold the homes to the homesteaders at a loss. The legacy of Arthurdale is complicated. Many historians have declared Arthurdale as a failure, claiming that the communal structure increased dependence on the federal government and discouraged self-sufficiency. Others, including Eleanor Roosevelt, who had made Arthurdale a pet project, claimed it was a success. In the context of current conversations about a Green New Deal, it is essential to note that New Deal–era experiments in communal living such as Arthurdale required an actual act of Congress. The exceptional degree of federal support and overt racism made this solution to absentee land ownership problematic. While government ownership is often considered different from absentee ownership, it is also far from the ideal of local control, a requirement for a just transition.[10]

Homesteading

The response of Detroit, Michigan, to deindustrialization is an interesting example that might provide guidance to the postindustrial Appalachian coalfields. The city of Detroit was faced with an extraordinary number of vacant and blighted properties due to massive out-migration in the wake of job losses in the automobile and related industries. In response, it established the Detroit Land Bank Authority in 2013 to help solve the problem of the thousands of abandoned homes it had acquired for back taxes. The city began auctioning some of these houses for sale, with bids starting at $1,000. Central to this measure was that purchasers had to be Michigan residents or commit to moving to the state to occupy their home. Owners also had to commit to rehabilitating the houses and to ensure that they be occupied. These steps, sometimes referred to as "urban homesteading," were intended to populate abandoned neighborhoods and ensure that absentee ownership did not take over the city. While this program did not single-handedly fix Detroit's economic downturn, it did keep downtown neighborhoods together. However, these efforts have been criticized for leading to gentrification and for supporting a corrupt culture of backroom deals between local officials and real estate developers.[11]

Applying the concept of urban homesteading to rural Appalachia, journalist and philanthropist Jim Branscombe proposed an Appalachian Homestead

Act in a series of opinion pieces leading up to the 2016 presidential election. His idea was for the federal government to purchase unreclaimed mine lands from absentee corporations and turn them over to local use. Branscombe did not offer many details about how this transfer of land would work, but we can look to the example of urban homesteading in Detroit as an example. First, an Appalachian Land Bank Authority would need to be established. This agency would use a combination of tax foreclosure and federal funds (perhaps the Abandoned Mine Lands [AML] funds administered by the Office of Surface Mining and Reclamation Enforcement) to acquire former surface mine sites from absentee corporations and make them available to coalfield residents.[12]

Branscombe envisioned his Homestead Act as a way to bring mountain people out of poverty: "The Appalachian Homestead Act may be today's single best solution to the enduring problem of mountain poverty. And it may well be the most important opportunity for a new generation looking for a place to build an economy and a community that makes sense in a time of global warming and economic dysfunction."[13] While homesteading has a historic precedent of redistributing land in the United States, previous federal efforts, such as the Homestead Act of 1862, added to systemic oppression of Native Americans, removing Indigenous people from their lands and cultures. These consequences are in opposition to the principles of just transition, which connects self-determination and ecological health to larger issues of justice, including addressing systemic racism and other forces of oppression. Indigenous "land back" movements aim to "get Indigenous lands back into the hands of indigenous peoples." While similar to the ideas proposed by Branscombe and others, Indigenous claims to land across the United States, and indeed in Appalachia, precede any claims by non-Indigenous Appalachians to the land. Yet this history is not addressed in these homesteading proposals. In order to be effective, the Appalachian Homestead Act must redistribute land through a democratic process designed to increase local control of resources, as well as take into account Indigenous claims to Appalachian land. Branscombe's idea is not clearly defined enough to ensure a just transition, but there is room to build on his ideas.[14]

The major unresolved question with the Appalachian Homestead Act is how to ensure that land is redistributed in order to break the extractive cycle that has dominated the coalfields for more than a century. The original incarnation of the Community Action Agencies formed during the Johnson administration's "War on Poverty" may provide one example. The mandate for these agencies was to encourage "maximum feasible participation of the poor." If the goal of the Appalachian Homestead Act is to promote economic diversification, then actively engaging low-income residents is necessary to achieve this vision.[15]

The Commons Communities Act

In his 2017 book *Ramp Hollow: The Ordeal of Appalachia*, historian Steven Stoll combines the ideas of communal living and homesteading into a proposal called the Commons Communities Act. Stoll's intention is to redistribute land to residents of the Appalachian coalfields. Stoll writes, "I wrote the Commons Communities Act after months of thinking about how the people of the southern mountains might find work with dignity, working for themselves and their families without owing their existences to corporations. I thought that government could help to solve this problem and do what it should do: stand between citizens and the power of capital."[16]

Citing the failure of federal agencies that focus exclusively on a capital driven model of development, such as the Appalachian Regional Commission, Stoll proposes that the federal government increase taxes on the top 1 percent of earners. This, combined with an "Industrial Abandonment Tax" on absentee corporations would be used to purchase land to "provide the ecological base for hunting and gathering, cattle grazing, timber harvesting, vegetable gardening, and farming."

He proposes further that the federal Department of Agriculture be charged with organizing communities not just in Appalachia but across the United States. Despite the federal oversight, Stoll believes that each community should develop its own governing principles. While acknowledging the similarity of his proposal to Arthurdale, he points out important differences between the New Deal experiment and his proposed commons communities: "It has no factory, no originating debt, and no presumption that people must subsist entirely from gardens. It emphasizes scientific conservation, cultural expression, entrepreneurship, and democracy."[17]

Many of Stoll's ideas for his commons communities echo preindustrial life in Appalachia, such as small-scale food production and hunting and gathering from the forest commons. He highlights that ecological principles designed to conserve the diverse ecosystem of the Appalachians are directly connected to economic diversity and to principles of a just transition. While Stoll considers this as "more of a thought experiment than a ready-made policy," his ideas might inspire more feasible methods to increase communal control of land.[18]

Federal Legislation and a Just Transition

In the past decade, a series of federal policies have been put forward that have the potential to support a just transition in the Appalachian coalfields. The RECLAIM Act was originally proposed in 2017. It proposed the use of AML funds to support local economies through the development of projects focused on renewable energy, agriculture, wildlife habitats, and recreational tourism. Similarly, the nationally focused Green New Deal was intended to address the need for job opportunities and the need to address global climate change at the same time. However, both of these acts failed to pass Congress.

Important elements of both policies, including extra funding for reclamation and investment in green jobs, were included in the Infrastructure Investment and Jobs Act that passed in 2022. This increased funding has the potential to provide direct support for a just transition in the coalfields, but questions remain: Will it be enough, and will it be democratically distributed?

One can imagine that, like the RECLAIM Act, a first step toward community land ownership might be providing the funding for communities to use the land in new and sustainable ways. Perhaps once work is being done on abandoned mine lands, then the argument to transfer land ownership from private holdings to local communal ownership would be more palatable for those who balk at the idea of communal ownership.

These examples of federal legislation demonstrate that there is a clearly recognized need to address the lack of economic opportunity and environmental sustainability in the region. Perhaps this is an encouraging sign that there might be some economic help on the way to the region; however, without ownership of the means and modes of production, Appalachian people will remain beholden to the same capitalist forces that have created inequitable livelihoods through extractive industries. Both Branscombe and Stoll argue that land ownership must be redistributed, and for Stoll this is essential for returning dignity to residents. To date federal legislation has not guaranteed that private interests will not extract profit from people in Appalachia—something that both Branscombe and Stoll attempt to address in the transfer of land ownership to communities.

The Not-So-Tragic Commons

In the Global South, where many communities still face the overt detrimental effects of colonialism and imperialism, scholars have noted the ways that communal ownership of land and other natural resources can increase quality of life and the agency of local residents. While the idea of Appalachia as an "internal colony" has been debunked, there are still useful lessons from communities around the world in thinking about the utility of communal ownership of natural resources.[19]

In response to the "tragedy of the commons" thesis that ecologist Garret Hardin popularized in 1968, political economist Elinor Ostrom and others have challenged this critique of the commons, suggesting that Hardin did not take into account the agreements that most commons communities implement to inhibit resource depletion. In fact, as anthropologist Arun Agarwal argues, multiple broad-based studies have demonstrated that "small local groups can design institutional arrangements to help manage resources sustainably." Anthropologists Amanda Lee Stronza and Katja Neves-Graca have similarly argued that communities in the Global South are best suited to manage their own common-pool natural resources, in part because of their traditional ecological knowledge of resource management and in part because of the direct benefits to communities in terms of economics and organizational capacity. Agarwal further argues that state and private ownership have failed to protect natural resources and provide equitable employment opportunities for communities. Might Appalachian communities argue that private owners (i.e., coal companies) have not done their due diligence in protecting natural resources? In the Global South, these arguments have made their way into policy decisions, allowing people to increase ownership over their own resources and therefore increase control over their own lives.[20]

Where Do We Go from Here?

Examples from the Global South are instructive in thinking about how communities that have been exploited can begin to regain control over their own lives and livelihoods. In his Appalachian Homestead Act, Branscombe argues that people in Appalachia need access to land—land for farming, reforesting, and recreation. He sees land as key to a diversified economy and thriving agricultural communities in Appalachia. What needs to be better parsed out is a democratic process for deciding how the land will be used as well as ideas for reparations for Indigenous populations who have been forced off their land or those who are otherwise marginalized in Appalachia. Furthermore, it will be important to consider safeguards that will make sure that new types of private interests are not able to take control of the regions' natural resources or labor. In his idea for commons communities, Stoll rightly acknowledges that private interests are not going to invest in a new kind of economy based on communal landownership. But he also realizes that the government has the funds and power to help make these communities a reality—there is hope that new federal legislation will pave the way for such a shift in government funding and transfer of land ownership. One issue that both Stoll and Branscombe fail to address is that people in Appalachia may not want to return to agricultural lifestyles but may have other viable ideas for what to do with the land. There should be space for this kind of flexibility in public policy.

Land reform in Appalachia is a difficult and complex subject. The displacement and genocide of Indigenous peoples by European colonizers started a cycle of absentee ownership, inequity, and wealth disparity. The process of industrialization continued this legacy. Speaking to the 2017 conference of the Appalachian Studies Association, Elandria Williams of the Highlander Center challenged scholars and activists to think deeply about how connections to the land inform efforts toward a just transition: "I want us to hold what colonization means. And if we want a just transition, it might mean something we don't actually want . . . because it would mean putting the land back into the hands of people who were here before. I want to go beyond just transition, to talk about beautiful solutions that have values at the core that honor our humanity, that honor our soul."[21]

Finding these place-based solutions that honor the complex connections between the Appalachian Mountains and the people who live there may be the single most important step toward building a better future for our region.

Privately owned land is deeply ingrained in the US legal system, and critics of communal land ownership point to the tragedy of the commons as a reason to continue promoting the neoliberal values of private ownership. However, lessons from the Global South show that communal ownership can work to provide local communities with control over their own livelihoods and futures. Several of the solutions to land inequity we discussed rely on government intervention, but we note that government intervention (especially through processes such as eminent domain) has historically resulted in disenfranchising Indigenous people and perpetuating inequitable distribution of land and power. While we cannot pretend to have the perfect solution to the problems of inequitable land ownership, our goal in this chapter is to advance public discussion and spark new ideas. Clearly a diverse group of people, including Indigenous, low-income, and people of color, will need to be involved in creating equitable solutions to land ownership and supporting a just transition for Appalachia.

Notes

1. Anne Lewis, dir., *On Our Own Land* (Whitesburg, KY: Appalshop Films, 1988).

2. Shaunna L. Scott and Kathryn Engle, "Introduction," in *Just Transitions* (Lexington: University of Press of Kentucky, 2025).

3. Freeman Owle, interview in *Appalachia: A History of Mountains and People: Part 2 New Green World*, dir. Ross Spears (James Agee Film Project, 2009).

4. West Virginia Department of Arts, Culture, and History, "Dr. Thomas Walker and the Loyal Company," 2019, http://www.wvculture.org/history/settlement/loyalcompany02.html; Wilma A. Dunaway, *The First American Frontier: Transition to Capitalism in Southern Appalachia, 1700–1860*, Fred W. Morrison Series in Southern Studies (Chapel Hill: University of North Carolina Press, 1996); Like Manget, "Nature's Emporium: The Botanical Drug Trade and the Commons: Tradition in Southern Appalachia, 1847–1917," *Environmental History* 21, no. 4 (2016): 660–87.

5. Ronald D. Eller, *Miners, Millhands, and Mountaineers: Industrialization of the Appalachian South, 1880–1930* (Knoxville: University of Tennessee Press, 1982); John Alexander Williams, *Appalachia: A History* (Chapel Hill: University of North Carolina Press, 1982/2002).

6. Tom Miller, "Who Owns West Virginia?," *Huntington Herald-Dispatch*, December 1974.

7. Ben A. Franklin, "Appalachian Regional Study Finds Absentee Ownership of 43% of Land," *New York Times*, April 5, 1981, sect. I, p. 28.

8. West Virginia Department of Arts, Culture, and History, "Dr. Thomas Walker and the Loyal Company"; Danielle Dulkin, "A Black Kingdom in Postbellum Appalachia," *Scalawag Magazine*, September 9, 2019, https://scalawagmagazine.org/2019/09/black-appalachia-kingdom.

9. C. J. Maloney, *Back to the Land: Arthurdale, FDR's New Deal, and the Costs of Economic Planning* (Hoboken, NJ: Wiley, 2011).

10. Richard Haid, *Arthurdale: An Experiment in Community Planning 1933–1947* (Morgantown: West Virginia University Press, 1975).

11. Detroit Land Bank Authority, "Second Amended and Restated Articles of Incorporation of Detroit Land Bank Authority," December 23, 2013; Erick Trickey, "How Detroit Is Beating Its Blight," *Politico Magazine*, May 18, 2017.

12. James Branscombe, "Create a Homestead Act for Appalachia's Rebirth," *Lexington Herald-Leader*, May 20, 2016.

13. Branscombe, "Create a Homestead Act."

14. Land Back, "Land Back Manifesto," https://landback.org/manifesto, accessed December 2, 2020.

15. United States Congress, The Economic Opportunity Act of 1964, Pub. L. 88-452 (August 20, 1964).

16. Steven Stoll, *Ramp Hollow: The Ordeal of Appalachia* (New York: Hill and Wang, 2017), 272.

17. Stoll, *Ramp Hollow*, 274.

18. Stoll, *Ramp Hollow*, 272.

19. Mary Anglin, "Toward a New Politics of Outrage and Transformation: Placing Appalachia within the Global Political Economy," *Journal of Appalachian Studies* 22, no. 1 (2016): 51–56; Dwight Billings, "Rethinking Class beyond Colonialism," *Journal of Appalachian Studies* 22, no. 1 (2016): 57–64; Stephen L. Fisher and Barbara Ellen Smith, "Reinventing the Region: Defining, Theorizing, Organizing Appalachia," *Journal of Appalachian Studies* 22, no. 1 (2016): 76–79.

20. Elinor Ostrom, *Governing the Commons: The Evolution of Institutions for Collective Action* (Cambridge: Cambridge University Press, 1990); Arun Agawal, "Sustainable Governance of Common Pool Resources: Context, Methods, and Politics," *Annual Review of Anthropology* 32 (2003): 248; Amanda Lee Stronza, "Commons Management and Ecotourism: Ethnographic Evidence from the Amazon," *International Journal of the Commons* 4, no. 1 (2010): 56–77; Katja Nevez-Graca, "Revisiting the Tragedy of the Commons: Ecological Dilemmas of Whale Watching in the Azores," *Human Organization* 63, no. 3 (2004): 289–300.

21. Elandria Williams, "Extreme Appalachia! Rage and Renewal" (paper presentation, the Appalachian Studies Association Annual Conference at Virginia Polytechnic Institute and State University, Blacksburg, VA, March 11, 2017).

7

Seeding Just Transitions through Local Food and Agriculture Systems

KATHRYN ENGLE, ELYZABETH W. ENGLE, CANDACE MULLINS, MARTIN RICHARDS, AND MAGGIE SMITH MOSLEY

Local foods and agriculture have emerged as central components of a renewed Appalachian economy. Government and development agencies—for example, the Appalachian Regional Commission (ARC)—see the cultivation of local foods as a mechanism for community economic development and as a potential alternative to coal mining. The ARC identified local food as a targeted investment sector in its 2016–2020 strategic plan and has supported dozens of community-based projects in partnership with other federal agencies through the "Local Foods, Local Places" program. The 2022 ARC report "Agriculture and Local Food Economies in the Appalachian Region" further highlighted ways agriculture and local food present opportunities for economic development.[1] At the state level, Kentucky's SOAR (Shaping Our Appalachian Region) initiative has regional food systems as part of its "blueprint."[2]

Citizens' groups have also renewed interest in centering post-coal futures on agriculture. Over the past few decades, regional and subregional agricultural organizations have grown in strength and number. Organizations including Appalachian Sustainable Agriculture Project (ASAP), headquartered in Asheville, North Carolina; Appalachian Sustainable Development (ASD), in southwest Virginia; the West Virginia Food and Farm Coalition, headquartered in Charleston; the Appalachian Resource Conservation & Development Council, in east Tennessee; and Rural Action, in southeast Ohio, work to make connections between producers and consumers and promote sustainability. These organizations and networks offer programs promoting economic diversification and food and agriculture in the region.[3]

Local foods promise a variety of benefits, including increased income for farmers, fresher and healthier food for consumers, and less fuel consumed during transportation. Local foods have the potential to help mitigate climate change impacts and can promote more just economic arrangements and labor practices. In the coalfields, agriculture has been proposed as a different way to use or reclaim abandoned mine land. Such projects have the potential to address health disparities and obesity, increase food security, build social capital, and create local jobs.[4]

Direct sales, farmers' markets, community-supported agriculture (CSA), food hubs, farm-to-school programs, community gardens, gleaning programs, food preservation programs, local foods networking organizations, community kitchens, local processing facilities, farm-to-table restaurants, and organic production programs have sprung up across the region. Regional branding programs, like Kentucky's "Appalachia Proud," seek to capitalize on renewed interest in "buying local." National interest in regionally unique cuisine has highlighted Appalachian foodways and local traditions, as initiatives like the Appalachian Food Summit seek to expand networks supportive of localized agricultural and food systems. The diversity of food and agricultural traditions found in the region complicate essentialist notions of Appalachia as a white, homogenous place. Food has the potential to play an important part in just transitions in the region.[5]

This chapter examines the intersecting work of three grassroots organizations that promote local food-systems development in Central Appalachia: Community Farm Alliance (CFA), Grow Appalachia, and the Knox County Farmers' Market (KCFM). Written collaboratively by local food activists and researchers, this chapter examines both policy and on-the-ground practices to explore how local foods and agriculture relate to economic and community development and present possibilities for just transitions in the region. These case studies offer suggestions for local food-systems development: building grassroots dialogue, creating successful models, and influencing public policy; centering community capacity building and working together across organizations; and promoting relocalization, presenting different representations, and expanding access.

Community Farm Alliance

Community Farm Alliance was formed in 1985 during the 1980 Farm Crisis by Kentucky farmers to bring grassroots voices to public policy in support of Kentucky's small, disadvantaged family farmers and the communities that depend on them. By (1) elevating constructive grassroots dialogue, (2) building successful models, and (3) securing good public policy, CFA has supported the development of a sustainable local food and farm system for forty years.

In the 1990s, Kentucky's tobacco farming families were coming to a crisis point over the future of tobacco. CFA members began to think about a just transition for farming's future beyond tobacco. CFA leaders saw local food systems as the best opportunity to maintain family-scale agriculture and rural communities. Through model market development, such as four urban, low-income farmers' markets and farm-to-school demonstration projects, CFA members quickly learned firsthand that local food systems have the potential to create jobs, improve health, alleviate poverty, and create community resilience.

Through this work, they also saw the disparity between populations who could access fresh, local, and healthy food and those who could not. By 2000, food justice, access, and security became an integral part of CFA's work to support not only good family farm policy but also good food policy. Through research and publications such as *The Greenprint: A Long Term Plan for Kentucky's Agricultural Economy* (2001), *Bringing Kentucky's Food and Farming Economy Home* (2003), *and Bridging the Divide* (2007), CFA laid the groundwork for building an organization in which urban folks, especially people of color, low-income, and other disadvantaged groups, have equity. As Cassia Heron, CFA's first urban woman of color board chair (2012) succinctly summarized at a leadership gathering, "For Kentuckians, the conditions in 'hoods and hollers aren't much different." Just transition is not just about transforming extractive economies into something else; it's about preserving a culture and including the history of a place into a new vision for the economy. Urban or rural, the histories have clear geographic differences, but the issues communities face are systematic.[6]

The connections between poverty, nutrition, and community economics are becoming increasingly apparent across the state of Kentucky. Agriculture in all its forms, but especially those tied to the development of local and regional food systems, has emerged a bright spot for eastern Kentucky as it transitions from its dependency on coal. As in much of Central Appalachia, openly discussing the future of eastern Kentucky is often difficult because of the social, economic, cultural, and political dominance of the coal industry. Much like communities dependent on tobacco, coal-dominated communities are fearful of losing not only an economic base but also a cultural identity. Nevertheless, CFA's organizing efforts in eastern Kentucky show that the people remain resilient and, when given real, viable options for improving their lives, they can commit to shared community and economic development goals. CFA's efforts are proving what has been suspected: food and local agriculture offer nonpolarizing pathways to economic opportunities. Often at odds over coal and economic issues, people are willing to come together around food, leading to far-reaching, productive conversations—conversations that can ultimately address the creation of a sustainable future for eastern Kentucky and Appalachia.

CFA's mission is to organize and encourage cooperation among rural and urban citizens, through leadership development and grassroots democratic processes, to ensure an essential, prosperous place for family-scale agriculture in our economies and communities. In other words, an economic and social transition begins with constructive grassroots dialogue, is built on successful models, and is secured with good public policy.

Grassroots Dialogue

People know their problems and have a pretty good idea of how to address them but typically don't know where to begin to create change. CFA helps people organize to define the problem, identify barriers, find needed resources, create a plan to make change, and build leadership to give a voice and face to the problem. CFA utilizes a story-based communications strategy, using personal stories to define problems and solutions, and has conducted grassroots dialogues within eastern Kentucky through the "Breaking Beans: Food Story Project" to illuminate issues and offer solutions. These stories highlight the conversations and work occurring throughout the region and tell the personal stories of practitioners and advocates working in food and agriculture in eastern Kentucky.[7]

Successful Models

Because of an inequity of opportunity and resources, people are challenged to overcome poverty. The poor are circumstantially and often intentionally marginalized from society, with little representation or voice in public policy. With the onset of the Great Recession in 2008, farming reemerged in eastern Kentucky—often out of necessity. Not surprisingly, from these efforts people began looking to agriculture as a way to make a living. CFA's role has been to collaboratively work with other organizations and beginning farmers to identify their needs, connect them to resources, and network them with existing farmers to build models for programs and frameworks that can enact change.

In November 2010, CFA and Mountain Association (formerly Mountain Association for Community Economic Development) began exploring how the two organizations could work together to support emerging sustainable agriculture efforts. CFA, Mountain Association, and the Appalachian Center at the University of Kentucky launched the Eastern Kentucky Food System Collaborative (EKY FSC) in 2011 to bring together organizations and individuals interested in realizing the benefits of a food system in eastern Kentucky. The collaborative determined that the priority issues in eastern Kentucky were:

a. Supporting farmers, especially new farmers
b. Developing markets, especially supporting farmers' markets
c. Creating community gardens to educate and building food security, with a special focus on children
d. Educating the public about food, nutrition, and economic impact.

The EKY FSC laid the foundation for defining CFA's program of work in eastern Kentucky and helped cultivate a collaboration of allied organizations and funding partners to support:

- The needs of new and beginning farmers through the Ag Legacy Initiative (ALI), which today is seen in the Central Appalachian Family Farm Fund and the Kentucky Black Farmer Fund[8]
- Equitable food system entry at farmers' markets for farmers and consumers through the Farmers Market Support Program (FMSP), including the Kentucky Double Dollars Program for SNAP (Supplemental Nutrition Assistance Program) / WIC (Women, Infants, and Children) / SFMNP (Seniors Farmers' Market Nutrition Program), and piloting the first rural farmers' market in the nation as a USDA Summer Feeding Program site[9]
- The EKY Farm Table Program for institutional market food hub development[10]
- Technical assistance for the creation of community food system assessments that have facilitated communities to inventory how their current food and farm system is functioning and identify areas of growth to make it stronger[11]
- Peer-to-peer learning opportunities such as the Eastern Kentucky Farmers Conference and the Central Appalachian Network's 2022 virtual series "A Fair Food System: A Summit on Scalable Solutions to Creating Community Food Systems," which included sessions relating to healthy food access, climate change, and crisis management due to pandemic impacts and flooding[12]

Public Policy

CFA members believe that the people most affected should have a say in addressing their social, economic, and environmental problems. Transformational, systematic change typically happens incrementally, the result of the persistent pursuit of incremental wins that eventually add up to a whole greater than the sum. However, incremental reinforcing change depends on the creation of a democratic, transparent process with supportive resources. With renewed federal, state, and local political leadership, what has been largely a grassroots movement supported by private philanthropy is becoming sustainable.

CFA organizes for policy change by lending an ear to the community and seeking patterns that point to the need for political action. Once identified,

CFA begins working with the community to develop a model project that then serves as an example for how policy could make a larger more sustainable impact. Since 1985, CFA members have influenced over two dozen pieces of legislation to support Kentucky farmers and the rural and urban communities that depend on them.[13] CFA members successfully applied this approach in helping Kentucky create a transition process, supportive policies, and programs for tobacco communities under Kentucky HB 611 and the creation of the Kentucky Agriculture Development Fund (KADF) to disburse $1.7 billion over twenty-five years. Utilizing grassroots voices, CFA has helped create the Kentucky Food Action Network and, advocating for a permanent state fund, the Healthy Farm and Food Innovation Fund, to sustainably address Kentucky's persistent food insecurity and nutrition related health crisis.

Pathways to Change

In the face of the COVID-19 pandemic, continued systemic inequity, and ongoing climate impacts like flooding and drought, CFA's work cuts across everything that is dividing Kentucky and America. These crises require finding short- and long-term solutions and critically evaluating and addressing the social and economic systems that disadvantage the most vulnerable among us. This journey has created the Central Appalachian Family Farm Fund and the Kentucky Black Farmer Fund as evergreen funds to support farmers and is moving CFA forward on its strategic plan, the *Pathway to Change,* and toward our long-term priority of ensuring that "Kentucky has an organized and diverse family farm, food, and fiber coalition that effectively influences and creates political, social, and economic change."[14]

The physical and human infrastructure developed for Kentucky Double Dollars and the FMSP helped to mitigate recent crises by providing both consumers and producers in Kentucky important safety nets. Our ultimate goal is to build an equitable and accessible food system that provides fresh, nutritious food to all while generating community wealth by investing in both the physical and the social infrastructure.[15]

Grow Appalachia

Since 2010, Grow Appalachia has addressed food insecurity in Central Appalachia through home and community garden initiatives, foodways, farming, and hunger relief programming. Grow Appalachia, a Strategic Initiative of Berea College, began in 2010 with a mission to "help as many Appalachian families grow as much of their own food as possible," initially supporting the installation of backyard and community gardens in four eastern Kentucky counties. In its first year, Grow Appalachia worked with one hundred families who produced 120,000 pounds of food for their families and communities. Ten years later, Grow Appalachia has worked with more than six thousand families in six Central Appalachian states to produce more than four million pounds of food.[16] While "just transition" may not be the specific phrase used to describe the mission of Grow Appalachia, the principle is embedded in its core as it enables place-based initiatives that support human and environmental flourishing by promoting organic food production, community food security, local economic opportunity, and relationship building.

The following section knits together two insider-outsider perspectives to (1) provide a brief history of the Grow Appalachia organization, (2) detail the evolution of its mission and scope, and (3) provide lessons learned about how the organization's garden grants program has contributed to just transitions in Central Appalachia through building community capacity and organizational networks.[17] The reflections shared in this section are from the perspective of Candace Mullins, who began as Grow Appalachia's associate director in 2012 and transitioned to executive director in 2021. In addition, further reflections are gleaned from a collaborative research project (2016–2018) between Grow Appalachia headquarters and Elly Engle, then a doctoral student in rural sociology at Pennsylvania State University. Drawing on interviews, field observations, and program-wide surveys, Elly sought to understand how Grow Appalachia programming was translated from the Berea headquarters to their partner sites to their participants' gardens, as well as how the programming contributed to community development throughout the coal-impacted regions of Central Appalachia.

Ten+ Years of Growing Appalachia

Since Grow Appalachia started in 2010, the organization's core programs have been centered on access to resources and education around backyard gardening. This work involves subgranting funds to Appalachian community-based organizations that provide social services to their communities. The partnering organizations are provided with financial, educational, and technical assistance; and garden grants are used to establish organic home, community, and institutional gardening sites. This framework supports a network of organizations in the Appalachian coalfields (and beyond) to address their local food security needs and new economic opportunities with their own leadership and outreach.

Grow Appalachia has continued evolving to include a greater breadth of programming aimed at short-, medium- and long-term approaches to food security. Grow staff and partners quickly realized that while home and communal gardening is the best long-term approach to addressing food insecurity at the household level, there are many steps along the way that can be elevated to support a healthy, viable, and just agricultural economy for Central Appalachia overall. Addressing one part of the food system without addressing the others would leave out important opportunities to build from work that has been ongoing for decades, including agricultural initiatives as well as those in other sectors. To support thriving and just transitions, "Grow Appalachia partners with families, communities, and organizations in Appalachia to create healthy, resilient, and economically viable food systems."[18]

From Grow Appalachia's perspective, addressing rural food insecurity requires an examination of the whole food system in order to tailor programs and resource distribution to individual and community needs. Food insecurity is experienced differently, and while backyard growing areas are abundant for many residents of Central Appalachia, that is not the case for everyone. Further, food insecurity has a variety of origins, including un- and underemployment, lack of access to produce and grocery stores, and transportation challenges. While Grow Appalachia does not primarily seek to address unemployment, labor wages, transportation, or the prevalence of food markets, its programs have evolved to acknowledge and adapt to these issues while still meeting the initial goal of increasing access to nutritious food. In this way, Grow Appalachia sees small-scale food production as not just a means to household food security but also a necessary step and exciting opportunity for laying the foundation for just transitions.

For example, after its initial years of investing in garden programming and resources for families throughout the region, Grow Appalachia began to encourage market garden development in 2011 as a means to provide supplemental income for households. To date, Grow Appalachia has invested in a dozen farmers' markets, supported infrastructure purchases for market gardeners and farmers' markets, and created programming to help transition home gardeners to produce goods for sale as well as subsistence. Since 2010, market gardeners in the program have seen more than $710,000 in sales across the region. For many market gardeners, value-added products have been a critical component to year-round sales, which is why Grow Appalachia has also supported the development of more than eight commercial community kitchens across the region. These spaces allow market gardeners to create shelf-stable products year-round.

Supporting market garden ventures helped Grow Appalachia see the need for affordable and accessible growing supplies and equipment for small-scale producers. Many growers were unable to source affordable soil amendments, high-quality farm infrastructure, or other growing supplies in their respective geographic areas. Additionally, although small-scale farmers had access to some technical assistance for marketing, business development, and capital through community development financial institutions, state departments of agriculture, nonprofits and university extension agencies, there was a lack of production planning to support scaling up to increase efficiency. These gaps led Grow Appalachia to develop a social enterprise initiative to increase farmers' access to resources, infrastructure, and technical assistance. Since 2010, Grow Appalachia has built more than 150 high tunnels for farmers and nonprofit agencies in order to support year-round production of food throughout Central Appalachia.

Additionally, through their work with community partners, Grow Appalachia observed that many families struggled to afford food costs when school was out of session. Due to increased costs of fresh foods, limited cooking experience, and time constraints, many families must choose food quantity over quality. Subsequently, Grow Appalachia developed the Berea Kids Eat program as a means to support immediate hunger relief initiatives in Berea, Kentucky. Since 2016, Berea Kids Eat has operated a year-round feeding program that has served more than 128,000 meals, started a Junior Farmers' Market, and provided critical support for nutrition education for families in Berea. These initiatives are also being implemented at Grow Appalachia partnering sites, such as the Cowan Community Center in Letcher County, Kentucky. The Letcher County Farmers' Market has supported a summer feeding program for more than five years while also facilitating a vegetable prescription program in partnership with a local health-care provider, Mountain Comprehensive Healthcare, for residents to access produce at the farmers' market via a "Veggie Prescription" from their doctors.

These initiatives target varied needs throughout the region by supplying the resources, assistance, and experience necessary to support household food security and professional development of beginning farmers. By weaving together these programs, Grow Appalachia takes a full-system approach to addressing community food security and food-systems development, making just transitions through food and agriculture possible at the community level throughout the Appalachian region.

Growing Capacity by Growing Gardens

While Grow Appalachia's programming has expanded to include many different food systems–based initiatives, the garden grants program remains the backbone of Grow Appalachia's community outreach work. Annually, Grow Appalachia headquarters solicits applications from community-based nonprofit organizations throughout Central Appalachia that wish to establish or expand garden programming. Since 2010, Grow Appalachia has worked with a diverse array of partner sites, including social service organizations, extension offices, educational institutions, cultural heritage centers, and economic development organizations. Partner sites have also varied widely in size, serving anywhere from 10 to over 150 households on an annual basis. When accepted into the garden grant program, partner site organizations are provided with financial, technical, and educational resources. Each partner site also has an appointed site coordinator who manages reporting, grant applications, workshops, and the distribution of resources.

Grow Appalachia intentionally designed—and redeveloped over time, based on experience—their garden grant program to build short- and long-term household and community resilience. When reviewing proposals for partner sites, Grow Appalachia prioritizes applications from organizations and coordinators that can demonstrate a history of connection, trust, and experience within their home community. Once awarded the garden grant, the site coordinators are given broad latitude in how they choose to set up their partner site, from the recruitment of gardener participants to development of educational workshops to the creation of local social enterprise initiatives. Headquarters does provide a basic backbone for implementation, including a commitment to garden through the growing season, hosting six required gardening/food workshops, avoiding income caps for gardener participants, and providing ongoing support for single-parent households, grandparents doing caretaking as parents, and disabled or elderly gardeners. Otherwise, partner sites are encouraged to translate the programming in ways that build on and adhere to local assets, history, and biophysical context.

For example, some partner sites have an abundance of volunteer resources that help them carry out other initiatives within their nonprofit programs. At partner sites like Red Bird Mission, a nonprofit organization that has been in Bell County, Kentucky, since 1921, many of these volunteers help to organize bulk seed orders for gardeners, sort plants, support the farmers' market, provide weeding or planting support for elderly gardeners, or teach classes. Volunteers allow Red Bird Mission to use time and resources elsewhere that would have otherwise been part of the Grow Appalachia budget. That said, a volunteer-based model would not work in all partner site locations and has even sometimes been to the detriment of local programs when volunteer turnover has led to program instability.

Land is another asset that some partner sites may utilize in their programs. Pine Mountain Settlement School, for instance, is a nonprofit organization that has been in Harlan County, Kentucky, for more than a hundred years; it has had a long-standing history of focusing on education and support within the community. Founded with a strong working farm, Pine Mountain Settlement School had decreased agricultural programming until becoming a Grow Appalachia partner in 2010. The farm not only has grown in productivity but also serves as a demonstration farm for Grow Appalachia participants to learn new practices directly in the field. Not all partner sites have access to abundant land, but when it is available, it has been found to lead to invaluable in-person learning opportunities.

Additionally, Grow Appalachia strives to build local resilience by creating flexible funding channels and opportunities for leadership development. Unlike other community food grant programs, Grow Appalachia allows their garden grants funds to be used for nontraditional, but necessary, resources like travel and labor. While the garden grant funds are often used to purchase equipment and other gardening and food processing resources (e.g., seeds, fertilizer, pressure cookers for canning), they can also provide social networking and education through garden visits and community gatherings. By allowing for funds to be spent on labor, Grow Appalachia aims to create sustainable part-time jobs for their partner site coordinators and others who maintain the programs at the community level. Since 2010, Grow Appalachia has supported 697 full- and part-time positions across the region. Site coordinators are almost always from the communities in which they work. Some site coordinators even began as participants in the program, learning the key pieces of garden programming from the basic level and then transitioning to garden mentors and eventually site coordinators. One site coordinator, for example, began as a participant, transitioned to site coordinator, and was promoted to associate director and then executive director of his nonprofit organization. It's clear that Grow Appalachia is a leadership and community development catalyst. Most coordinators are plugged into their communities and often know the best places to source resources as well as find community partners and leaders to help teach classes and till gardens.

Local resilience is also built by Grow Appalachia's regional approach to leadership and food-system development. To support professional development as well as networking, collaboration, and resource sharing on a regional level, Grow Appalachia hosts an annual gathering of its site coordinators and staff at Berea College. This annual gathering includes orientation activities for new partner sites as well as ongoing professional development and program-planning activities for returning partner sites. In the spirit of colearning and celebration, senior partner sites also share presentations on lessons learned in the creation of successful site initiatives. Additionally, Grow Appalachia organizes its partner sites into regional groups that work together in breakout groups during the annual gathering and also lean on one another throughout the growing season to share in goals, challenges, and wins.

These collaborations have been encouraged from the beginning. Most regional groups facilitate bulk supply purchases, regional policy work, and shared educational instructors. Some evolve into larger projects and partnerships. For example, a multistate regional group made up of three Grow Appalachia partner sites focused in eastern Tennessee and southwestern Virginia partnered on a federal grant to support the growth and development of market gardeners and beginning farmers. The program provides training for beginning farmers on small-scale farming practices; the training operates in two sessions that include both classroom learning and on-farm experience. In five years, the program has worked with more than 160 beginning farmers. Collaborating across county and state lines helps leverage resources that some Grow sites might not have previously been able to access due to geographic boundaries or lack of experience or relationships. In this way, leadership and community development work together to support a stronger regional food system.

Conclusions from Grow Appalachia

Grow Appalachia's mission is—and has always been—centered on food. Its programs all promote food security but not from a standpoint of deficiency or charity. Instead, Grow Appalachia uses food as a way to celebrate and leverage the assets of Central Appalachian communities and people toward creating a more sustainable future that embraces cultural traditions, economic justice, and a connection to the land and to each other. Through site-driven programming, flexible resource channels, professional development of local leaders, and regional network building, Grow Appalachia strives to build self-sufficient, resilient, and connected organizations and communities that can feed themselves and each other. In this way, Grow Appalachia builds foundation community capacity for building *further* capacity, using household and community food security initiatives as well as broader food-systems development as a transitional pathway to brighter, more just futures for the region overall.

Knox County Farmers' Market

Farmers' markets—a primary feature of local food systems nationally and in Appalachia—are on the rise. According to the Kentucky Department of Agriculture, in 1993 there were only 43 farmers' markets registered with the state. In 2003, there were 85; by 2013, there were 149; and, in 2022, there were 174 registered farmers' markets in Kentucky—covering nearly every county in the state. The Kentucky Department of Agriculture's "Appalachia Proud" program began in 2014 to highlight and promote agriculture in Kentucky's fifty-four

Appalachian counties. There are now farmers' markets in every Appalachian county in the Commonwealth. Knox County, located in southeastern Kentucky, is one of them. Begun in 2014 with support from both Grow Appalachia and the Community Farm Alliance, the Knox County Farmers' Market (KCFM) has grown into a vibrant community institution that promotes local food and agriculture. The development and work of the KCFM shows the importance of (1) relocalizing food systems, (2) providing new representations of agricultural and economic possibilities, and (3) expanding access through partnerships.[19]

Knox County, like many communities in Central Appalachia, has been impacted by the long, steady decline of the coal industry. Knox County has a rich history of logging and coal mining, although these sectors currently make up a small percentage of the total employment of the area. The county is considered economically distressed by the Appalachian Regional Commission (ARC) and has a poverty rate of 39.2 percent and a population of 31,687. Many depend on government assistance programs, with 35.1 percent of the county participating in SNAP, also known as food stamps. Obesity and other chronic health concerns as well as food access continue to present challenges.[20]

At the same time, southeastern Kentucky has a rich history of gardening and agriculture. Although direct marketing and roadside stands have always been present in the county, previous attempts at establishing a formal farmers' market have not been successful. In June 2014, the idea for KCFM emerged from conversations between local farmers and folks affiliated with the Knox County Health Department, Union College (now Union Commonwealth University), and the Lend-A-Hand Center Grow Appalachia Gardening Program. Earlier that year, the Lend-A-Hand Center, a nonprofit community service organization working in the Stinking Creek area of the county, became a Grow Appalachia partner site. The program set up community gardens at local schools, assisted home gardeners in the Stinking Creek area of the county, and provided workshops and gardening materials for gardeners.[21]

Seeing a need for a market, community members formed a committee and researched how to start a market, looking at options for the market in the county seat of Barbourville. This grassroots committee worked to cultivate strategic partners in the community, find sponsors, and recruit vendors, including farmers, gardeners, crafters, and people offering prepared foods. The group made plans for a grand opening and full market season. The committee created marketing materials, selected a location for the market, created market rules, purchased necessary equipment, and planned for entertainment and special activities. The opening market was met with enthusiastic support from the community and continued every Thursday evening through the month of October.

Relocalization and Community Building

As KCFM continued to grow during its first year, the committee formalized into a board of directors, and the market incorporated into a 501(c)(3) nonprofit organization. The board developed vendor regulations, bylaws, and other governing documents, as well as the following mission statement: "The Knox County Farmers' Market's purpose is to provide an opportunity for local food and craft producers to market high-quality products directly to the consumer."[22] The board came up with a set of goals for the market, focusing on networking, economic development, access, education, and sustainability.

Through this process, the board worked to help relocalize agriculture in Knox County and the surrounding area. KCFM provided a venue to help build back some of the local connections, trading arrangements, and relationships that characterized agriculture in the community in the past. It provided an alternative to supermarket chains and encouraged people to meet their needs locally. One of the goals of the market is "to strengthen and promote the growth of local foods in Knox County and beyond, building a network connecting producers and consumers through the production, marketing, financing, and distribution of fresh, local products." Functioning as a nonprofit organization, KCFM provides a weekly place to buy and sell goods and also supports the local food system through education and outreach to both producers and consumers. It finds ways to help support local farmers and build a customer base. It also hosts vendor development programs, encourages young and beginner farmers, shares information about grants and opportunities, hosts cooking demonstrations, hosts agricultural demonstrations, and participates in community events and festivals.[23]

KCFM quickly became an important community institution—a place for people to gather, buy from their neighbors, have a meal, hear local music, buy local crafts, and learn about community organizations and nonprofits set up at the market. People linger after they finish their shopping to develop friendships. As the market continued to grow, relationships of collaboration and reciprocity that were once commonplace became reestablished. The market helped build social capital while providing a place for direct-to-consumer marketing, helping relocalize the food system.

(Re)presentation and Education

In June 2015, Barbourville was selected as one of twenty-six communities nationwide to participate in the "Local Foods, Local Places" program sponsored by the ARC and other federal and state partners. Participation in the program included funding for different KCFM projects and a facilitated strategic-planning process that featured a two-day workshop.[24]

During this workshop, KCFM, community partners, and representatives from state and federal agencies crafted an action plan with goals and plans for the market and local food-systems development in the community. The group stated their aspirations for local foods and defined the steps needed to reach their goals. In the face of the continuing decline of the coal industry and national stereotypes about eastern Kentucky, the community (re)presented agriculture as an integral part of the community. The report showed the possibilities for food and agricultural enterprises to meet needs and spur economic activity. The action plan showed the farmers' market as part of a larger agenda for local food-systems development; it revealed how food related to other issues, including economic development, tourism, health, and equity. The action plan provided a blueprint for the continued growth of the market, many elements of which have been accomplished in the past several years. These included setting up an online presence and finding a permanent site for the market at the Knox County Cooperative Extension pavilion. With the help of the "Local Foods, Local Places" program, KCFM set goals and charted a course for the future.[25]

Many of the elements of the action plan focused on education, already a key aspect of the market. KCFM educates customers about healthy food options, shows the importance of buying locally, and presents the history and impacts of agriculture in the area. KCFM connects farmers and gardeners to resources by identifying grants, best practices, and networking opportunities. It works on behalf of vendors to promote and advertise the market, showing possibilities for both producers and customers. During the height of the pandemic, the market worked to continue to provide assistance to local farmers and a safe venue for customers. Through education and outreach, KCFM represents new possibilities for a post-coal future in the southeastern Kentucky coalfields. By advocating for farming and gardening, and by bringing attention to producers in the area, KCFM centers agriculture as a viable, important, and growing part of the economy.

Expanding Access and Partnerships

In addition to offering a variety of programs, events, and educational opportunities to the local community, KCFM focuses on access and affordability in order to expand its reach to underserved sectors. In order to expand the customer base and provide a service to the community, KCFM began accepting SNAP benefits at the market. It received equipment to process SNAP EBT cards and developed an accounting system that allowed customers to use their card to receive tokens for fresh fruit and vegetables. The vendors could then return the tokens and be reimbursed by the market. The market also applied for WIC Farmers' Market Nutrition Program vouchers and SFMNP vouchers to be distributed in Knox County so that low-income seniors and mothers could more easily purchase produce and other goods at the market.

In order to further increase access for low-income customers, in 2016, KCFM began participating in Community Farm Alliance's FMSP "Double Dollars" program. The program doubles the value of SNAP transactions and state-issued WIC and Seniors vouchers for customers at the market. Customers scan their EBT cards and are issued tokens at twice the value deducted from their EBT cards or represented by their WIC or Seniors vouchers. This has been a boon to the market, helping both farmers and low-income customers. These partnerships have been able to leverage resources and show real impact at the local level, stimulating thousands of dollars of extra economic impact in the county.[26]

Farmers' Markets, Local Food Systems, and Community

Small Appalachian farmers' markets like KCFM have become important community institutions as well as essential elements of the local food system. The development and success of KCFM illustrates how relocalization of food systems and different representations of community narratives are important elements of just transitions. KCFM has cultivated social connections and economic alternatives that demonstrate the potential for local food in the county while expanding access to underserved populations. Not only the market's economic impact but also its community- and relationship-building demonstrate its worth. In an area impacted by the coal industry, KCFM has reframed the conversation about the economy to center collaboration over competition and small local producers and low-income customers over corporations. Faced with continued disruptions including climate change, inequality, and the long-term impacts of the pandemic, grassroots institutions like KCFM are all the more vital in shortening the value chain and promoting sustainability and connection at the local level.

As the experiences of these three organizations show, local agriculture and food-systems development present diverse possibilities for seeding just transitions in the Appalachian region. The decades-long work of CFA shows the need for building grassroots dialogue, creating successful models, and influencing public policy. The region-spanning initiatives of Grow Appalachia show how change can be made by centering community capacity building and working together across organizations. The local-level activities of the KCFM show the importance of promoting relocalization, presenting different representations, and expanding access. Additionally, as can be seen from how these organizations have supported the development of one another's programs, these cases point to the importance and impact of building regional networks of support and growth. Collaboration on food-related initiatives both enables and is enabled by breaking down geopolitical barriers to share resources, networks, and insights.

Looking forward, the work of these organizations can also point to a variety of ways in which food- and agriculture-related community development must continue to grow and adapt in order to support truly just transitions. Flooding, fires, hurricanes, and other climate-related disasters, as well as the COVID-19 pandemic have exacerbated issues of social and economic justice in all parts of society but particularly within our food systems. This has created an opportunity to reenvision what it really means to build resilient and just food systems, including increasing support for producers and consumers of minoritized identities and improving access to financial and physical resources, adaptability in a changing climate, and the continued necessity of regional collaboration to support sustained local impacts. By addressing the gaps and weaknesses of our food systems, both existing ones and those we are cobuilding, we can continue to make meaningful contributions to just futures for all.

Notes

1. Appalachian Regional Commission & KK&P, "Agriculture and Local Food Economies in the Appalachian Region," April 2022, https://www.arc.gov/wp-content/uploads/2022/04/Agriculture-and-Local-Food-Economies-in-the-Appalachian-Region-April-2022.pdf.

2. Steven C. Deller, David Lamie, and Maureen Stickel, "Local Foods Systems and Community Economic Development," *Community Development* 48, no. 5 (October 20, 2017): 612–38; Jean Haskell, "Assessing the Landscape of Local Food in Appalachia," May 1, 2012, https://www.arc.gov/report/assessing-the-landscape-of-local-food-in-appalachia; Charlie Jackson, Allison Perrett, and Katie Descieux, "Agriculture and Food Systems Trends in the Appalachian Region: 2007–2012," Appalachian Regional Commission, Appalachian Sustainable Agriculture Project (ASAP), July 2015, https://www.arc.gov/report/data-maps; Kathryn Webb Farley and Carrie Blanchard Bush, "Using Relationships as Resources in Social Impact Investing: Examining a Local Food Movement in Appalachia," *Journal of Appalachian Studies* 22, no. 2 (2016): 224–44; Joseph "Jody" Holland, "Examining Capacity within the Local Food Economy: Lessons Learned from the Appalachian Region in Mississippi," *Journal of Appalachian Studies* 22, no. 1 (2016): 31–44; Lucy M. Long, "Culinary Tourism and the Emergence of an Appalachian Cuisine: Exploring the 'Foodscape' of Asheville, NC," *North Carolina Folklore Journal* 57, no. 1 (2010): 4–19; Mae Humiston, "2014–2015 Breaking Beans: The Appalachian Food Story Project Final Report," Community Farm Alliance, September 10, 2015, http://cfaky.org/test/wp-content/uploads/2015/09/Breaking-Beans-Report-FINAL-with-stories.pdf; Jairus Rossi, A. Lee Meyer, and Jann Knappage, "Beyond Farmers Markets Local Food Opportunities in Southeastern Kentucky's Retail and Institutional Industry," Community Farm Alliance, University of Kentucky College of Agriculture, Food and Environment, Community & Economic Development Initiative of Kentucky, March 2018, http://cedik.ca.uky.edu/files/beyond_farmers_markets_final.pdf; See also https://www.arc.gov/investment/central-appalachia-growing-opportunities-through-local-food, accessed March 26, 2025; https://www.epa.gov/smartgrowth/local

-foods-local-places, accessed March 26, 2025; http://www.soar-ky.org/blueprint, accessed March 26, 2025.

3. See https://asapconnections.org, accessed March 26, 2025; https://asdevelop.org, accessed March 26, 2025; https://www.wvfoodandfarm.org, accessed March 26, 2025; https://arcd.org; and http://ruralaction.org, accessed March 26, 2025. See also ACEnet, https://acenetworks.org, accessed March 26, 2025.

4. Deller, Lamie, and Stickel, "Local Foods Systems and Community Economic Development."

5. See https://www.facebook.com/appalachianfood/, accessed March 28, 2025; Elizabeth S. D. Engelhardt and Lora E. Smith, eds., *The Food We Eat, the Stories We Tell: Contemporary Appalachian Tables*, New Approaches to Appalachian Studies (Athens: Ohio University Press, 2019), Wilkinson, Crystal, *Praisesong for the Kitchen Ghosts: Stories and Recipes from Five Generations of Black Country Cooks* (New York: Penguin Random House, 2024).

6. See "The Greenprint: A Long Term Plan for Kentucky's Agricultural Economy," 2001, https://cfaky.org/wp-content/uploads/2018/01/greenprintcomplete.pdf; "Bringing Kentucky's Food and Farming Economy Home," 2003, https://cfaky.org/wp-content/uploads/2018/01/bringing-ky-home.pdf; and "Bridging the Divide," 2007, https://cfaky.org/wp-content/uploads/2018/01/bridgingthedivide.pdf.

7. See https://cfaky.org/programs/breaking-beans-the-appalachian-food-story-project, accessed March 28, 2025, and "Breaking Beans Final Report, 2014–2015," https://cfaky.org/wp-content/uploads/2018/01/breaking-beans-report-final-with-stories.pdf, accessed March 28, 2025.

8. Impacts for the Central Appalachian Family Farm Fund and Kentucky Black Farmer Fund can be viewed in the *Our Covid-19 Investment* report at https://cfaky.org/reports, accessed March 28, 2025.

9. See https://cfaky.org/fmsp, accessed March 28, 2025.

10. See https://cfaky.org/reports, accessed March 28, 2025.

11. Full reports for each assessment Community Farm Alliance has supported can be found at https://cfaky.org/reports, accessed March 28, 2025.

12. See https://cfaky.org/eastern-kentucky-farmer-conference/, accessed March 28, 2025, and https://www.cannetwork.org/community-food-systems, accessed March 28, 2025.

13. See https://cfaky.org/history, accessed March 28, 2025.

14. See https://cfaky.org/what-we-do/pathway-to-change-2, accessed March 28, 2025.

15. "Food as Medicine," https://www.agriculture.senate.gov/download/farm-bill/mr-martin-richards-testimony, accessed March 28, 2025.

16. See https://growappalachia.berea.edu, accessed March 28, 2025.

17. Elyzabeth W. Engle, "Community Capacity Building, Context, and Everyday Environmental Injustices: Rural Community Gardening and Organizational Networks in Central Appalachia" (PhD diss., Pennsylvania State University, 2018), Elyzabeth W. Engle, "'Coal Is in Our Food, Coal Is in Our Blood': Everyday Environmental Injustices of Rural Community Gardening in Central Appalachia," *Local Environment* 24, no. 8 (2019): 746–61.

18. See the strategic plan: C. Mullins et al., "Planting the Seeds: Grow Appalachia's Three Year Strategic Plan," July 1, 2021, https://indd.adobe.com/view/6e7a1c2e-ffe4-4aeb-9a65-529bea496936.

19. Deller, Lamie, and Stickel, "Local Foods Systems and Community Economic Development," 612–38; Kentucky Department of Agriculture, Direct Farm Marketing Division.

See https://www.kyproud.com/programs/appalachia-proud, accessed March 28, 2025, and https://www.facebook.com/knoxcountyfarmersmarket, accessed March 28, 2025.

20. Knox County is located in what is now known as southeastern Kentucky on colonized land that was originally stewarded by a number of Indigenous peoples, including the Cherokee and Shawnee. See the Community and Economic Development Initiative of Kentucky's Knox County Agriculture and Food Profile, https://blueprintkentucky.ca.uky.edu/county-data-profiles/census-agriculture, accessed March 28, 2025. County Economic Status, based on 2018 ARC data, is available online at https://www.arc.gov/research/Data Reports.asp, accessed March 28, 2025. The poverty rate estimate based on 2016 Small Area Income and Poverty Estimates and the population estimate based on the 2016 US Census Bureau, Population Estimates Program (PEP), are both available at https://www.census.gov/quickfacts/fact/table/knoxcountykentucky/PST045216, accessed March 28, 2025. The 2012–2016 American Community Survey 5-Year Estimates are available at https://www.census.gov/programs-surveys/acs/technical-documentation/table-and-geography-changes/2016/5-year.html, accessed March 28, 2025.

21. Kathryn Engle, "Stinking Creek Stories: Memory, Agriculture, and Community in Rural Southeastern Kentucky," *Register of the Kentucky Historical Society* 116, no. 3 & 4 (Summer/Autumn 2018): 457–508. See https://lendahandcenter.wordpress.com, accessed March 28, 2025/. The Lend-A-Hand Center Grow Appalachia Gardening Program was a Grow Appalachia partner site through the 2016 growing season, with Kathryn Engle serving as the site coordinator. For more information see Kathryn Engle, "Cultivating Community Economy on Stinking Creek: The Lend-A-Hand Center Grow Appalachia Gardening Program," *Journal of Appalachian Studies* 27, no. 1 (Spring 2021): 10–33.

22. See Local Foods Local Places Technical Assistance Program, "Strengthening the Local Foods System: Actions and Strategies for Barbourville, Kentucky," September 15, 2015, https://www.ams.usda.gov/sites/default/files/media/lflpcapbarbourville.pdf, accessed March 28, 2025.

23. See https://www.facebook.com/knoxcountyfarmersmarket, accessed March 28, 2025

24. See https://www.epa.gov/smartgrowth/local-foods-local-places, accessed March 28, 2025.

25. See Local Foods Local Places Technical Assistance Program, "Strengthening the Local Foods System: Actions and Strategies for Barbourville, Kentucky," September 15, 2015, https://www.ams.usda.gov/sites/default/files/media/lflpcapbarbourville.pdf. See also Rossi, Meyer, and Knappage, "Beyond Farmers Markets Local Food Opportunities," for a discussion of potential for the growth of local food in retail and institutional markets in southeastern Kentucky. Appalachia is often presented as a barren, unproductive, backward place. Initiatives such as these re-present the region as a place of possibility and becoming.

26. KCFM is also a summer feeding program site through a partnership with the KCEOC Community Action Partnership.

8

Health in the Quest for Appalachia's Just Transition

RACHEL E. DIXON AND F. DOUGLAS SCUTCHFIELD

"Dirty" Coal and Appalachia's Silent Suffering

In 2018, Blackley and colleagues reported a substantial increase in progressive massive fibrosis (PMF) among coal miners in Kentucky and West Virginia. PMF is an advanced form of coal workers' pneumoconiosis (CWP), known colloquially as "black lung." It develops in the process of mining when workers inhale coal dust and silica. As particles enter alveoli and other pulmonary structures, they accumulate, inflaming tissues, creating irreversible scars, and choking out healthy space for oxygen exchange. The result, as Berkes and Lancianese note, is "a kind of mining disaster in slow motion," a sluggish suffocation that can take up to ten years to diagnose. By then, there are no options for full recovery, short of a transplant.[1]

It was not that epidemiologists and health officials were unaware of black lung in 2018; they had been searching for it in the wrong places. Although programs existed to monitor *employed* miners, those who were unemployed or health care–avoidant fell through the cracks. Decades prior, when occupational hazards were more visible, union efforts had spurred the 1969 Federal Coal Mine Health and Safety Act (the "Coal Act"), which created a new organization to oversee underground mining safety (the Mining Enforcement and Safety Administration; later the Mining Safety and Health Administration, or MSHA). The subsequent Occupational Safety and Health Act of 1970 established both the National Institute for Occupational Safety and Health (NIOSH) and the Occupational Safety and Health Administration (OSHA) to help ensure healthy working conditions via timely research, information, education, and training. Together with provisions from OSHA, the Coal Act created a program to address occupational lung disease in miners: the Coal Workers' Health Surveillance Program (CWHSP). Through this initiative, NIOSH regularly surveilled coal workers for signs of pneumoconiosis via X-rays at local black lung clinics. Between 1990 and 1999, NIOSH found only thirty-one unique cases of PMF across the United States.[2]

Though the program continued, regular reviews of working miners' health records lulled federal health experts into false confidence that PMF had been controlled. Yet the advent of new dust-generating surface-mining techniques in the 1990s, coupled with a systemic lack of monitoring of *out-of-work* miners and employed miners' hesitancy to seek medical care, allowed the disease to proliferate in darkness.[3]

The canary in the coal mine was an alert from a Kentucky physician, who contacted NIOSH in 2016 after tracking sixty PMF cases at his practice in Pike County. National Public Radio picked up his story later that year and estimated that the true incidence of black lung was "more than 10 times" what NIOSH had previously indicated. Subsequent studies, such as a 2016 investigation of eastern Kentucky and one of three clinics in Virginia in 2018 demonstrated that there was a substantial problem: in Central Appalachia, hundreds of miners exhibited PMF on radiograph, with the youngest patients only in their thirties. This discovery triggered a national debate on protections for coal miners—employed, laid-off, and retired—and activists argued that the protections were woefully inadequate despite decades of research. If NIOSH had known since the 1970s that silica and other coal dust wreaked havoc on workers' lungs, why didn't MSHA place strict limits on silica exposure? Further, given that miners spend years fighting to receive their entitled black lung benefits, why is access to compensation still so limited?[4]

In addition to these concerns, the national debate over PMF's resurgence has thus far lacked attention to intersectionality in its discussion of miners' health. The dearth of data by race on PMF and other mining-related respiratory diseases raises troubling questions, among them: why have national bodies failed to consider the experiences of Black Appalachians in navigating occupational disease? Part of this oversight lies in the fact that academic research on potential racial disparities related to CWP and PMF are virtually impossible to locate (Brigham, Albright, and Harris 2020 excepted). Additionally, CWHSP reports fail to explore potential gaps in health outcomes between white miners and miners of color. This oversight is glaring, given both the evidence of racial discrimination in pulmonary screening (and health care generally) and the region's legacy of segregated coal towns, among other racial injustices. After all, Trotter Jr. notes, Black miners have disproportionately shouldered the health burden of mining, having been overrepresented in more hazardous positions inside the mines.[5]

National conversations have not spurred meaningful action to reduce vulnerability among miners; requests for additional black lung funding have so far been stonewalled. Exemplifying this is a 2017 letter in which eight congressmen requested a 50 percent increase in budgeting for black lung clinics, citing the urgency of addressing the PMF epidemic. The Trump administration was silent on this point and declined to increase appropriations, according to budget figures released by the Health Resources and Services Administration in 2018. Policymakers continue to sweep Appalachian health under the proverbial rug, particularly where ailments are less visible. Ron Carson, who directs the Stone Mountain black lung clinic in Appalachian Virginia, put it more bluntly in his interview with NPR: "Mining disasters get monuments. Black lung deaths get tombstones."[6]

Environmentalists uphold such stories as evidence of the imperative to transition away from "dirty" coal. They argue that in decarbonizing the Appalachian Region, its inhabitants free themselves from coal-related diseases. Yet health improvement is not an inevitability in post-coal transition. Put frankly, the tendency to subjugate health concerns to other social and economic imperatives permeates the just transition discourse, and this can perpetuate ill health via means other than mining. If coal is dirty (in the sense of jeopardizing health), so, too, are many plans to move beyond it.

While better health outcomes are not guaranteed in the move beyond coal, they are desperately needed to help Appalachia achieve health parity with the rest of the United States. Policymakers and communities, therefore, have the difficult task of addressing the root causes of regional health disparities *alongside* efforts to decarbonize. As Scutchfield and Wykoff's *Appalachian Health* shows, occupational diseases like PMF form only half of the picture in Appalachia; the other half is a complex web of ideological, political, and social processes with which a truly just transition must grapple.[7]

This chapter considers how communities and their leaders might design transition policies to achieve both environmental and health justice. In outlining a path forward through embedding health in all policies, it explores the links between coal mining and health, the political landscape for health reform, and pitfalls and promise in current just transitions plans.

The Coal Conundrum: A Catch-22 for Health

Appalachia's substantial health problems result from a complex web of factors driving disparity, some environmental but others related to the region's economic stagnation, educational gaps, and social context. Public health scholars call these factors that influence well-being the *social determinants of health* (SDOH). As Kaiser Permanente Vice President Kathie Gerwig reminds, "Health issues do not stay within the walls of an exam room or a healthcare facility . . . addressing the social, economic and environmental determinants of health includes helping people access affordable housing, reliable transportation, and employment," among other resources. Thus, achieving good health is not as simple as setting up a clinic or eliminating environmental pollutants; the Healthy People 2020 initiative notes that it must also include attention to education, economic stability, and community context—and how each of these factors interact.[8]

The role of race in explaining gaps at population level is another central concern of SDOH, and it is key to reaching a more nuanced understanding of Appalachia's coal-related health disparities. When Evans, Barer, and Marmor first posed the question "Why are some people healthy and others not?" part of the answer came from ethnicity and its relation to other social factors, especially class and status. Subsequent research has more clearly demonstrated the link between race and well-being: in 1997, epidemiologist David Williams called for closer attention to differences in health by race; just two decades later, Mays, Cochran, and Barnes highlighted "persistent and vexing health disadvantages" among African Americans in the United States; and Bailey and colleagues more recently explored how structural racism perpetuates ill health. It is clear that racism continues to drive health inequality. In Appalachia, this racism often overlaps environmental injustice, whereby marginalized groups are more likely to face pollution and other ecosystem degradation due to a lack of social and political power. In *Ailing in Place*, Morrone explores the siting of a toxic landfill in a predominantly Black community in Warren County, resulting in national outrage and a call for environmental justice in local planning.[9]

Because health depends on many factors, a transition away from coal will have complicated effects on population well-being, some positive and others negative. One is that coal-related pollution suppresses health across the region, as numerous studies have shown. Yet moving away from coal is a double-edged sword: decline in mining catalyzes structural unemployment and increases material deprivation. In turn, poverty exacerbates health disparities. Furthermore, environmental justice scholars have criticized the "mining-to-prison pipeline" in Central Appalachia, in which several post-coal plans have involved construction of penitentiaries. Decarbonization strategies built on unjust systems, such as the penal system, compound racial disparities and introduce negative health effects. Owing to these complex considerations, just transition plans must carefully evaluate the wider health implications of their specific policy proposals. This section explores the impact of coal on health to make a start in this effort.[10]

Coal's Negative Effect on Health

Studies have unequivocally demonstrated that coal-related pollutants harm health. *The Lancet*'s 2021 *Countdown on Health and Climate Change* estimates that over one million deaths are directly attributable to air pollution from coal-fired power. The OECD (Organisation for Economic Co-operation and Development) notes that while most of those deaths take place in industrializing countries (e.g., China and India), air pollution affects those in advanced economies as well. In Appalachia, silica exposure drives the PMF epidemic, adding additional complications to COVID-19 relief efforts. The 2018 federal study on respirable coal mine dust found that in 1960, at the height of the previous black lung epidemic, over 30 percent of miners who had worked for twenty-five years or more contracted CWP and PMF. Today, those who work in smaller mines experience higher-than-expected rates of these diseases. Blackley and colleagues explain this increase with the relationship between social conditions and health: smaller mines typically lack union protections and thus more frequently expose employees to silica dust. Graber and colleagues' follow-up study of over nine thousand former miners linked mining to excess mortality from CWP, chronic obstructive pulmonary disease, and lung cancer. These health outcomes persist despite policy advancements (such as the EPA's Clean Air Act of 1963), in part because of the narrow remit of federal agencies in monitoring and punishing noncompliance. As we explore in more depth later, this lack of regulation often results from capture of federal agencies by the powerful coal lobby.[11]

In addition to air pollution, the people of Appalachia face watershed crises related to contamination from mining byproducts and significant landscape changes. Ducatman and Dixon explain that valley-fill practices—whereby coal sludge and other waste is dumped into the lowlands surrounding mine sites—risk toxic runoff into nearby streams. Pollution of watersheds can impact digestive functioning, producing diarrhea, rash, tooth erosion, and kidney stones. Flooding is also common in Appalachia, where inadequate infrastructure and poor land-use practices increase surface water runoff. In August 2022, eastern Kentucky experienced catastrophic flooding that was characterized as a "one-in-1,000-year event" and which killed forty-four people across six counties. Documentaries such as *Mountaintop Removal* and *Coal Rush* follow grassroots efforts to rectify watershed contamination in Appalachian communities and demonstrate how convoluted the pathway to justice can be when citizens combat coal companies in the fight to save streams and ward off floods. Though federal reclamation programs exist to mitigate such effects, they are underresourced and ineffective.[12]

Perhaps most concerning are emerging studies that suggest an association between coal mining, primarily mountaintop removal mining (MTR), and cancer risk. Hendryx and Hitt found a significant negative correlation between stream integrity (a measure of ecological health) and total cancer mortality per one hundred thousand people in West Virginia. Areas with higher levels of contamination from coal mining (i.e., lower stream integrity) also had higher rates of respiratory, digestive, breast, and other types of cancer. Laboratory studies have demonstrated that dust generated from MTR accelerates the progression of cancer in both human and other animal lung tissue. Illustrating a case of "dueling epidemiologists," some have criticized literature linking coal mining and cancer, stating that most studies are associational, display an ecological bias, and are inadequate to demonstrate causation.[13]

Unintended Harms and Blind Spots in the Move toward Just Transitions

Despite the clear health risks of coal dependence, mining provides some measure of well-being among residents of Appalachia. Historically, industry jobs have paid well and required little formal education. This is a boon for coal communities, where levels of educational attainment are often lower relative to their non-Appalachian counterparts (in part due to those historically good wages in mining with little formal education required). When mines close and jobs disappear, laborers fail to find replacement work at similar wages, which intensifies poverty and drives out-migration. The Appalachian region is particularly vulnerable to such structural unemployment because of its lack of economic diversity. A loss of coal mining jobs impacts other businesses, erodes the tax base, and harms other aspects of society as well. Due to coal employment's direct effects on these social determinants, any plan to move beyond mining could actually be *regressive* for population health.[14]

The just transition and environmental justice literatures partly consider unintended consequences of climate policies but do not pay adequate attention to the specific health effects of transition. In 2021, the Italy-based Eni Enrico Mattei Foundation (FEEM) published a working paper comparing just transition policies in China, the European Union, and the United States. Though pursuing different "philosophies" in just transition—stabilizing employment for better living standards (China), leaving no one behind (European Union), and effecting environmental justice (US)—the policy examples of all countries focused more on economic stabilization and retraining than on the health effects of transition. This absence carries over into academic research, as well. Tribaldos and Kortetmäki lament the "marginal attention given to food security in sustainability transition studies" even where such studies purport a basis in justice principles. Where food systems are considered in research and policy development, the nuance is "underdeveloped" and often inattentive to "serious health impacts [of food systems] including malnutrition . . . non-communicable diseases, and mental health impairments."[15]

As Munro, Boyce, and Marmot warn, "Climate change mitigation policies are uniquely wide-ranging and systemic in their impacts: they have the potential to impact on many of the determinants of health," both positively and negatively. Markkanen and Anger-Kraavi push for more research on what they call the *negative* coimpacts of climate change policies, and they emphasize issues of equity in these discussions. Their definition of equity as allocation "according to the level of need" resonates with discussions in the health literature about correcting disparities in health-care access, an issue of utmost importance in Appalachia, where medical and social systems are already inadequate and badly strained. If just transition plans do not attend to equity, they risk further intensifying barriers to health-care access. For example, some green policies force people to relocate, which may have negative impacts on mental health. In the table 8.1, we consider a few initial impacts on health—both positive and negative—of transition pathways that have been considered for communities in Appalachia.[16,17]

Weighing up the health impacts of transition pathways is necessary to unlock justice, especially in light of the documented tendency to discount future health benefits in the presence of more immediate effects (such as job loss) of phaseout. This "future discounting" can weaken overall support for green policies at the core of just transitions—or work in reverse to popularize pathways that would have deleterious future health effects. While one cannot predict how Appalachia's residents would weigh the health impacts of a *specific* transition proposal, research on regional health-care mindsets provides some clues about potential policy reception. For example, Vanderpool and colleagues find that Appalachian individuals self-report much higher levels of health-care avoidance—waiting to see physicians until after symptoms become burdensome—than individuals in the rest of the United States. Though this research does not suggest that Appalachians care less about their health than other Americans, it does indicate that economic and social concerns often take priority over health.[18]

In that vein, research on the underreporting of PMF incidence suggests that miners will avoid chest radiography if they fear results might endanger their employment status. In Appalachian Kentucky, for example, only 17 percent of miners participated in NIOSH's free PMF screening program from 2011 to 2016. Stansbury confirms this health-care avoidance, based on anecdotal evidence from his clinic in Morgantown, West Virginia. Furthermore, this tendency mirrors behavior found in a 2016 study of "exposure experience" in Appalachian Ohio—one study participant analogized factory work to mining: "Coal miners . . . go in the coal mines every day knowing that there is a danger there . . . but we got to make a living."[19]

Table 8.1. Weighing Health Impacts of Common Transition Proposals

Transition Pathway	Policy/Industry Example(s)	Potential Health Impacts (nonexhaustive)	
		Positive Effects (+)	Drawbacks (–)
Agritech	Sustainable farming B Corp **AppHarvest** (APPH) has produced large-scale indoor farms to increase crop yields and reduce agricultural runoff while employing Appalachian people.	**Better access to nutritious food:** Expansion of the agricultural industry addresses some aspects of food insecurity across the region, providing nutrient-rich, locally grown produce.	**Waterborne disease:** With hydroponics systems, the risk of waterborne diseases increases, and special measures must be taken to ensure disinfection (see note 17, Mori and Smith).
	Hemp production has been touted as a way to improve economic conditions in Central Appalachia, where the climate is particularly suited to the crop.	**Medicinal benefits:** Specific crops can offer new medicinal benefits. For example, hemp is a precursor to CBD, which has been used efficaciously in chronic pain management (see, e.g., note 17, Strickland et al.).	**Occupational exposures:** A 2020 special issue on the health effects of cannabis and hemp production (see note 17, Simpson) highlights that the move to agritech is not without health-related challenges. Lack of research into the health effects of cannabis and hemp may mean exposure-related risks are hidden. Furthermore, agricultural workers face increased risk of disease from parasites, UV exposure, and pesticides, where used (see note 17, Salman Butt et al.).

(Continued)

Table 8.1. Weighing Health Impacts of Common Transition Proposals (*Continued*)

Transition Pathway	Policy/Industry Example(s)	Potential Health Impacts *(nonexhaustive)*	
		Positive Effects (+)	Drawbacks (–)
Clean energy development	The multistate **Marshall Plan for Middle America** (see note 17) argues for the need to leverage public and private investments to bring renewable energy generation to the Ohio River valley.	**Improvements in air and water quality:** Limiting carbon-associated pollution through a move to wind, solar, and other renewable-energy technologies improve air quality, water quality, and other measures of ecological health.	**Potential for toxic components:** Solar thermal technologies—which convert solar energy to heat—rely on absorption fluids that can be toxic. Research into "eco-friendly fluids" is still advancing (see note 17, Kosinska, Balakin, and Kosinski). Health injustices are still associated with a variety of other technologies, as well (see note 17, Bell).
	The **Ruhr Valley** area of Germany has emerged as a leader in environmental technology and **renewable energy research**.	**Increased life expectancy:** A 2021 analysis of panel data from twenty-nine European countries from 2005 to 2018 (by Rodriguez-Alvarez; see note 17) showed an increase in potential life expectancy with investment in renewable energy.	**Community relocation:** New development plans may endanger local communities within site boundaries. Forced relocation, where it results, can negatively impact mental and community health, particularly in rural communities where place attachment is higher (see note 17, Bukvic et al.).

(*Continued*)

Table 8.1. Weighing Health Impacts of Common Transition Proposals (*Continued*)

Transition Pathway	Policy/Industry Example(s)	Potential Health Impacts (*nonexhaustive*)	
		Positive Effects (+)	*Drawbacks (−)*
Manufacturing	In the 1980s, the Thatcher government introduced policies to promote foreign direct investments in **manufacturing in Wales** following mine closure.	**Economic boost:** Most arguments for a transition to manufacturing center on job creation and wealth building as central to well-being.	**Ecosystem impacts:** Manufacturing can have deleterious ecosystem effects, as evidenced by the water crisis in Flint, Michigan. **Occupational risks:** Manufacturing involves physical labor and long working hours, which present myriad occupational hazards not unlike those seen in the coal industry, such as physiological stress (see note 17, Salman Butt et al.).
Natural resource management	**ReImagine Appalachia's** blueprint for "A New Deal that works for us" pitches a revival of the Depression-era Civilian Conservation Corps, employing Appalachians in natural restoration.	**Improved food security:** A study of community-based natural resource management found that such efforts significantly improved household food security (see note 17, Pailler et al.).	**Zoonotic disease exposure:** There is a small risk that with increased interaction between humans and animals, potential for zoonotic disease increases. Management of these risks is thus central to strong natural resource management policy (see note 17, Debnath et al.).

(*Continued*)

Table 8.1. Weighing Health Impacts of Common Transition Proposals (*Continued*)

Transition Pathway	Policy/Industry Example(s)	Potential Health Impacts (*nonexhaustive*)	
		Positive Effects (+)	*Drawbacks (−)*
Prison management	Proposals to construct prisons in post-coal communities have both succeeded (**US Penitentiary, Big Sandy**) and drawn widespread critique. (A 2019 proposal to locate a prison in Letcher County was revived in 2022, spurring additional protests.)	**Economic boost:** As with manufacturing proposals, job creation and wealth building from prisons are touted as pathways to regional well-being, though research does not bear this out.	**Disease proliferation:** As exhibited during the COVID-19 pandemic, congregate living facilities make disease containment difficult. **Health inequity:** Evidence suggests that US prisons are often sited in areas with high levels of pollution—as in Appalachia. This increases exposure for incarcerated individuals, widening disparities in health outcomes compared to nonincarcerated populations (see note 17, Toman and also Schept

(*Continued*)

Table 8.1. Weighing Health Impacts of Common Transition Proposals (*Continued*)

Transition Pathway	Policy/Industry Example(s)	Potential Health Impacts (*nonexhaustive*)	
		Positive Effects (+)	*Drawbacks (−)*
Recreational tourism	Neighboring cities **Gatlinburg and Pigeon Forge** (Tennessee) have remodeled themselves as tourist destinations, with their Great Smoky Mountains National Park drawing 14.1 million visitors to become 2021's most popular.	**Long-term well-being:** A study of Spain (see note 17, Godovykh and Ridderstaat) found that while tourism can negatively impact health in the short term, it has an overall positive effect on local populations in the longer term, boosting social interactions.	**Crime levels:** Tourist destinations typically experience higher-than-average rates of crime, though the underlying causes of this are debated (see note 17, Mawby and Vakhitova). **Air quality impacts:** Pollution may intensify due to increased traffic into communities. **Ecosystem impacts:** Degradation of local ecosystems may result due to increased footfall, where resources are not properly managed and protected. **Motor vehicle accidents:** Increase in ATV-related fatalities could result as Appalachian communities become tourist destinations. (see note 17, Psarras, Panajiotidis, and Andronikidis, on the relationship between tourism and traffic accidents.)

(*Continued*)

Table 8.1. Weighing Health Impacts of Common Transition Proposals (*Continued*)

Transition Pathway	Policy/Industry Example(s)	Potential Health Impacts (*nonexhaustive*)	
		Positive Effects (+)	*Drawbacks (−)*
Retraining in IT and other knowledge-based sectors	**BitSource**, an Appalachia-based software development company, moves individuals from coal mining to coding in Pikeville, Kentucky.	**Less physical stress:** Reductions in strain associated with physical laboring in the mines would occur.	**Electronic waste:** The question of what to do with "e-waste" has become a global crisis, and externalities associated with IT development are often shifted to low- and middle-income countries.
			Occupational risks: Different physical skill set required; new strains related to increase in screen time mean specialist care needs may increase (e.g., vision screenings).

(*Continued*)

Table 8.1. Weighing Health Impacts of Common Transition Proposals (*Continued*)

Transition Pathway	Policy/Industry Example(s)	Potential Health Impacts (*nonexhaustive*)	
		Positive Effects (+)	*Drawbacks (–)*
Services and hospitality	The introduction of **retail shops, call centers, and hospitality-related roles** are just a few of the transition pathways some advocate for areas like Central Appalachia (see note 17, Semuels).	**Flexible work arrangements:** Flexibility inherent in some hospitality and service-sector work may provide new employment opportunities for those in Appalachia who are aging, disabled, or less able to work full-time jobs, alleviating poverty and other precursors to ill health. More research is needed in this area.	**Poor mental health among workers:** The quick pace and stringent demands required of service and hospitality workers result in poorer self-reported wellness, especially mental (see note 17, Zhang, Torres, and Jahromi). Burnout has been especially well documented across the industry (see note 17, Ayachit and Chitta). **Precarious work:** See note 17: Bhattacharya and Ray's finding that workers in precarious positions (e.g., gig-economy work, on nonstandard contracts, or in part-time positions) experience higher job stress and more days in poor physical and mental health.

The point is this: advocates of just transition cannot take the health benefits of phasing out coal as a given without teasing out the nuances of a specific proposal situated in an Appalachian context. To many, less pollution may not outweigh the health-related impacts (both physical and mental) of joblessness and poverty from mine closures, for example. Instead, policymakers must work *alongside communities* to advance sound plans that anticipate the numerous potential effects on health determinants of a transition away from coal.

The Political Economy of Appalachian Health Reform

The politics of health advocacy in Appalachia complicate efforts to embed health equity in environmental policy proposals, even where benefits and drawbacks have been weighed. This section draws on Appalachian studies literature to explore the region's political landscape and its implications for just transition work. It first summarizes key governmental players in Appalachian policymaking before addressing both the regulatory capture of these bodies by the coal industry and citizen-led resistance efforts.

The Political Landscape of Rural Health

In late 1963, just one year after the publication of Harry Caudill's famous *Night Comes to the Cumberlands*, the federal government announced plans "to fight Appalachian poverty." As Steven Stoll describes in *Ramp Hollow*, this was the genesis of the Appalachian Regional Commission (ARC), a partnership between the federal government and thirteen states with counties in Appalachia. Today, the ARC continues to assist regional development efforts, coordinating actions among the thirteen governors, administering federal grant programs (such as the Partnerships for Opportunity and Workforce and Economic Revitalization [POWER] initiative) and working with states to devise strategies for poverty alleviation and health-care expansion. It serves as a bridge between national-, state-, and county-level governments while also conducting research on health and economic disparities.[20]

ARC works alongside federal bodies like the Department for Health and Human Services (DHHS). The DHHS administers programs that intersect Appalachian health, such as the Black Lung Clinics Program. In 2020, at the urging of the Trump administration, it released its *Rural Action Plan*. The plan identified critical Appalachian health disparities and highlights work—such as initiatives to address the opioid epidemic and unhealthy diets—that it would prioritize in coming years. Ultimately, funding appropriated by Congress for rural health interventions ended up under DHHS care in its Office of Rural Health Policy. Via the office's Rural Health Service Centers, the federal government would then partner with ARC in some grant administration and research efforts. From there, money would find its way to state governments, where governors and legislators decide how to best use it to promote health among Appalachia's residents. This is a winding and complex process, reliant on the cooperation of a variety of organizations for success.[21]

The region's use of state–federal partnerships for development means that health policy governance can be disjointed. Morrone specifically notes that efficacy of local public health efforts is predicated on cooperation between all levels of government and the constrained resources at their disposal. When organizations do not work well together, as Ducatman and Dixon detail, community well-being is sidelined. In our earlier example of the PMF epidemic, a screening program defined and funded at the federal level (by NIOSH, under the DHHS) was ultimately inattentive to realities within Appalachian counties.[22]

Yet the disorganization runs deeper. Consider the example of black lung benefits: the 1969 Coal Act, which developed NIOSH and its screening program, included a provision for miner compensation. The Black Lung Benefits program, as noted in a 1971 federal briefing, "provides for monthly cash benefit payments from general tax funds to coal miners total disabled due to pneumoconiosis arising out of employment" and to their widows. Though the DHHS may both flag miners who qualify for the program and fund black lung clinics, the Department of Labor (DOL)—specifically its Division of Coal Mine Workers' Compensation—actually administers benefits to individuals. It requires miners to apply separately for the benefits, even if they have already been diagnosed with CWP or PMF stemming from past work. This application process then requires them to meet with a DOL-approved physician (from a predetermined list of providers in their area) for a pulmonary evaluation. Coal companies who are liable for claims then have the right to demand miners be evaluated by *another* physician—this time of the company's choosing—before confirming benefits. Additional complexity arises from the fact that Appalachian states have their own black lung benefits programs that supplement payments from the federal government's Black Lung Disability Trust Fund. Lawmakers at the state level often change rules for eligibility and payment processes. In 2018, for example, Kentucky came under fire after lawmakers tightened restrictions on benefits by shortening the list of radiologists qualified to diagnose CWP and PMF (introduced as "House Bill 2"). The result of all this red tape is that many miners die before their benefits are secured.[23]

Regulatory Capture and the Power of the Coal Lobby

The powerful "Coal Lobby" (famously studied by Bell and York and discussed as "King Coal" by earlier scholars) is partly responsible for the disjointed system to claim black lung benefits and other forms of health-related compensation. When Kentucky passed House Bill 2 to limit qualified CWP diagnosticians, critics noted that the Kentucky Coal Association, an industry-run lobbying firm, had actively supported the legislation, knowing it would frustrate miners' efforts to secure compensation. Ties between lawmakers and coal representatives are often strong, the result of decades of successful political action by groups advocating for continued mining. The result is regulatory capture, in which agencies tasked with overseeing industry are heavily influenced (and in some cases run) by the industries themselves. Bell and York detail how "Friends of Coal," an industry-organized initiative, presents itself as a grassroots effort, advancing a "coal-dependent" cultural identity to reduce support for mining regulations. Even more sinister, Big Coal's enmeshment in federal policymaking works to suppress health research on the effects of mining. In 2017, for example, the Trump administration canceled a National Academy study on the links between MTR, higher cancer incidence, and birth defects.[24]

These lobbying efforts coalesce into formidable opposition for just transition policies—not just for coal-related compensation. Mayer's study of transition proposals in the US Mountain West region found that Big Coal can derail proposals even when they garner widespread support from community members. The expansive coffers of coal corporations also impact political campaigns, as Goodell contends happened in the 2000 presidential election: "Coal industry executives knew that if [Al] Gore was elected, regulations to limit or tax carbon dioxide emissions wouldn't be far behind. So Big Coal threw its money and muscle behind George W. Bush, helping him gain a decisive edge in key industrial states, including West Virginia, a Democratic stronghold [at the time]."

Subsequent developments in the Bush administration—particularly Big Coal's involvement in the vice president's National Energy Policy Development Group—led to a rise in "clean coal" rhetoric, the argument that companies can mitigate the negative health effects of mining by utilizing scrubbers and other technologies at processing plants. The push for "clean coal" persists today, undermining serious efforts to discuss frameworks that actually center justice and equity for the people of Appalachia.[25]

Appalachia Fights Back: Micromobilization for Improved Health

Grassroots movements have been able to use health concerns as a window into transition discussions, despite immense resistance from the Coal Lobby. In her autoethnography, *Coal in Our Veins*, Thomas explores the intersection of health activism and just transition. She describes the formation of the Coal

River Mountain Watch, a community-based environmental protection group focused on stopping air pollution. At the turn of the century, a new coal processing plant by Massey Energy decimated air quality in a small West Virginian town. As Thomas describes it, two residents of the community, Pauline Canterberry and Mary Miller, fought to collect evidence of this pollution in the hopes of winning a citizen lawsuit against the corporation: "They filmed the coal dust that covered their cars, clogged the screens on their windows, and billowed in black clouds over their homes. They then presented this to the Surface Mining Board, which unanimously voted that the plant was violating its permit." Yet it would be over a decade before these "Dustbuster Sisters" and their neighbors won rightful compensation. By then, Massey Energy's subsidiaries had enabled one of the worst watershed disasters in Appalachian history (the Martin County, Kentucky, slurry spill) and the Upper Big Branch mine disaster, in which twenty-nine West Virginian miners perished.[26]

Bell finds that the "micromobilization" of Appalachian community leaders is not as common as one might expect, given the severity of the pollution from coal. In *Fighting King Coal*, in which she draws on her own experience as a rural health worker in West Virginia, she hypothesizes that "the influx of non-locals into the coalfield region" for environmental organizing work actually disincentivizes local residents from speaking out against mining or considering just transition plans. Historically (and, for several reasons, rightfully) distrustful of outside perspectives, many in Appalachia are wary of those from outside the region who place mining jobs in jeopardy with criticisms of the coal industry. It can be difficult, then, to rally residents around initiatives tinged with anti-coal sentiment. Forcing mine closure without a guaranteed economic alternative is not palatable for the majority of Appalachians, even if transition in the abstract stands to significantly improve health.[27]

Despite the difficulty inherent in micromobilization, grassroots efforts may be strengthened if they work to become "nested" in local communities and predicated on specific proposals. Borrowing Ostrom's concept of "nestedness," Lukacs, Ardoin, and Grubert explain that when nonprofit groups and leaders act as neighbors, "giving and receiving neighboring acts," they move beyond paternalism toward partnership. In this way, self-organized, nested watershed protection groups have made the biggest strides in governing water quality in Appalachian communities. Groups such as Appalshop (Letcher County, Kentucky), Mountain Association (eastern Kentucky and southwestern Virginia), Generation West Virginia (Charleston), and Appalachian Voices (Boone, North Carolina) can successfully introduce conversations about health and just transition precisely because they are viewed as neighbors. These organizations grew from within the mountains and can productively couch discussions in the language of community development and achieving prosperity rather than opposing coal.[28]

Pitfalls and Promise in Current Just Transitions Policy

While micromobilization work is promising, it cannot shift the systemic health disparities gripping Appalachia without support from government interventions. Thus we turn to extant systemic reforms to better understand the extent to which they consider health equity and embody a road map for truly just transition that centers health. As illustrated by recent work from the Stockholm Environment Institute, governments across the globe are modeling and deploying just transition policies. These schemes consider who benefits from decarbonization and aim to provide what Green and Ghambir call "transitional assistance" to those most vulnerable to losing out. They advocate broad social policies that complement environmental aims by recognizing the full spectrum of losses that an out-of-work miner or mining community might face. However, it is worth noting that even this pair only mentions "health" thrice in twenty-one pages.[29]

Like just transitions scholarship, existing policy designs have not fully incorporated health concerns in their assessments of compensation-worthy losses. To illustrate this point, we briefly outline two cases: the creation of the Coal Workforce Transition Program in Alberta, Canada, and proposed decarbonization legislation in the United States. Both case studies draw on the work of Dixon, who conducted extensive fieldwork and legislative tracking in each region in late 2019 and early 2020. Her review of seventy policy documents and seventeen elite interviews illuminates pitfalls and possible paths forward in developing just welfare systems in coal-supported regions.[30]

Case One: Alberta's Coal Workforce Transition Program

When the environmentally focused National Democratic Party of Alberta announced in 2015 its intention to accelerate the province's phaseout of coal-fired power generation, Albertans were shocked. Many of the province's rural areas were coal towns, completely reliant on the industry for economic vitality and survival. In making this announcement, Premier Notley couched her plans in many tenets of just transition and promised the move would "improve both the environment and health of Albertans." The Notley administration quickly got to work developing a Coal Workforce Transition Program (2017) and Coal Community Transition Fund (2018) to offset the harm for coal-dependent people. The Transition Program included a $40 million investment in three components: a "Bridge to Retirement," "Bridge to Re-employment," and "Bridge to Relocation." The Transition Fund provided one-time payments for community development projects, many of them focused on infrastructure enhancement.[31]

Despite rhetoric related to health, each of these programs viewed compensation rather narrowly, in terms of economic losses incurred in the move away from coal. None of the programs explicitly addressed Alberta's health infrastructure (which has been historically underfunded) or issues related to health that might arise from industry loss. Instead, representations of just transition in policy documents and leaders' statements most often focused on an overreliance on coal, the need to diversify Alberta's economy, and a lack of skills among workers, which would preclude future employment. While some programs intersected the social determinants of health—such as vouchers for miners' reeducation—Alberta's proponents of just transition lacked a comprehensive understanding of how health concerns interact with environmental and economic aims.[32]

Case Two: *The US POWER+ Plan and Its Successors*

Appalachia has seen its own push for just transition, though no programs have been as explicitly focused on climate justice as the work in Alberta. In 2012, President Obama announced his intention to build "an economy built to last" and shortly thereafter unveiled the Universal Displaced Worker Program (UDWP) to provide retraining and reemployment services for out-of-work miners. Appalachian communities have since received National Dislocated Worker Grants (NDWG), which provide direct benefits for jobless miners. Both of these measures set the stage for the administration's Clean Power Plan (CPP) in 2015, "the first-ever national standards that address carbon pollution from power plants." Obama's justification for the CPP included a note on the negative health effects of mining, though the administration did not say coal should be phased out completely. By pairing the CPP with a suite of social investments (the POWER+ Plan), the administration hoped to make its regulations more palatable and promote aspects of a Green New Deal.[33]

Ultimately, these efforts were stalled by the Trump administration, which repealed the CPP in favor of "clean coal" technology. Curiously, Trump kept some supports from Obama's POWER+ Plan, though he reduced a proposed $9 billion investment to $30 million in one-time Assistance to Coal Community grants and $600 million in funds administered by the ARC. As in Alberta, extant Appalachian transition policies focus narrowly on recouping financial losses from coal's decline. They involve compensation for retraining miners or corporate tax breaks for investing in former coal towns. Where social programs exist, they are modest. Dixon found that in Appalachia, the dominant foci of policy documents and conversations are the loss of coal jobs, a resistance to "over-regulation," and the desire to boost education levels across the region. Nevertheless, many powerful entities still advocate a return to coal mining. Neither option wrestles with Appalachian health disparities or considers the indirect impacts of transition policies on population health.[34]

In both Canada and the United States, officials cited health concerns and justice-related principles to spur conversations about transition, but this discourse did not spur coherent pro-health programs. There were several obstacles to achieving this goal. Resource constraints and the pressure for immediate returns on investment were cited by leaders as reasons for this policy failure. However, Dixon observed that an inattention to process, tendency toward top-down decision-making, and dismissal of citizen agency often hindered even the best visions for a decarbonized future. Therefore, in thinking about healthy and just transition, leaders must consider how grassroots cooperation can enable policies that better integrate health concerns into environmental discussions.[35]

Health at the Core of Just Transitions? Toward a HiAP Approach to Transitional Assistance

Scholars have made convincing arguments for the need to consider post-coal transition as a key population health policy. However, few studies frame health policy as a central component of a *just transition*. A recent exception comes in commentaries on "sustainable welfare" by Gough, who urges governments to find "synergies between the environment and welfare" and contended that "public service provision is an essential part of a green new deal." Health provision, he clarified, is one half of successful public services.[36]

Gough's words are reminiscent of budding scholarship on health equity, which frames health effects as the key consideration in any policy to promote welfare. The literature dubs this a "health in all policies" (HiAP) approach, which stresses that "health is an important enabler and prerequisite for attaining . . . society's social and economic goals." HiAP decision-making utilizes participatory, intersectoral processes and encourages "health impact assessments" in evaluating transitional assistance policy. Woolf, one of the foremost writers on the social determinants of health, contends "that social policy is health policy." Anyone following a HiAP approach, he says, should "systematically consider the health consequences before making choices about policy options." The American Public Health Association celebrates the HiAP approach as a more efficient way to enact social and environmental change. It argues that centralizing health concerns increases the odds of climate-forward policies and produces cobenefits across sectors. In simpler terms, when we keep health at the forefront of just transition, we simultaneously advance environmental and economic well-being.[37]

What might a HiAP approach to just transitions look like in Appalachia? To start, it will engage the nested groups that are already doing great work across the region. Rather than just attacking the coal industry for its legacy of ill health, policymakers must focus on the sacrifices miners have made in working to keep the lights on across America. They should simultaneously understand that to secure better quality of life in retirement, workers need easier access to health services, built environments to sustain healthy lifestyles, and the income supports to keep poverty from blocking well-being. Though state governments have made numerous mistakes in rural policy, recent efforts provide reason to hope that truly just transitions are possible. For instance, "Farmacy" programs have sprung up in West Virginia and Kentucky to start prescribing fruits and vegetables and combat nutritional deficiencies. These initiatives are supported via collaboration between governments, local health-care providers, farmers' markets, and corporations. They not only reduce incidence of chronic disease but also enable a return to subsistence-based agriculture. Additionally, the Kentucky Broadband Initiative, seen as a boon for workforce development and education, could also improve population health by increasing access to digital health tools and connecting Appalachians with health-care providers.[38]

It is clear from this review that health equity and environmental justice complement one another. While the effects of air pollution, water contamination, and fractured health infrastructure have resulted in a cycle of ill health for Appalachia's people, these patterns need not continue. Just transitions can provide pathways out of deprivation and illness, but only if we stop relegating health to an aside in larger discussions about Appalachia's future. By attending to the complex web of regional health determinants and the specific effects that transition proposals have on those factors, proponents of decarbonization within Appalachia can work from the coalfields to congressional halls to create a future that is both healthy *and* just for all.

Notes

1. Committee on the Study of the Control of Respirable Coal Mine Dust Exposure in Underground Mines, *Monitoring and Sampling Approaches to Assess Underground Coal Mine Dust Exposures* (Washington, DC: National Academies Press, 2018); Elaine Sheldon McMillion and Howard Berkes, *Coal's Deadly Dust* (Arlington County, VA: PBS Frontline, 2019), https://www.pbs.org/wgbh/frontline/film/coals-deadly-dust; David J. Blackley et al., "Resurgence of Progressive Massive Fibrosis in Coal Miners—Eastern Kentucky, 2016," *CDC Morbidity and Mortality Weekly Report* 65, no. 49 (2016): 1385–89; Howard Berkes and

Adelina Lancianese, "Black Lung Study Finds Biggest Cluster Ever of Fatal Coal Miners' Disease," NPR, February 6, 2018, https://www.npr.org/2018/02/06/583456129/black-lung-study-biggest-cluster-ever-of-fatal-coal-miners-disease; David J. Blackley et al., "Progressive Massive Fibrosis in Coal Miners from 3 Clinics in Virginia," *JAMA* 319, no. 5 (2018): 500–501.

2. Carrie Arnold, "A Scourge Returns: Black Lung in Appalachia," *Environmental Health Perspectives* 124, no. 1 (2016): A13–A18; John Alexander-Williams, *Appalachia: A History* (Chapel Hill: University of North Carolina Press, 2002), 351–52; Christian Wright, *Carbon County USA: Miners for Democracy in Utah and the West* (Salt Lake City: University of Utah Press, 2020), xxv–xl; "Coal Workers' Health Surveillance Program," CDC, last reviewed February 19, 2020, https://www.cdc.gov/niosh/cwhsp/about/?CDC_AAref_Val=https://www.cdc.gov/niosh/topics/cwhsp/default.html; Centers for Disease Control and Prevention, "Pneumoconiosis and Advanced Occupational Lung Disease among Surface Coal Miners—16 States, 2010–2011," *Morbidity and Mortality Weekly Report* 61, no. 23 (2012): 431–34; Blackley et al., "Resurgence of Progressive Massive Fibrosis in Coal Miners."

3. Blackley et al., "Resurgence of Progressive Massive Fibrosis in Coal Miners."

4. Blackley et al., "Resurgence of Progressive Massive Fibrosis in Coal Miners"; Howard Berkes, "Advanced Black Lung Cases Surge in Appalachia," NPR, December 15, 2016, https://www.npr.org/2016/12/15/505577680/advanced-black-lung-cases-surge-in-appalachia; Blackley et al., "Progressive Massive Fibrosis in Coal Miners from 3 Clinics"; Carolyn Crist, "Resurgence of Crippling Black Lung Disease Seen in U.S. Coal Miners," Reuters Health, August 23, 2018, https://www.reuters.com/article/us-health-coalminers-idUSKCN1L82FT; McMillion and Berkes, *Coal's Deadly Dust*, 2016; Noemi B. Hall et al., "Current Review of Pneumoconiosis among US Coal Miners," *Current Environmental Health Reports* 6, no. 3 (September 2019): 137–47; Jeff Young, *Appalachian Fall: Dispatches from Coal Country on What's Ailing America* (New York: Tiller Press, 2020); Jeff Young, "Remembering a Miner Who Personified Coal's Contributions and Costs," *Ohio Valley ReSource*, WFPL, September 13, 2020, https://wfpl.org/remembering-a-miner-who-personified-coals-contributions-and-costs; Howard Berkes and Huo Jingnan, "Coal Miners to Demand Congress Restore Full Black Lung Benefits Tax," NPR, July 23, 2019, https://www.npr.org/2019/07/23/743152782/coal-miners-to-demand-congress-restore-full-black-lung-benefits-tax.

5. Emily Brigham, Kassandra Albright, and Drew Harris, "Health Disparities in Environmental and Occupational Lung Disease," *Clinics in Chest Medicine* 41, no. 4 (2020): 623–39; For the most recent CWSHP report, see CWSHP, "Advanced Pneumoconiosis among Working Underground Coal Miners—Eastern Kentucky and Southwestern Virginia, 2006," *Mortality and Morbidity Weekly Report* 56, no. 26 (2007): 652–55; an important study on racial injustice in pulmonary care is that of Michael Lake et al., "Black Patients Referred to a Lung Cancer Screening Program Experience Lower Rates of Screening and Longer Time to Follow-Up," *BMC Cancer* 20 (2020): 561; For further information about the erasure of the Black Appalachian experience, read the other chapters in this book and the following sources: William H. Turner, *The Harlan Renaissance: Stories of Black Life in Appalachian Coal Towns* (Morgantown: West Virginia University Press, 2021); Wright, *Carbon County USA*, 10; and William H. Turner, "The Canaries in Appalachian Coal Mines Were Black," *Now & Then: The Appalachian Magazine* 32, no. 2 (2016): 18; Joe William Trotter Jr., "The Dynamics of Race and Ethnicity in the US Coal Industry," *IRSH* 60 (2015): 145–64.

6. H. Morgan Griffith et al. to President Donald Trump, March 29, 2017, https://ohiovalleyresource.org/wp-content/uploads/2017/03/Black-lung-clinics-letter.pdf; Ron Carson, quoted in Berkes and Lancianese, "Black Lung Study Finds Biggest Cluster Ever."

7. F. Douglas Scutchfield and Randolph W. Wykoff, eds., *Appalachian Health: Culture, Challenges, and Capacity* (Lexington: University Press of Kentucky, 2022).

8. Steven H. Woolf and Paula Braveman, "Where Health Disparities Begin: The Role of Social and Economic Determinants—and Why Current Policies May Make Matters Worse," *Health Affairs* 30, no. 10 (2011): 1852–59; Kate Beatty and Melissa White, "The Social Determinants of Health," in Scutchfield and Wykoff, *Appalachian Health*; "Social Determinants of Health," HealthyPeople.gov, US Office of Disease Prevention and Health Promotion, updated October 8, 2020, https://wayback.archive-it.org/5774/20220413203948/https://www.healthypeople.gov/2020/topics-objectives/topic/social-determinants-of-health#two; Kathie Gerwig, cited in Theresa M. Wizemann, "Creating a Pipeline of Financing for Population Health: Exploring Sin Taxes and Tax Credits," in *Exploring Tax Policy to Advance Population Health, Health Equity, and Economic Prosperity: Proceedings of a Workshop, Oakland, California, December 7, 2017* (Washington, DC: National Academies Press, 2018).

9. Robert G. Evans, Morris L. Barer, and Theodore R. Marmor, *Why Are Some People Healthy and Others Not? The Determinants of Health Populations* (Boca Raton, FL: Routledge, 1994); David R. Williams, "Race and Health: Basic Questions, Emerging Directions," *Annals of Epidemiology* 7, no. 5 (1997): 322–33; Vickie M. Mays, Susan D. Cochran, and Namdi W. Barnes, "Race, Race-Based Discrimination, and Health Outcomes among African Americans," *Annual Review of Psychology* 58 (2007): 201–25; Zinzi D. Bailey et al., "Structural Racism and Health Inequities in the USA: Evidence and Interventions," *Lancet* 389, no. 10077 (2017): P1453–63; Courtney D. Cogburn, "Culture, Race, and Health: Implications for Racial Inequities and Population Health," *Milbank Quarterly* 97, no. 3 (2019): 736–61; Michele Morrone, *Ailing in Place: Environmental Inequities and Health Disparities in Appalachia* (Athens: Ohio University Press, 2020), 11.

10. Judith M. Graber et al., "Respiratory Disease Mortality among US Coal Miners: Results after 37 Years of Follow-Up," *Occupational and Environmental Medicine* 71, no. 1 (January 2014): 30–39; Michael Hendryx and Melissa M. Ahern, "Mortality in Appalachian Coal Mining Regions: The Value of Statistical Life Lost," *Public Health Reports* 124, no. 4 (July/August 2009): 541–50; David C. Holzman, "Mountaintop Removal Mining: Digging into Community Health Concerns," *Environmental Health Perspectives* 119, no. 11 (November 2011): A476–83; Anthony C. Gatrell and Susan J. Elliot, *Geographies of Health: An Introduction* (West Sussex: Wiley, 2015), 22, 146–48; Rachel E. Dixon, "Social Policy for Transitioning Regions: Resilience and the Future of Work in an Era of Post-Coal Risk" (MPhil diss., University of Oxford, 2020); Robert Todd Perdue, "Linking Environmental and Criminal Justice: The Mining to Prison Pipeline in Appalachia," *Environmental Justice* 11, no. 5 (2018): 177–82; Judah Schept, *Coal, Cages, Crisis: The Rise of the Prison Economy in Central Appalachia* (New York: NYU Press, 2022).

11. Nick Watts et al., "The 2020 Report of the *Lancet* Countdown on Health and Climate Change: Responding to Converging Crises," *Lancet* 397 (January 2021): 130; OECD, *Policy Highlights: The Economic Consequences of Outdoor Air Pollution* (Paris: OECD Publishing, 2016); Willie Dodson, "Black Lung Service Providers Shift in the Face of COVID-19," Appalachian Voices, March 24, 2020, https://appvoices.org/2020/03/24/black-lung-service-providers-shift-in-the-face-of-covid-19; Crist, "Resurgence of Crippling Black Lung Disease"; Committee on the Study of the Control of RCMD Exposure, *Monitoring and Sampling Approaches*, 1; David J. Blackley et al., "Small Mine Size Is Associated with Lung Function Abnormality and Pneumoconiosis among Underground Coal Miners in Kentucky, Virginia and West Virginia," *Occupational and Environmental Medicine* 71, no. 10 (October 2014): 690–94; Graber et al., "Respiratory Disease Mortality among US Coal Miners."

12. Ducatman and Dixon, "Appalachian Environment"; Carl Werntz, quoted in Caitlyn Greene and Patrick Charles McGinley, "Yielding to the Necessities of a Great Public Health Industry: Denial and Concealment of the Harmful Health Effects of Coal Mining," *Environmental Law and Policy Review* 43, no. 3 (2019): 748; Buddhi Gyawali et al., "Assessing the Effect of Land-Use and Land-Cover Changes on Discharge and Sediment Yield in a Rural Coal-Mine Dominated Watershed in Kentucky, USA," *Water* 14, no. 4 (2022): 516; Chelsea Harvey, "Three Reasons Appalachia's Risk of Deadly Floods Keeps Rising," *Scientific American*, August 3, 2022, https://www.scientificamerican.com/article/three-reasons-appalachias-risk-of-deadly-floods-keeps-rising; Holzman, "Mountaintop Removal Mining," A480; Michael Cusack O'Connell, dir., *Mountaintop Removal* (Washington, DC: PBS, 2007), DVD; Filippo Piscopo and Lorena Luciano, dir., *Coal Rush* (New York: Film2 Productions, 2012).

13. Nathaniel P. Hitt and Michael Hendryx, "Ecological Integrity of Streams Related to Human Cancer Mortality Rates," *EcoHealth* 7, no. 1 (2010): 91–104; Sudjit Luanpitpong et al., "Appalachian Mountaintop Mining Particulate Matter Induces Neoplastic Transformation of Human Bronchial Epithelial Cells and Promotes Tumor Formation," *Environmental Science & Technology* 48 (2014): 12912–19; Christina Umbright et al., "Pulmonary Toxicity and Global Gene Expression Changes in Response to Sub-Chronic Inhalation Exposure to Crystalline Silica in Rats," *Journal of Toxicology and Environmental Health, Part A* 80, no. 23–24 (2017): 1349–68; Michael Hendryx, Keith J. Zullig, and Juhua Luo, "Impacts of Coal Use on Health," *Annual Review of Public Health* 41 (2020): 397–415; Wiley D. Jenkins et al., "Population Cancer Risks Associated with Coal Mining: A Systematic Review," *PLoS One* 8, no. 8 (2013): e71312.

14. Beatty and White, "Social Determinants of Health"; Dixon, "Social Policy for Transitioning Regions," 2; Nate W. Kratzer, "Coal Mining and Population Loss in Appalachia," *Journal of Appalachian Studies* 21, no. 2 (Fall 2015): 173–88.

15. Erpu Zhu et al., *Towards an Inclusive Energy Transition Beyond Coal—A Comparison of Just Transition Policies Away from Coal between China, the EU and the US* (Milan: FEEM, 2021); Theresa Tibaldos and Teea Kortetmäki, "Just Transition Principles and Criteria for Food Systems and Beyond," *Environmental Innovation and Societal Transitions* 43 (2022): 244–45.

16. Alice Munro, Tammy Boyce, and Michael Marmot, *Sustainable Health Equity: Achieving a Net-Zero UK* (London: Institute of Health Equity, 2020); Sanna Markkanen and Annela Anger-Kraavi, "Social Impacts of Climate Change Mitigation Policies and Their Implications for Inequality," *Climate Policy* 19, no. 7 (2019): 828–29; Richard C. Ingram et al., "The Availability of Health Care in Appalachia," in Scutchfield and Wykoff, *Appalachian Health*; Carlos Dora, Michaela Pfeiffer, and Francesca Racioppi, "Lessons from Environment and Health for HiAP," in *Health in All Policies: Seizing Opportunities, Implementing Policies*, ed. Kimmo Leppo et al. (Helsinki: Ministry of Social Affairs and Health, Finland, 2013), 259.

17. Sources for information in the table:

- **AgriTech:** App Harvest, https://www.appharvest.com; Justin C. Strickland et al., "Cross-sectional and Longitudinal Evaluation of Cannabidiol (CBD) Product Use and Health among People with Epilepsy," *Epilepsy & Behavior* 122 (2021): 108205; Christopher Simpson, "Occupational Health and Safety in the Cannabis Industry," *Annals of Work Exposures and Health* 67, no. 7 (2020): 677–78; Jameson Mori and

Rebeca Smith, "Transmission of Waterborne Fish and Plant Pathogens in Aquaponics and Their Control with Physical Disinfection and Filtration: A Systematized Review," *Aquaculture* 504 (2019): 380–95.

- **Clean Energy Development:** Leslie Marshall et al., *Marshall Plan for Middle America: Roadmap* (Pittsburgh, PA: Center for Sustainable Business, University of Pittsburgh, 2020); Ana Rodriguez-Alvarez, "Air Pollution and Life Expectancy in Europe: Does Investment in Renewable Energy Matter?," *Science of the Total Environment* 792 (2021); A. Kosinska, B. V. Balakin, and P. Kosinski, "Use of Biodegradable Colloids and Carbon Black Nanofluids for Solar Energy Applications," *AIP Advances* 11, no. 055214 (2021); Shannon E. Bell, "Environmental Injustice and the Pursuit of a Post-Carbon World: The Unintended Consequences of the Clean Air Act as a Cautionary Tale for Solar Energy Development," *Brooklyn Law Review* 82, no. 2 (2017): 529–58; Jennifer Castor, Kaylyn Bacha, and Francesco Fuso Nerini, "SDGs in Action: A Novel Framework for Assessing Energy Projects against the Sustainable Development Goals," *Energy Research & Social Science* 68 (2020): 101556; Anamaria Bukvic et al., "Understanding Relocation in Flood-Prone Coastal Communities through the Lens of Place Attachment," *Applied Geography* 146 (2022): 102758.
- **Manufacturing:** Muhammad Salman Butt et al., "Climate Change Vulnerability, Adaptation Assessment, and Policy Development for Occupational Health," *Avicenna* 2022, no. 2 (2022).
- **Natural Resource Management:** ReImagine Appalachia, *ReImagine Appalachia Blueprint*, 2021, https://reimagineappalachia.org/wp-content/uploads/2021/03/ReImagineAppalachia_Blueprint_042021.pdf; Sharon Pailler et al., "Impacts of Community-Based Natural Resource Management on Wealth, Food Security and Child Health in Tanzania," *PLoS One* 10, no. 7 (2015): e0133252; Falguni Debnath et al., "Increased Human-Animal Interface and Emerging Zoonotic Diseases: An Enigma Requiring Multi-Sectoral Efforts to Address," *Indian Journal of Medical Research* 153, no. 5–6 (2021): 577–84.
- **Prison Management**: Elisa L. Toman, "Something in the Air: Toxic Pollution in and around U.S. Prisons," *Punishment & Society* 25, no. 4 (2022): 1–22; Schept, *Coal, Cages, Crisis.*
- **Recreational Tourism:** "Annual Park Ranking Report for Recreation Visits in: 2021," National Parks Service, 2022, https://irma.nps.gov/STATS/SSRSReports/National%20Reports/Annual%20Park%20Ranking%20Report%20(1979%20-%20Last%20Calendar%20Year); Maksim Godovykh and Jorge Ridderstaat, "Health Outcomes of Tourism Development: A Longitudinal Study of the Impact of Tourism Arrivals on Residents' Health," *Journal of Destination Marketing & Management* 17 (2020); Rob I. Mawby and Zarina I. Vakhitova, "Researching the Relationship between Tourism, Crime and Security: The Tourism Industry and the Disenfranchised Citizens," in *The Handbook of Security*, 3rd ed., ed. M. Gill (London: Palgrave, 2022); Andreas Psarras, Theodore Panajiotidis, and Andreas Andronikidis, "The Role of Tourism in Road Traffic Accidents: The Case of Greece," *Current Issues in Tourism* 27, no. 4 (2024): 567–83.
- **IT and Knowledge-Based Sectors:** Lauren Smiley, "Can You Teach a Coal Miner to Code?," WIRED Backchannel, November 18, 2015, https://www.wired.com/2015/11/can-you-teach-a-coal-miner-to-code/; BitSource website, https://bitsourceky.com.

- **Services and Hospitality:** Alana Semuels, "Imagining a Post-Coal Appalachia," *Atlantic*, April 8, 2015, https://www.theatlantic.com/business/archive/2015/04/imagining-a-post-coal-appalachia/389817; Tingting Christina Zhang, Edwin Torres, and Melissa Farboudi Jahromi, "Well on the Way: An Exploratory Study on Occupational Health in Hospitality," *International Journal of Hospitality Management* 87 (2020): 102382; Madhura Ayachit and Shyamsunder Chitta, "A Systematic Review of Burnout Studies from the Hospitality Literature," *Journal of Hospitality Marketing & Management* 31, no. 2 (2022): 125–44; Anasua Bhattacharya and Tapas Ray, "Precarious Work, Job Stress, and Health-Related Quality of Life," *American Journal of Industrial Medicine* 64 (2021): 310–19.

18. Robert Pollin and Brian Callaci, "The Economics of Just Transition: A Framework for Supporting Fossil Fuel–Dependent Workers and Communities in the United States," *Labor Studies Journal* 44, no. 2 (2019): 94; Robin C. Vanderpool et al., "Health Behaviors in Appalachia," in Scutchfield and Wykoff, *Appalachian Health*; Barbara Ellen Smith, *Digging Our Own Graves: Coal Miners & the Struggle over Black Lung Disease*, updated ed. (Chicago: Haymarket Books, 2020).

19. Blackley et al., "Resurgence of Progressive Massive Fibrosis in Coal Miners," 500; Robert C. Stansbury, "Progressive Massive Fibrosis and Coal Mine Dust Lung Disease: The Continued Resurgence of a Preventable Disease," *Annals of the American Thoracic Society* 15, no. 12 (2018): 1394–96; J. Matthew Judge et al., "The Exposure Experience: Ohio River Valley Residents Respond to Local Perfluorooctanoic Acid (PFOA) Contamination," *Journal of Health and Social Behavior* 57, no. 3 (September 2016): 336.

20. Harry Caudill, *Night Comes to the Cumberlands: A Biography of a Depressed Area* (Boston: Little, Brown, 1962); Homer Bigart, "U.S. Reveals Plan to Fight Appalachian Poverty," *New York Times*, November 13, 1963, archived online: https://www.nytimes.com/1963/11/13/archives/us-reveals-plan-to-fight-appalachian-poverty-franklin-roosevelt-jr.html; Steven Stoll, *Ramp Hollow: The Ordeal of Appalachia* (London: Macmillan, 2017), 260; "ARC's POWER Initiative," Appalachian Regional Commission, updated 2021, https://www.arc.gov/newsroom_topic/power-initiative/#:~:text=Appalachian%20Regional%20Commission%20Awards%20Nearly,opportunities%20in%20coal%2Dimpacted%20communities; "Power Initiative," US Economic Development Administration, https://www.eda.gov/archives/2016/power, accessed 2021.

21. "Black Lung Clinics Program," Health Resources and Services Administration, reviewed July 2020, https://www.hrsa.gov/get-health-care/conditions/black-lung; US Department of Health and Human Services, *Rural Action Plan* (Washington, DC: US DHHS, 2020), https://www.hhs.gov/sites/default/files/hhs-rural-action-plan.pdf.

22. Morrone, *Ailing in Place*, 32; Ducatman and Dixon, "The Appalachian Environment."

23. "Black Lung Benefits: An Administrative Review," *Bulletin of the Social Security Administration*, October 1971, 1, https://www.ssa.gov/policy/docs/ssb/v34n10/v34n10p11.pdf; Office of Workers' Compensation Programs, "Black Lung Program," OWCP, 2021, https://www.dol.gov/agencies/owcp/dcmwc; Office of Workers' Compensation Programs, "Guide to Filing for Black Lung Benefits," OWCP, 2021, https://www.dol.gov/agencies/owcp/dcmwc/filing_guide_miner; Howard Berkes and Benny Becker, "Kentucky Lawmakers Limit Black Lung Claim Reviews Despite Epidemic," NPR, March 31, 2018, https://www.npr.org/2018/03/31/598484688/kentucky-lawmakers-limit-black-lung-claims-reviews-despite-epidemic.

24. Daniel Boswell, "Workers' Compensation Reform Complicating the Black Lung Epidemic," *Miami Business Law Review*, January 26, 2019, https://business-law-review.law.miami.edu/workers-compensation-reform-complicating-black-lung-epidemic; Shannon E. Bell and Richard York, "Community Economic Identity: The Coal Industry and Ideology Construction in West Virginia," *Rural Sociology* 75, no. 1 (2010): 111–43; Eric Lipton, "Behind the Coal Industry's Trump-Era Lobbying War," *New York Times*, October 5, 2020, https://www.nytimes.com/2020/10/05/us/politics/coal-trump-industry-lobbying.html; Timothy Cama, "Trump Administration Halts Research on Mountaintop Removal Coal Mining," *Hill*, August 21, 2017, https://insideclimatenews.org/news/21082017/mountaintop-mining-coal-health-study-scrapped-trump.

25. Adam Mayer, "A Just Transition for Coal Miners? Community Identity and Support for Local Policy Actors," *Environmental Innovation and Societal Transitions* 28 (September 2018): 1–13; Jeff Goodell, *Big Coal: The Dirty Secret behind America's Energy Future* (Boston: Houghton Mifflin, 2006), XVII–XVIII.

26. Erin A. Thomas, *Coal in Our Veins: A Personal Journey* (Boulder: University Press of Colorado, 2012), 166; Shannon E. Bell, *Our Roots Run Deep as Ironweed: Appalachian Women and the Fight for Environmental Justice* (Champaign: University of Illinois Press, 2013).

27. Shannon E. Bell, *Fighting King Coal: The Challenges to Micromobilization in Central Appalachia* (Cambridge, MA: MIT Press, 2016), 5–7.

28. Heather Lukacs, Nicole M. Ardoin, and Emily Grubert, "Beyond Formal Groups: Neighboring Acts and Watershed Protection in Appalachia," *International Journal of the Commons* 10, no. 2 (2016): 878–901; Elinor Ostrom, *Governing the Commons* (Cambridge: Cambridge University Press, 1990); "Who We Are," Appalshop, updated 2021, https://appalshop.org/story; "Our History," Mountain Association, updated 2021, https://mtassociation.org/about/our-history/; "About," Generation West Virginia, originally published 2016, https://generationwv.org/about; "About Us," Appalachian Voices, updated 2021, https://appvoices.org/about.

29. Georgia Piggot et al., *Realizing a Just and Equitable Transition Away from Fossil Fuels* (Stockholm: Stockholm Environment Institute, 2019); Fergus Green and Ajay Gambhir, "Transitional Assistance Policies for Just, Equitable and Smooth Low-Carbon Transitions: Who, What and How?," *Climate Policy* 20 (2020): 902–21.

30. Dixon, "Social Policy for Transitioning Regions."

31. These sources are quoted in Dixon, "Social Policy for Transitioning Regions"; Rachel Notley, *Alberta's NDP: Leadership for What Matters, Election Platform 2015* (Edmonton, AB: National Democratic Party, 2015); "Support for Albertans Affected by Coal Phase Out," Government of Alberta, 2019, https://www.alberta.ca/support-for-coal-workers.aspx; "Coal Community Transition Fund," Government of Alberta, 2019, https://www.alberta.ca/coal-community-transition-fund.aspx.

32. Dixon, "Social Policy for Transitioning Regions."

33. These sources are quoted in Dixon, "Social Policy for Transitioning Regions"; White House, "White House Announces Details on President's Plan to Provide Americans with Job Training and Employment Services," March 12, 2012, https://obamawhitehouse.archives.gov/the-press-office/2012/03/12/white-house-announces-details-president-s-plan-provide-americans-job-tra; White House, "Remarks by the President in State of the Union Address," January 24, 2012, https://obamawhitehouse.archives.gov/the-press-office/2012/01/24/remarks-president-state-union-address; "Fact Sheet: Overview of

the Clean Power Plan," US Environmental Protection Agency, 2015, https://19january2017snapshot.epa.gov/sites/production/files/2015-08/documents/fs-cpp-overview.pdf; Barack Obama, "Remarks by the President in Announcing the Clean Power Plan," speech to the United States of America, August 3, 2015, https://obamawhitehouse.archives.gov/the-press-office/2015/08/03/remarks-president-announcing-clean-power-plan; "Fact Sheet: Administration Announces New Economic and Workforce Development Resources for Coal Communities through POWER Initiative," White House, August 24, 2016, https://obamawhitehouse.archives.gov/the-press-office/2016/08/24/fact-sheet-administration-announces-new-economic-and-workforce.

34. These sources are quoted in Dixon, "Social Policy for Transitioning Regions," 38–47; "US Department of Energy Announces $64M for Components of Coal FIRST Power Plants," National Energy Technology Laboratory (NETL), May 18, 2020, https://www.netl.doe.gov/node/9752; "DOE Announces Intent to Commit $81 Million for Coal FIRST Design Development," NETL, February 7, 2020, https://www.netl.doe.gov/node/9484; "Coal Communities Commitment: Diversifying Coal Communities for a Resilient Future," US Economic Development Administration (EDA), October 11, 2017, https://www.eda.gov/funding/programs/american-rescue-plan/coal-communities-commitment.

35. Dixon, "Social Policy for Transitioning Regions," 86.

36. Hendryx, Zullig, and Luo, "Impacts of Coal Use on Health"; Ian Gough, "Climate Change: The Myopia of Social Policy," speech to the University of Oxford Department of Social Policy and Intervention, March 11, 2021.

37. Eeva Ollila, Fran Baum, and Sebastián Peña, "History of HiAP," in Leppo et al., *Health in All Policies*, 4; Steven H. Woolf, "Progress in Achieving Health Equity Requires Attention to Root Causes," *Health Affairs* 36, no. 6 (2017): 986; Linda Rudolph et al., *Health in All Policies: A Guide for State and Local Governments* (Washington, DC: American Public Health Association and Public Health Institute, 2013).

38. Ducatman and Dixon, "Appalachian Environment"; "About," Farmacy West Virginia, 2021, http://farmacywv.com/about/; "MCHC Farmacy—2015–2018 and Beyond," Mountain Comprehensive Health Corporation, 2020, https://www.mchcky.com/farmacy; Kentucky Education and Workforce Development Cabinet, "Kentucky Broadband Initiative," Team Kentucky, 2021, https://educationcabinet.ky.gov/Initiatives/Pages/KBI.aspx.

Strategies for Advancing Just Transitions

9
Building Networks for Just Transitions

Ivy Brashear, Peter Hille, and Betsy Whaley

The challenges eastern Kentucky faces are deep-seated, long-standing, and systemic. A lack of economic diversification that could have fueled just transitions has meant that the region's economic systems were fundamentally broken long before the collapse of the coal industry. The mono-economy of the coal industry helped create and maintain this system for more than 150 years. Job scarcity and low educational attainment helped ensure a ready workforce, and reliance on coal jobs created significant social and political protection against opposition to the industry's environmental impacts, labor practices, and health and safety issues.

Just transition in eastern Kentucky means justice for former coal industry workers, and a broad transition toward economic justice for the communities and all people living there. The framework of Appalachian just transition is built on the understanding that these communities fueled the growth of the entire nation while sacrificing lives, health, economies, and ecosystems to do so. The extraction economy in this region contributed significantly to generational poverty, leaving many families unable to weather economic shifts and climate disasters such as the July 2022 floods. The coalfields now bear the brunt of global changes in the energy economy coal miners helped to build. Crises like the COVID-19 pandemic and the unprecedented flooding continue to fully reveal the deep economic hardship faced by many in eastern Kentucky. Justice here demands major investment to build a new economy and demands that it be done in a way that doesn't just benefit the few. The new economy must be more diverse, sustainable, equitable, and resilient.

A just transition in eastern Kentucky is bold and complicated and requires a set of complex interconnected strategies that work across a wide range of fronts. The resources needed are enormous and can't all flow through any one channel. This means that the nature of the problems and the scope of the solutions are well suited to a networked approach—in fact, they demand it.

In this chapter, we explore some of the most active Central Appalachian just transition networks operating today. We focus on the Central Appalachian Network, the Appalachia Funder's Network (AFN), and What's Next, East Kentucky?! (WNEKY). We explain how they differ and where they are situated along the continuum of structure and formality. We draw on these examples to illustrate how elements of networked capacity make economic transition work and consider the role that philanthropic funders play in creating, shaping, and sustaining networks.

The Mountain Association (formerly known as the Mountain Association for Community Economic Development, or MACED) has worked toward an ambitious vision of just transitions for post-coal Appalachia since 1976. We believe the people of eastern Kentucky and their communities hold the keys to transforming the region. We work in partnership with people and support their ideas and goals to diversify the region's economies. We define just and equitable community economic development as a community-led, action-oriented approach to regenerating local economies and strengthening democracy. This approach recognizes that the economic, environmental, and social challenges eastern Kentucky faces are interconnected and complex and that solutions must simultaneously address issues on individual, community, and regional levels. To be effective, solutions must be inclusive, particularly of people and groups that have been historically excluded from decision-making and wealth building. The solutions must be rooted in place, culture, and local knowledge. Such an undertaking goes well beyond the capacity of any one entity. It can't even be fully addressed with the resources of the largest philanthropies or the federal government itself. It is certainly beyond the reach of any single regional nonprofit alone. However, networks help connect the various individual groups, entities, and funding sources in ways that allow just transition to happen more efficiently and effectively.

Networks differ in operation from single organizations in a variety of ways. They are generally not owned and directed by any one entity, they may not have one strong, clear center, and while they are generally aligned around some set of shared interests, they often also encompass and allow for diversities of mission, analysis, alliances, strategies, and tactics. There is a range of networks and degrees of interconnection, alignment, and formality. Some are loose, informal networks of association in which the entities involved might recognize their interconnections, but there is no formal structure, membership, or stated purpose. Networks can also be highly structured, have very specific membership agreements, clear leadership structures, and agreed-upon mission, strategy, fundraising, and staffing. Networks can evolve along this continuum and begin to look and function more like organizations, but they retain key characteristics of networks, including decentralized leadership, multiple intersecting priorities, and a set of resources and capacities that are broader than those of a single organization.

Eastern Kentucky has many organic networks that have no name, no structure, no center, and no formal membership but are nevertheless effective in aligning shared work efficiently. Organizations that form organic networks have established relationships and shared interests and can effectively collaborate as a result. Such organic networks often overlap significantly with formal networks.

Mapping organic networks reveals multiple nodes rather than one center. Organizations with more disparate analysis and strategy may connect through different nodes, which illustrates the breadth of capacity brought to the work and the gaps where there are opportunities for more strategic alliance.

A network map of eastern Kentucky nonprofits working toward just transition was developed in 2016 by representatives of Mountain Association, Appalshop, Kentuckians for the Commonwealth (KFTC), Community Farm Alliance (CFA), and the Stay Together Appalachian Youth Project (STAY). The process helped us, as aligned organizations, advance our understanding of how nonprofit capacities intersect. Some focus on organizing and advocacy, some develop strategic communications for narrative change, and others work on tangible projects that demonstrate new economic opportunities. All the organizations are doing different work in connected and important ways, and those networked connections allow us all to leverage a much wider range of assets and capacities.

Compion et al. found that more than two hundred local economic development organizations in the fifty-four Kentucky Appalachian counties operate in a core-periphery manner. In other words, older, more established organizations act as central nodes of activity and information, while smaller, less-established organizations operate on the periphery in a loose partnership structure.[1] Mapping these economic development nonprofits allowed researchers to identify strengths and weaknesses of those organizations and their partnerships. Information revealed through network mapping can be valuable to organizations working toward a similar goal because it can show them how their unique skill sets work together.

Central Appalachian Network: How a Long-Standing, Highly Structured Network Works

The Central Appalachian Network (CAN) was established in 1992 after several nonprofits in Kentucky, Ohio, Virginia, and West Virginia explored intersections in their work.[2] Early conversations were supported by a program officer from a regional foundation that already supported several of the organizations. Today, CAN represents a well-established and highly structured network with members from six Central Appalachian states. Its structural elements include Memorandums of Understanding (MOUs), a leadership committee, an annual budget, and staffing provided by a third-party network coordinator.

CAN's strength has allowed the network to become more intentional in advancing identified economic sectors with specific, intersecting strategies. It accomplishes this work through formal working groups in four identified sectors: food systems, clean energy, reduce and reuse, and climate restoration. Work was led for many years by a steering committee of seven anchor member organizations. As CAN has shifted to more intentional emphasis on equity, the network transitioned to a more inclusive and representative model of governance, with a leadership team representing the working groups and rotating seats for other organizations. Members of the leadership team participate in fundraising for the network and receive stipends to support their CAN participation.[3] CAN is composed of more than fifty member organizations, including for-profit and nonprofit enterprises.

CAN's sector-based work in food systems, clean energy, reduce and reuse, and climate restoration seeks to create a just transition in ways that are locally based and inclusive. The food-systems work was built on foundational work completed by two network members. This work began in 2000 and has established networks of producers and a value chain of production, aggregation, and regional distribution. The working group builds value chains in a collaborative spirit, develops supportive policy work, and publishes educational campaigns for consumers and producers. They have also tracked the growth of local food systems since 2009. More recently, the group formed a subgroup to address land access for beginning farmers.

Clean Energy has emerged as a key economic sector in the region in recent years. The clean energy working group was launched in 2016, and it functions through three committees: policy and advocacy, communications, and investment. One of the first actions of the policy and advocacy subcommittee was to develop a rapid response fund for organizations to apply for minigrants to address emergent policy shifts that could negatively impact growth of clean energy in the region. The communications subcommittee creates clean energy communications campaigns to amplify important clean energy stories in the region, and the investment subcommittee fosters a pipeline of regional, investable clean energy projects that would be most ready to receive investment.

The most recent working groups—reduce and reuse and climate restoration—build cross-state networks to grow sectors focused on climate mitigation and increase collective impact of the network.

Without these working groups, individual organizations would create duplicative programming and communications campaigns, which would lessen their overall impact. In coming together, organization can share lessons learned, amplify each other's work, and be more effective and strategic. The network helps speed up the process of building a new economy by increasing the impact of our collaborations.

This approach is not without its challenges. In its early days, CAN often functioned as a think tank and mutual support group whose external functions were appearances at topical convenings and occasional research projects with published results.[4] As CAN has become more intentional through its working groups, it has also wrestled with equity implications between the structured steering committee and the informal network. CAN had long recognized that steering committee membership required significant time and effort, so it raised funds to support the shared work and pay for contract services for network management and facilitation. Those funds also paid stipends to steering committee members. This model helped keep the network strong and ensured a high level of active participation. However, it also raised questions about how steering committee membership was determined and the relationship between the steering committee and the broader network.

The working groups have become more formalized with their own MOUs. In 2019, CAN expanded its structure, practices, governance, and self-definition. It restructured in 2020 to include more members and define different types of memberships, including their specific benefits and expectations. With new structures and procedures to better define roles, responsibilities, and benefits for the leadership team, the working groups, and the broader network of networks, CAN is even better suited to help foster a just transition that works for everyone.

Appalachia Funders Network: How Philanthropy Can Build Networks

Funders often think networks of grantees can align the work they support and maximize the impact of their funding. At their best, these types of networks increase connectivity between organizations that already have significant alignment in mission and strategic work. Funder support for these networks often includes funding for meetings, training, travel, and shared work.

It's also true that funder-driven networks can also be artificial constructs that the organizations are compelled to do to access funding for their respective organizations. Such networks often exist only for the duration of a funder's specific programmatic initiative that created the network. Funder-created networks can also establish connections that might not otherwise exist. These may or may not bear fruit depending on whether there is shared interest and mutual benefit. Because there are many funders supporting work in Appalachia, there are multiple overlapping networks that represent groups of grantees.

Funder-driven networks with an interest in Appalachia organized the Appalachia Funders Network in 2010.[5] AFN has become an important forum that fosters shared analysis of the region's challenges and provides coordination of approaches to address them. AFN has supported regional CAN convenings and creative place making and energy projects in the region. AFN and CAN provide significant thought-leadership and advocacy for the Appalachian just transition framework.

What's Next, East Kentucky?!: How the Mountain Association Supports Grassroots Regional Networks

Mountain Association has focused more explicitly on developing and growing a network of local community groups across eastern Kentucky since 2017 through WNEKY, which demonstrates the possibilities created when interregional collaboration is centered. We helped form WNEKY and have worked with its steering committee to build its foundation and expand.[6]

WNEKY's goal has always been encouraging greater communication, cooperation, and collaboration across county lines in eastern Kentucky. This goal is a direct response to the observation that multiple organizations were leading various initiatives to support community economic development in each eastern Kentucky county, but there was little collaboration between those groups across county lines.

Representatives from Mountain Association, Appalshop, Brushy Fork Institute and AIR Institute of Berea College, Foundation for Appalachian Kentucky, and Community Farm Alliance convened in 2017 to determine how to better collaborate. The partners decided over several months of meetings that they would support development of a grassroots network of communities in eastern Kentucky. Initial goals included: build strong regional collaboration that connects communities so they can share what is working in their places; amplify successes; learn from one another; and advance community-led just economic transitions.

A group of leaders from the communities involved in these initial conversations came together at the Brushy Fork Institute Leadership Summit in Berea, Kentucky, in September 2017. The Institute is an annual convening at Berea College where workshops that train and build capacity for nonprofit, community, and government leaders are hosted. The group of community leaders that met through Brushy Fork was interested in network theory and how they could apply those ideas to the blossoming work they were doing together.[7] In thinking about next steps for their coalition, they formed a steering committee, and, later that year, the WNEKY network was born.

They were faced with an overarching question: Why build another network when several eastern Kentucky and Central Appalachian networks already existed among educators, business support organizations, and governmental entities, such as the Shaping Our Appalachian Region (SOAR) initiative (which began as a bipartisan, quasi-governmental initiative to support economic growth in eastern Kentucky)?[8] What could another network possibly accomplish that hadn't already been tried by all the others?

The answer was that many of the existing networks were built around professions or professionals rather than around grassroots community leaders. There was no grassroots regional network of community leaders committed to working together to build a just economic transition across lines and identities that often divide the region, including politics, city/county rivalries, religion, and/or socioeconomic status. Rivals are identified early in life through sports in the school systems, and the often-false notion of resource scarcity for community development persists, perpetuating a spirit of competition rather than collaboration between communities. In this environment of perceived scarcity, collaboration between communities seems counterintuitive. WNEKY aims to combat those notions of division and scarcity by focusing on collaboration, mutual decision-making, and the belief that collaboration and cooperation bring greater access to resources for all.

WNEKY came into being in the wake of the high-profile formation of SOAR.[9] WNEKY's original partners, however, identified a need for a broad-reaching grassroots network emphasizing a just transition framework. Mountain Association has played the important role of incubating the nascent WNEKY network, and Mountain Association's just transition definition—that community economic development efforts should be community-led and focused, that local assets should be at the center, and that whatever economy replaces extraction should be just, equitable, sustainable, and resilient—was adopted by WNEKY as a guiding principle. Mountain Association wanted to ensure that this network would operate from the bottom up, with community groups collaborating to build capacity for just transitions, and that its leaders would helm such efforts.

Mountain Association turned to two examples of successful Appalachian networks to help build WNEKY: CAN, and Try This West Virginia, a network of communities aimed at improving public health in West Virginia.[10]

Try This West Virginia is an inspiring example of what can happen when communities come together to share ideas of what is possible around a particular theme or economic sector. Their annual conference draws hundreds of people and is focused on empowering local leaders and shifting the narrative about the possibilities in Appalachia. They also offer a minigrant program for communities to build local health initiatives.

In 2019, the program supported community groups in building walking trails, starting community gardens, transforming unused properties into public exercise spaces, training trainers to lead health reset courses, offering yoga classes for children, and providing solar installations for community gardens. Groups funded through the minigrants have an opportunity to share their stories at the annual conference. Try This West Virginia proves that supporting ideas that work can shift the narrative in communities, encourage emerging leaders, and inspire change, and its example was instrumental in the foundation of WNEKY.

Rural Support Partners (RSP) has extensively researched rural networks and has identified "building blocks" for successful networks. These building blocks include trusting relationships, shared vision and values, clear benefits for local people, shared power and accountability, and strong backbone support.

Mountain Association and WNEKY leaned heavily on this research in building WNEKY.[11] Using the RSP research "Rural Networks for Wealth Creation" as a guide, considerable time was spent on creating a shared vision and defining WNEKY values and principles.[12] That vision and those values serve as a foundation that guided the work that followed.

WNEKY's vision and mission is to build relationships, connect communities, celebrate successes, and collaborate to support a thriving eastern Kentucky. The values that guide the work are:

- Communities taking the lead when determining what works best for their place.
- Inclusion.
- Mutual respect.
- Accountability.
- Equity.

The steering committee outlined the following objectives to clarify network priorities:

- Put feet on ideas to get stuff started and/or done.
- Connect communities to allies and resources for support, training, skill sharing, and skill building.
- Provide learning opportunities in communities across the region.
- Deploy shared communication about opportunities, events, training, and regional collaboration.
- Tell stories of innovation and success.
- Answer questions and connect inquiries to and within the network.
- Honor communities that are making progress and are actively engaged in the network.

- Build the next generation of eastern Kentucky leadership by emphasizing youth involvement and leadership development.

While the network is still very young, it is already adding value for participants. WNEKY provides information about resources, including funding opportunities, and connects members to those resources.

For example, in 2021, WNEKY launched a pilot program with funding from the USDA to test the concept of a "Community Accelerator" in Grayson, Kentucky. The Accelerator would support grassroots organizing, leadership capacity building, and resource development for community-based projects that support community economic development. In the first year, Grayson leaders helped the city become recognized as a "gig city," turned an empty and overgrown lot on Main Street into a "pocket park," and admitted the city into Kentucky's Main Street Program. Participants said the Community Accelerator program was integral in each of these initiatives and likely would not have happened without the program. WNEKY has received Appalachian Regional Commission funding to expand the pilot to two more communities in 2022 and 2023.

Collaboration is hard and requires time, energy, and resources. It requires a significant investment from all parties to build trust and relationships, and this is challenging in eastern Kentucky, where the perception of scarcity is felt most keenly. Many networks fail because participants don't have the capacity to ensure the work is getting done. Frequently, network members believe the work of the network is important, but it's not their primary responsibility, so network projects get pushed to the back burner. The RSP rural network research shows that networks need backbone support and coordination to become and remain successful. As an example, RSP provides backbone support for CAN through network coordination, which includes logistical support to the steering committee and working groups, organizing fundraising efforts, and managing communication among members—work that might not happen without RSP's support.

Having a network coordinator whose top priority is the work of the network ensures members have the support they need to move from good ideas to completed projects. Mountain Association received funding from the Catholic Campaign for Human Development in 2018 to support WNEKY start-up and cover costs of coordination, meeting expenses, and small participation stipends for steering committee members. Mountain Association had the help of an Appalachian Transition Fellow, who served as the WNEKY network coordinator in 2018. The Appalachian Transition Fellowship program was operated by the Highlander Research and Education Center.[13] The program trained and placed young Appalachians in organizations across Central Appalachia to grow those organizations' capacity to help deepen and strengthen the Appalachian just transition.

Mountain Association provided funding for Brushy Fork Institute to hire a coordinator for WNEKY in 2019. The coordinator facilitates communication with the steering committee, prepares agendas, follows up on action items, arranges logistics, and supports the network's working groups. This coordination is invaluable and ensures the work moves forward without the steering committee feeling overwhelmed or overburdened, which can create burnout and high turnover.

Since WNEKY began, more than forty community groups and entities from twenty eastern Kentucky counties have participated in network activities. These activities have included community conversations, public gatherings about specific topics, and steering committee meetings.

A recent evaluation by researchers at the University of Kentucky using ripple effects mapping found that WNEKY is providing benefit to individuals and communities in a variety of ways.[14] Specifically, the network is:

- Building more trust and stronger relationships across the region.
- Supporting the growth of stronger leaders and organizations.
- Leveraging more funding for communities.
- Increasing influence on policy and necessary systemic change.
- Accelerating change through collaboration and regional initiatives.[15]

WNEKY has grown so much that the network is now independently identifying and pursuing funding sources for their work.

It is clear from Mountain Association's years of building, fostering, and being a part of networks that they are essential in building a new, thriving economy in eastern Kentucky and beyond. They bring together members with a diverse set of strengths in various areas of expertise, which are then used to support a common vision of a brighter future. They allow us to be more than the sum of our parts, and help build and organize broader networks to catalyze, guide, and sustain eastern Kentucky's future. They help support anchor organizations and community groups that bring best practices and local knowledge into the network, which then are transferred back out into their respective communities and used for the collective betterment of those places. And, equally importantly, these many varied networks help articulate, advocate, and demonstrate the just economic transition needed in the region through coordinated storytelling and narrative efforts. This work helps accelerate just transition beyond the scope of any one entity's individual work and allows us all to build region-wide coalition toward a more sustainable and just economic future in Central Appalachia.

Mountain Association's goal of achieving a just and equitable economic transition to a post-coal economy in eastern Kentucky cannot be achieved by us alone. Nor can it be reached if each individual community group, nonprofit, institution, or entity dedicated to this work attempts to do so alone. We must work together in intersecting networks of connection to reach this ambitious goal. Some of those networks will be formal, like CAN and AFN; others will be informal, like the partnerships Mountain Association has with other eastern Kentucky–based organizations. Still others, like WNEKY, will be created at the grassroots level and carried forward by people living and working within communities.

We must also look beyond our Appalachian region for inspiration. Some networks of which the Mountain Association is a part are national in focus and include nonprofit groups from other frontline communities across the country where fossil fuel extraction and production have had a monopoly on the local economy for generations. These communities—which include Alaska; Buffalo, New York; Richmond, California; the Navajo Nation; southern Louisiana; and the Deep South—have borne the brunt of the economic exploitation that extraction causes and are now on the forefront of ushering in a just economic transition to a post–fossil fuel economy as a result. Appalachia has emerged as a leader in these national networks, and organizations working toward a just transition in eastern Kentucky have become a consistent voice for the just transition movement more broadly. These organizations, of which Mountain Association is a key member, have decades worth of knowledge and expertise from which to draw; because of that, our collective insight is often sought out by other communities.

Networks are dynamic, living things, and they evolve over time. Inevitably, by the time these words are printed, much of the detail may be out of date, but the networks themselves, and the principles and values that guide them, will continue to carry the work of just transition in Central Appalachia forward.

Notes

1. Sara Compion et al., "The Collaboration Networks of Economic Development Organizations in Eastern Kentucky," *Journal of Appalachian Studies* 21, no. 1 (2015):105–27.

2. Central Appalachian Network, https://www.cannetwork.org, accessed March 10, 2021,

3. Anchor organizations in CAN are: Coalfield Development, Appalachian Sustainable Development, NCIFund, Rural Action, Mountain Association, ACEnet, and Community Farm Alliance.

4. More information about the Central Appalachian Network can be found on their website: https://www.cannetwork.org. Further archival information about CAN, compiled

in 2011, is housed on an internal online server at Mountain Association and can be shared upon request.

5. Appalachia Funders Network, https://www.appalachiafunders.org, accessed March 10, 2021.

6. What's Next EKY?! https://whatsnexteky.org, accessed March 10, 2021.

7. Brushy Fork Institute was founded in 1998 by Berea College President John B. Stephenson, a leading Appalachian scholar, to meet what he saw as a need to bring local leaders together for networking, noting that they themselves had "the wisdom, the vision and the commitment to guide the development of their own communities." Brushy Fork's role has always been that of a convener and a catalyst, building on those local perspectives and assets, and was built on Berea College's long tradition of outreach and regional engagement. The work of the Institute builds on the history of Berea's support of the Council of the Southern Mountains (which operated as the premier network of regional organizations from 1913 to 1989) and the work of the Berea College Appalachian Fund (which was founded in 1950 and continues to support and connect organizations working in the region), showing the long tradition of outreach and regional engagement. Loyal Jones, founder of the Berea College Appalachian Center and former executive director of the Council of the Southern Mountains, helped guide the development of the fledgling Institute during Brushy Fork's early years. The Council, the Fund, and the Institute all utilized intentional network building to advance their respective missions in the region.

8. Shaping Our Appalachian Region, https://www.soar-ky.org, accessed March 10, 2021.

9. SOAR was founded by Republican US Representative Hal Rogers and then-Governor Steve Beshear, a Democrat, at the point when the collapse of the coal industry became impossible to ignore. It was meant to move the region toward a more diversified economy. Its founding in 2013 came on the heels of the Appalachia's Bright Future gathering, hosted by a loose network of nonprofit organizations in the region, of which Mountain Association was a part. At that time, when the coal industry began its precipitous decline in eastern Kentucky, many entities and institutions were attempting to work together to design a path forward for the region. While SOAR has built a far-reaching network and strategy for growth in the region, some groups that were not included in the initial planning of SOAR and who have not been represented on its executive committee have described it as a "top-down" effort to support economic development that isn't always focused on just and equitable transition. SOAR has largely championed traditional approaches such as industrial recruitment, whereas many grassroots groups in the region favor more locally driven approaches. The effort's focus and bipartisanship can vary with each new election.

10. Try This West Virginia, https://trythiswv.com, accessed March 10, 2021.

11. Paul Castelloe, Thomas Watson, and Katy Allen, "Rural Networks for Wealth Creation: Impacts and Lessons Learned from US Communities," Rural Support Partners, 2011, https://www.ruralsupportpartners.com/wp-content/uploads/2018/04/RuralNetworksforWealthCreation.pdf, accessed January 21, 2025.

12. Castelloe, Watson, and Allen, "Rural Networks for Wealth Creation."

13. Appalachian Transition Fellowship, https://highlandercenter.org/programs/appfellows, accessed March 10, 2021.

14. Nicole Breazeale and Heather Hyden, "Summary of Ripple Effect Mapping Process and Analysis with the Community Impact Office" (private archive of Mountain Association, 2020), 1–2.

15. Breazeale and Hyden, "Ripple Effects Mapping," 1–2. The report noted that WNEKY is "creating a new culture of development in the region" and that "all of their investments are about modeling and supporting members to do a different kind of development, namely one that is participatory and rooted in the rich arts and natural resource base of the region. It is a network of border defying individuals who can safely challenge each other's philosophy and approaches to community-based economic development. They are changing the culture of individualism and competitiveness within the region and creating consensus that pushes beyond political gridlock and negative narratives of EKY at the national level."

10

"Prisons Are Not Innovation"

Abolitionist Interventions for a Just Transition

SYLVIA RYERSON AND JUDAH SCHEPT

Central Appalachia today remains one of the most concentrated regions of rural prison and jail expansion nationwide. The region now hosts sixteen prisons in total, half of which are in eastern Kentucky. These facilities disproportionately incarcerate people of color from low-income communities, who are often sent hundreds of miles from home to serve time in the mountains. And while critical interventions into dominant narratives of Appalachia as a geography of monolithic whiteness demonstrate that the region is home to complex multiracial histories and contemporary communities, these prisons are located in counties that today are overwhelmingly white, revealing the profoundly racialized spatial contours of the US carceral state.[1]

The recent explosion of incarceration in the coalfields cannot be divorced from the long decline of the coal industry. Since the late 1980s, local, state, and national leaders have promoted prisons as rural jobs programs that can replace the ongoing loss of employment in the coal industry, despite dubious and contrary evidence of this economic strategy. From 2011 to 2018, eastern Kentucky lost 73 percent of its coal jobs. Statewide, the number of coal jobs in Kentucky is at its lowest since the nineteenth century, with 3,760 workers in the industry. In a telling comparison, there are now far more corrections jobs in the state—6,640—although that number does not include the medical, clerical, and mental health workers who also work inside prisons.[2] In short, prison and jail jobs have overtaken coal jobs in Kentucky by *thousands* of positions. Several eastern Kentucky counties have also turned toward jails as solutions to the twin crises of skyrocketing incarceration rates and severe declines in county revenue. As of late 2020, the Kentucky state prison population includes approximately 24,000 people, but there are only 11,700 state prison beds. Because of this severe overcrowding, the Kentucky Department of Corrections incarcerates almost half of state prisoners in county jails, paying those counties per diem rates. This arrangement has become particularly notable in the last decade as the number of people held in local jails in Kentucky increased 39 percent precisely during the same period in which coalfield communities suffered a precipitous drop in contributions from the coal severance tax, a once-reliable source of significant revenue. As cash-strapped eastern Kentucky counties are thrown deeper into crisis and are forced to eliminate jobs and close or dramatically reduce social and emergency services, they have increasingly looked to jails to shore up severe revenue shortages.[3]

The construction and expansion of prisons and jails constitute the state's response to the myriad crises generated by the decline of coal. As the dominant development efforts in the region, they serve as a key component of Central Appalachia's economic restructuring in this moment of transition. This predatory and pernicious approach fails to address the actual crises in Appalachian communities while building out a geography of racialized class war.

Importantly, this carceral regime has not gone uncontested. Local actors have challenged the logics of this growth, radically changing perceptions of the US carceral state and recognizing people incarcerated in the region as a part of the community. This chapter focuses on the long fight against the proposed 1,200-bed maximum security US Penitentiary and 256-bed Federal Prison Camp (USP-Letcher) in Letcher County, Kentucky. Organized opposition resulted in the historic defeat of the prison project in June 2019, when the Federal Bureau of Prisons (BOP) officially withdrew its Record of Decision (ROD) to build the facility. Unfortunately, at the time of this writing, the Bureau of Prisons has recently resumed efforts to build a prison in Letcher County, this time proposing a medium security prison: Federal Correctional Institution (FCI) Letcher. These new plans were announced just two months after the devastating summer floods in eastern Kentucky in the summer of 2022. Examining the work of the first coalition of local organizers, landowners, national attorneys and advocates, and federal prisoners who opposed USP-Letcher, this chapter considers what lessons and strategies can be learned from this multiracial and multiscalar campaign, to inform the broader Appalachian just transition movement. This chapter concludes with a brief discussion of the now unfolding efforts to stop this prison *again*, arguing that they underline the crucial importance of building and sustaining ongoing opposition to racialized mass incarceration into the movement for a just transition.

Inspired by the tradition of political and intellectual collaborations between organizers, journalists, and scholar-activists, including within Appalachian studies, this chapter draws heavily on, and learns primarily from, many of the actors who were deeply involved in the fight against USP-Letcher.[4] We conducted interviews with ten individuals during the summer of 2019 and the winter of 2020. As two people involved in the campaign against USP-Letcher, we felt strongly that the people we interviewed for the research were our interlocutors and cotheorists, whose insights shaped our own understandings of the lessons of this fight.

"A Sense of Urgency": Local Opposition to USP-Letcher

US Representative Harold "Hal" Rogers's office first proposed USP-Letcher to a group of county elites in 2004. The project was poised to become the fourth federal prison built in eastern Kentucky since 1992, following Rogers's long established "pork barrel" strategy of building prisons to secure federal funding to his district.[5] The plan mirrored Rogers's process of bringing federal prisons to neighboring eastern Kentucky counties of Clay, Martin, and McCreary in 1992, 2003, and 2004, respectively. After nearly a decade of bureaucratic stops and starts, the project began to gain momentum in 2013 with the commencement of the BOP's official "scoping period," the first stage in a federal agency's movement through the environmental review process. Following the 1969 passage of the National Environmental Protection Act (NEPA), all federal agencies must conduct such a process, culminating in a series of Environmental Impact Statements (EIS), open public comment periods on those statements, and an official ROD. As the environmental review was still in process, on December 18, 2015, $444 million of funding was approved for the project as part of the fiscal year 2016 federal budget passed by Congress and signed by President Obama.

This federal funding allocation catalyzed local opposition with a heightened sense of urgency. In the winter of 2015–2016, local activists came together to form the Letcher Governance Project (LGP) and began formally organizing and holding meetings. LGP was composed primarily of young white people living in Letcher County and the surrounding area. Many were experienced organizers who already had an intimate relationship to, and understanding of, the violence of the carceral state. Several had family members who had served time in jail or prison, and some had relatives who worked in the prison system. Some lived in Wise County, Virginia, adjacent to Letcher County and home of the notorious supermax Wallens Ridge and Red Onion State Prisons. Some worked on issues related to criminalization and incarceration, including substance abuse counseling and advocacy for the restoration of voting rights for former felons in Kentucky. The majority of LGP members were involved with *Hip Hop from the Hill Top & Calls from Home* (CFH), a weekly radio show on WMMT 88.7, the community radio station of media arts and education center Appalshop, rooted in Letcher County since 1969. For over two decades, the station has broadcast toll-free messages and music requests from family members to their loved ones incarcerated in the eight prisons within WMMT's listening area.[6] LGP founding member Tanya Turner described how regularly hosting CFH for over seven years informed her personal commitment to opposing USP-Letcher.

> It makes you reckon with some of your own internal lies about who's in prison . . . It is an intimate thing and you build relationships with people who are experiencing this violent isolation from their loved ones, and thinking in your head about how fucked the Criminal Justice system is, and understanding intimately what people are missing out on and how it impacts families . . . and you know we're even progressive, radical leftists or whatever, but we had a lot to learn about what it means to serve time. And for the regular bluegrass listeners that tune into WMMT, it's really a push on them about who is serving time. When you have to hear kids sing their ABCs to their dads—like "oh Daddy, I learned my ABCS"—it's a really jarring, it's an almost unintentionally jarring and shocking piece of radio.[7]

If CFH and other movement work had already politicized people around incarceration, the 2014 and 2015 uprisings in Ferguson and Baltimore, part of the emergent Black Lives Matter movement, further inspired and influenced them. Together, these events and activities contributed to a rigorous analysis of the carceral state and the role of Letcher County in the struggle against it. As LGP founding member Tom Sexton explained,

> For a lot of us, [fighting USP-Letcher] was the natural extension of Calls from Home. It put a sense of urgency behind the question of what are *we* going to do with the prison that's coming to *our* town that's going to be half a billion dollars? So big picture: Ferguson and the [BLM] protests activated people. . . . It got me to thinking about my own community, a disproportionately white community, and how we look at incarceration. And we're not an elitist society here. Almost everybody, even if you've got money, has a cousin or something that is either addicted to drugs or got locked up for selling drugs or some sort of crime. So it got me thinking: How can we connect the plight of Black folks that are locked up to the plight of poor whites here? That was my starting point. And you know, we've gotten to the point: this whole idea of race and class, as either one or the other, is just ridiculous. They're inextricably linked, and we see that in the carceral state here.[8]

While Representative Rogers worked with the Letcher County Planning Commission, a volunteer group of county elites, to rally support for the prison, LGP members knew that local sentiment was more ambivalent and saw both a need and a space for organizing. As LGP member Lill Prosperino noted, "I think a lot of people in Letcher County felt kind of indifferent about the prison. I don't think anybody was like 'Yeah we really want a prison!' But people were like, 'Oh we really need jobs.' So I think folks realized that they needed to have a framing and a story of people from, or living in, Letcher County that didn't want the prison and concrete reasons as to why. And so for me, LGP was always important for that reason."[9]

Organizers anticipated that local elites would frame all opposition as coming from "outsider agitators." Thus the choice of the Letcher Governance Project as a name was a deliberate and strategic move to establish their credibility and commitment to the future of the county. From the beginning, even as they formally coalesced to fight the prison, LGP's larger vision was centered on challenging regional power structures and organizing for grassroots democratic decision-making and local self-determination. To that end, the group developed a campaign around reclaiming the monies allocated for the prison for "real economic alternatives that are not built on human suffering," expressed by the hashtag #our444million. As Turner described how they developed this framing, "When you are just seeing so intimately everyday what your community lacks, it's hard not to dream about what that much money could do.... And we landed on #our444mil and that hashtag campaign generated hundreds of local people sharing ideas that they had, for what they would spend that money on. And they were really big dreams.... People talked about rehab facilities, art centers, big maker spaces, all kinds of stuff. There were local high school teachers, artists, kids, and punk rockers all using the hashtag."[10]

LGP's reframing delegitimized the prison proposal and simultaneously demanded meaningful, community-controlled investment in Letcher County. The group's political strategy emerged out of both local conditions and in generative study and struggle with other social movement organizations in the South. In particular, Turner noted the influence of a grassroots campaign led by Black youth in Atlanta against $10 million dollars of funding for police in schools, called "10 Mil 4 Real?" Locally, #our444million opened up a discursive and political space for imagining alternative material proposals, powerfully disrupting and recharting the terms of local debate. Evidence of the success and reach of the campaign could be seen in the thousands of oppositional comments submitted during the NEPA process, as people from Letcher County, as well as places as distant as Oregon and Philadelphia, framed their analysis in the language of #our444million.[11]

"A Flashback of That Heyday": Connecting to Prior Struggles

As LGP mobilized locally to counter the swell of prison boosterism, national environmental attorneys and activists also joined the fight, lending their support through extensive challenges during the NEPA Process. Using the tools of environmental legal campaigns, the Abolitionist Law Center (ALC) and Prison Ecology Project/Fight Toxic Prisons (FTP) challenged each iteration of the EIS, forcing multiple revisions.[12] This was part of a larger strategy to delay the process in hopes that the political and economic conditions might shift enough over time for the project to lose credibility and momentum.

As all of this was unfolding, local landowner Mitch Whitaker had his own concerns. Whitaker's property was a part of the original seven hundred acres chosen by the BOP as the site for the prison. Even though plans had been in the works for USP-Letcher since 2004, Whitaker first heard about the BOP's interest in his property in 2015 through an article in the local newspaper, the *Mountain Eagle*. He described himself as also shocked by the elite-driven and closed nature of the process: "It was just gonna get run by us so fast. . . . and if we hadn't put just a little pushback on it—see, it was on a fast track, it really was. And I could see that, because as a landowner right in the thick of this, I was never contacted!"[13] Whitaker is a master falconer who rehabilitates birds of prey on his land, which has been in his family for four generations. He was deeply concerned about the impact prison lights and fences would have on his ability to train, hunt with, and rehabilitate his birds. But his opposition to selling his land to the BOP also had deeper roots. Whitaker's father and grandfather fought to protect the property from strip mining in the 1970s.[14] Whitaker connected his current opposition to his family's prior struggles to protect their land.

> My grandpa didn't own the mineral rights so he really didn't have a right to his coal. People would cut [through] their backyards to get a truckload of coal . . . that was the mentality of it back then: "It's coal, it's money so we're going to take it, we're going to rip your land all to pieces." They could've got that over on my grandpa had it not been for my dad. My dad was educated, him and his brother were the first two in their family to go [to college], and so they told grandpa, "Look, we've got rights here. They can't come and bust your property into pieces." And had it not been for that, this all would have been for *naught* anyway—they would've *already* tore it up. So this was to me a flashback of that heyday. . . . And had it not been for Dad telling him you've got the *right*, it would have busted right through my grandfather's cow pasture and just been the awfulest mess there ever was. . . . It would have been terrible to have seen it split down the middle—and that's what I thought was gonna happen again.[15]

Whitaker also saw similarities between the BOP's attempts to buy land for USP-Letcher and the deeper history of land agents buying people's mineral rights.

> I feel like back when those old folks sold their mineral rights to these coal companies, the coal company would send a land guy in, and say, "Hey we're gonna give you five thousand dollars for that old hill behind your house that you can't even till—we're not even gonna bother you, we're gonna get stuff out from under it—coal." Folks were desperate and needed money back then. They didn't see that they were selling theirselves off so *cheap*. . . . If they could have held out, or if they knew the *value* of it, they wouldn't have sold it for pennies. A lot of times they were told, "You can keep the land; we just want the coal." . . . They were all sort of snookered and lied to. Again—same thing is happening here. This was tried to [be] slid right through before anybody could do any research or see how these other prisons have done in the area, before you knew what the real consequence was. Boy, it was a real *take advantage* type business move and I feel like this prison here is the same thing.[16]

From his own family's experience, Whitaker had a concrete analysis of the connections between prisons and coal in the region. Both are driven by imperatives from outside of the region, predicated on a process that precludes fully informed community consent and relying on the presumption of local obedience and deference to elites—coal company executives, the Federal Bureau of Prisons, state and local politicians, and entrenched local power structures. Moreover, Whitaker's steadfast opposition was rooted in his own deep relationship with and understanding of his land as part of a larger ecosystem, providing an essential habitat for native species of plants and animals. With the support of the ALC, FTP, and LGP, Whitaker refused to sell his land to the BOP. This refusal forced the agency to redraw the boundaries of the site, which triggered the need for a revision of the EIS, critically buying the emerging coalition more time to organize.

"Prisons Are Not Innovation": Disrupting the Process of Planning as Usual

In the summer of 2016, LGP members staged a protest at a regional "innovation summit" hosted by Shaping Our Appalachian Region (SOAR), a bipartisan economic development initiative started by Governor Steven Beshear and Congressman Rogers in 2013. During Rogers's keynote address, the group

"Prisons Are Not Innovation" 167

US Congressman Harold "Hal" Rogers (KY-5) at the podium as LGP members and supporters hold signs and disrupt his address. Photograph by Mimi Pickering, 2016.

stood up in front of the audience holding signs that read "Prisons Are Not Innovation" and "#our444million." LGP member Tanya Turner recalled the group's decision to interrupt the summit.

> They were saying [that SOAR] would be the new way money goes to the region. It was happening before our eyes—we were locked out of this process of investment again. It was still the same good ol' boys system [of decision-making] and they were pretending like it was a participatory process—that's what was so upsetting.
>
> And it was just infuriating to think that [Rogers] is getting all this praise for his *innovation*—even *if* some of these were good ideas happening through SOAR—they were still only [receiving] a fraction of the money that was being funneled into the prison. And so, it just felt like "everyone look over here at this shiny thing and don't think about this monument of human misery that we're going to build." And they were live streaming it, so we knew—because we weren't getting any local

attention—but we knew they couldn't ignore it if we dropped a banner in front of his face, they could not ignore that.[17]

Headed by the very person at the root of the past quarter century of prison building in the region, the SOAR Summit offered LGP a public and symbolic space to disrupt existing narratives and interject their own. As a bureaucratic and top-down attempt to articulate economic transition, SOAR necessarily and deliberately excluded people, projects, and organizations that its leadership saw as challenging to its vision for the region. As LGP member Tarence Ray argued, "Many of us were drawn from the ranks of the Just Transition Movement, and to us, the prison was a perfect example of an *unjust* transition. It was an expansion of the carceral state, which we considered to be an integral part of this nation's white supremacist legacy; it was reactionary, because incarceration targets the poor without offering rehabilitative or restorative solutions. Opposing it was not only the moral thing to do: the legitimacy of the just transition message rested on opposing it."[18]

Importantly, the action at SOAR had a big impact on Mitch Whitaker. As he recalled, seeing coverage of the protest fortified his determination to not sell his land.

> I had felt like that lone boat out in the ocean with no one around. So, all of a sudden I've got some more boats tied to me. And it done me so good when I seen on the evening news, when they . . . stood right up you know with the signs [laughs], that was it! That's my pals, you know those are the ones that understand it the same way. They're actually in it for what's right. . . . And that's when I said, "This is my fight." And there was times I thought, "Well, Mitch, you're just selfish, it's your backyard. You know, you're the one that doesn't want this, everybody else wants it." But then when those guys got on board it let me know that it wasn't just me . . . it wasn't just *my* selfishness wanting it out of here, but there was a lot of good reasons why we didn't need that prison.[19]

Attorney Dustin McDaniel of the Abolitionist Law Center also understood the action at SOAR as particularly significant: "Politically speaking, the Letcher Governance Project was a big deal. If [the BOP and local prison boosters] were successful in establishing this [narrative] of you know 'It's the community against the outsiders,' then you know they're winning politically. And when LGP started organizing and specifically when they did the 'our 444 million' action and campaign, that made it clear that that narrative didn't work."[20]

While LGP members faced significant backlash for their action, the protest succeeded on multiple fronts.[21] By confirming the presence of a group of local people committed to fighting the prison, the action strengthened the resolve of people like Whitaker while publicly rejecting the notion that opposition to the prison was the product of "radical outsiders" meddling in Appalachia. The action also directly challenged the terms and terrain of the Appalachian transition debate more broadly. By expressing their vision at SOAR, the LGP rejected recruitment into an economic agenda dictated by hierarchical and exclusive development schemes predicated on the purported deputization of regional workers into a central site of racialized state violence. Instead, the LGP insisted on a future built in solidarity with other geographies of dispossession.

"Solidarity Politics": Forging New Alliances for a Just Transition in Appalachia and Beyond

Recasting the terms of the debate opened space for new alliances to be built. While Whitaker acknowledged that his opposition was initially rooted in his own self-interest ("it's your backyard"), through his collaboration with LGP, ALC, and FTP, his own politics around incarceration shifted. Whitaker reflected on this.

> If there would have been some way they could've squelched my voice, they would have. So that's what they're doing with these people in prison—they're squelching them out, [including] to where we don't hear from them . . . because they're not citizens anymore. And I never thought that before. I thought, if you was in prison, you needed to be in there. . . . And everyone [locally was saying] prisons are good, prisons are good.
>
> You have to research, you have to look at both sides, and the more I got to looking at it, the more it wasn't all I used to think it was. It just seemed like this was done to a *whole culture* of people. And since then, I've heard all these facts about, you know, no one in the world incarcerates people as much as we do here, and the ratio, we are getting terrible about putting people in there. . . . Yes, my ideas of prison changed.[22]

Whitaker reidentified his own experience of getting his voice "squelched" with those of people incarcerated. And indeed, people incarcerated had also not been consulted about the plan to build USP-Letcher. As part of the ALC's overall legal strategy, attorney Emily Posner had been working tirelessly throughout the EIS process to solicit comments from people incarcerated in the federal prison system across the country. If the prison were to be built, federal prisoners would have no legal protection against being transferred to the new facility and thus constituted potentially directly impacted parties. The ALC was developing the argument that people incarcerated in the federal prison system had been unlawfully excluded from the NEPA process, as the BOP had neglected to provide copies of the EIS to any federal prison libraries. As Manuel Gauna, who submitted a complaint from federal prison in Arizona, stated, "I believe that construction of this particular prison is neglecting the people in Letcher and the people in the prison system. We as prisoners should have had the opportunity to participate in this public comment period for this project."[23]

As LGP member Lill Prosperino underscored, reading these comments from people incarcerated across the country was meaningful and fortifying in return.

> When I read these letters from people who are in prison, the fact that they even consider people in Letcher County as a reason why the prison shouldn't be built is so incredible to me. You're on the frontlines of this huge problem, and you care about, you know, "redneck" people in eastern Kentucky—it just feels amazing. My hope is that feeling is reciprocated. I hope that folks who are locked up know that in this situation, we were trying to come together and help each other out. There was this one guy [Manuel Gauna] in Arizona; his letter was very moving to me. To me that was why it was important to keep going even when we felt like we had lost momentum or things were not looking good.[24]

Mitch Whitaker's refusal to sell his land combined with extensive legal challenges during the NEPA process resulted in a historic number of EIS revisions—five in all—effectively delaying the prison's progression by three years. When the BOP ultimately delivered its ROD to build in April 2018, ALC immediately filed a lawsuit on behalf of twenty-one incarcerated plaintiffs, arguing that they and everyone incarcerated within the federal prison system had been unjustly excluded from the environmental review process. During this time, the political context continued to shift dramatically, and contradictions at the highest levels of the federal government were intensifying. Between the Trump administration's funding priorities at the southern border, declining numbers of federal prisoners, and federal sentencing reform, there were noticeable and widening cracks in the foundation of support for the prison. The ALC continued to build their legal case and cultivated a local plaintiff to add to the lawsuit. Several individuals worked with the ALC to form Friends of the Lilley Cornett Woods and North Fork River Watershed (FOLC), a nonprofit organization dedicated to conservation and environmental protection in the county and region. As a local organization comprised of mostly Letcher County residents who stood to be adversely impacted by the prison, the FOLC constituted a traditional NEPA plaintiff and thus added legal legibility to the lawsuit built around the federal prisoners' complaints. Following the passage of the First

Step Act in December of 2019, the ALC seized the moment and refiled an amended lawsuit, further arguing that given these political developments, the prison was unnecessary according to the BOP's own projections. Crucially, this meant that as a federal project that would have a significant environmental impact, USP-Letcher did not meet the statutory requirement under NEPA that the purpose and need for the project be legitimate. Months later, in June 2019, the BOP officially withdrew the ROD to build USP-Letcher, citing the concerns of ALC's lawsuit in their decision. This reversal marked the first time the construction of a federal prison has been halted following the allocation of funding *and* the issuance of a ROD, effectively defeating what was slated to become the most expensive prison built in US history.

For attorney Emily Posner, this was evidence of both the success of the coalition's strategy and the vision that fighting against prisons is central to the work of building a just and sustainable and, eventually, regenerative future.

> This was a demonstration of a lot of organizing work, keeping people involved, not giving up, demonstrating that solidarity politics really *do* work and that it's a multipronged effort. You can't just rely on litigation, you have to organize, you have to do media work, people have to feel empowered and that they can make a difference. And we all have to do this together.... I'm not a resident of southeastern Kentucky, but ... we need to be putting money into transitioning our economy into a different and better world for our children and grandchildren that's not dependent on fossil fuel and resource extraction, and that is sustainable and locally based ... and that transition also includes transitioning away from an economy based on incarceration.[25]

Amid the decline of coal, Central Appalachia has turned to incarceration as a strategy of crisis management, despite the proven economic failure of this approach and the harm and cruelty it inflicts. But this strategy of building cages in the coalfields has not come without visionary opposition. In observing Letcher County as a key site of struggle against a carceral future for Appalachia, we conclude that the success of this coalitional organizing offers several key lessons for the just transition movement.

First, LGP's #our444million campaign and broader calls for transparent local democracy and self-determination delegitimized the prison as a path for economic development. This framing demanded community-controlled investment in a healthy future for Letcher County, crucially opening up space to imagine alternative material proposals beyond the narrow purview of elite-driven planning efforts. Second, building from Mitch Whitaker's personal history and analysis, the coalition located prison building as a continuation of prior and ongoing processes of dispossession, not a "transition" away from them. Tracing how the legacies of strip mining created the economic and spatial conditions of possibility for prison growth enabled organizers to connect their opposition to the prison to the deep genealogies of radical organizing *in* Appalachia. The success of this strategy demonstrates the political possibilities that emerge when these historical connections are made, and how a just transition must directly reckon with these legacies of dispossession, not build on top of them. Third, the coalition demonstrated how a just transition in Appalachia will require the continued forging of new identifications and alliances with communities of color that are the most subject to criminalization and organized abandonment. The lawsuit brought by twenty-one incarcerated plaintiffs offers a concrete strategy for claiming the legitimate standing people incarcerated should have on questions of carceral expansion. The alignment of their legal challenge with organized local opposition, and especially local landowner Mitch Whitaker's commitment—parties that are generally framed in opposition in dominant political and media discourses on rural prison building—underscores the political power of coalition building across time, place, strategy, and prison walls. But these unlikely alliances did not happen without tremendous effort and labor. They were forged in the process of struggle itself, rooted in Letcher County's long history of radical organizing, and nurtured through LGP, ALC, and FTP's creative and tireless work throughout the NEPA process and lawsuit. In the words of LGP member Lill Prosperino, who grew up in Letcher County just a few miles from the proposed site, the fight against USP-Letcher reaffirmed their commitment to antiracist and anticapitalist organizing, grounded in relationships built with people currently incarcerated and their families.

> To me the fight's not over just because there isn't a prison in Letcher county. There shouldn't be prisons anywhere. And that needed to happen yesterday. [It] needed to never happen. I want to celebrate this win, but for me, celebrating is really just taking a deep breath, and saying, "Wow, that happened, and I have to keep going." To me, I can't turn a blind eye to every other place because they didn't build a prison in the town I'm from. A lot of people showed up for me and for us during that time, and so I owe it to them. All of those people incarcerated—they should all get a letter from me. I want to express my gratitude to them.[26]

May 2023 Addendum

Three years after the victory over USP-Letcher, on September 28, 2022, the BOP announced plans to build a new Federal Correctional Institution in

Letcher County (FCI-Letcher), a 1,152-bed medium security prison with an adjacent 256-bed work camp. The announcement came just two months after floodwaters ripped through eastern Kentucky on July 27, 2022, causing devastation and death across six counties; Letcher County was in the heart of the flood zone. The legacies of mining—the loss of topsoil, trees, and plants from mountains, and the choking of streambeds with this "overburden"—exacerbated heavy rains and contributed to the unprecedented "1000-year flood." The construction of prisons on top of these same sites would preempt any kind of climate mitigation efforts while perpetuating the horrors of racialized mass incarceration.

A new coalition to oppose FCI-Letcher has now formed, the stakes of this fight laid all the more bare by the fatal flood. Building Community Not Prisons (BCNP) includes concerned local residents; people formerly incarcerated in the region; and local, regional, state, and national organizations fighting mass incarceration, climate change, and environmental injustice, all brought together by the shared objective of stopping the prison in Letcher County once again, and once and for all. As this next chapter of the struggle unfolds in Letcher County, it will build on the foundations of the previous fight, and Central Appalachia will continue to be a critical site of struggle in the global fights against coal, cages, and climate change. The work of the coalition against USP-Letcher shows us a path forward, one rooted in a politics of solidarity between poor communities impacted by the myriad harms of mass incarceration and on the frontlines of economic abandonment and climate disaster.

Notes

1. Karida L. Brown, *Gone Home: Race and Roots through Appalachia* (Chapel Hill: University of North Carolina Press, 2018) and https://www.blackinappalachia.org.

2. Kentucky Energy and Environment Cabinet, Kentucky Quarterly Coal Report, 2020—Q2; Coal Facts 2017; Bureau of Labor Statistics, Occupational Employment and Wages, May 2017: Correctional Officers and Jailers. https://www.bls.gov/oes/current/oes333012.htm#ind.

3. Jack Norton and Judah Schept, "Keeping the Lights On: Incarcerating the Bluegrass," Vera Institute of Justice, 2019, https://www.vera.org/in-our-backyards-stories/keeping-the-lights-on; Robert Perdue and Kenneth Sanchagrin, "Imprisoning Appalachia: The Socio-Economic Impacts of Prison Development," *Journal of Appalachian Studies* 22, no. 2 (2016): 210–33; Sylvia Ryerson and Judah Schept, "Building Prisons in Appalachia: The Region Deserves Better," *Boston Review*, 2018, http://bostonreview.net/law-justice/sylvia-ryerson-judah-schept-building-prisons-appalachia; Sylvia Ryerson, "Prison Progress?," *Daily Yonder*, February 20, 2013, https://dailyyonder.com/speak-your-piece-prison-progress/2013/02/20.

4. Charles Hale, ed., *Engaging Contradictions: Theory, Politics and Methods of Activist Scholarship* (Berkeley: University of California Press, 2008); Jordan Camp and Christina Heatherton, eds., *Policing the Planet: Why the Policing Crisis Led to Black Lives Matter* (London: Verso, 2016). In Appalachian studies, see Stephen Fisher, ed., *Fighting Back in Appalachia: Traditions of Resistance and Change* (Philadelphia: Temple University Press, 1993); Mary Beth Bingman, "Stopping the Bulldozers: What Difference Did It Make?," in Fisher, *Fighting Back in Appalachia*, 16–30.

5. Ryerson and Schept, "Building Prisons in Appalachia," 2018.

6. See https://wmmt.org/projects/restorative-radio, accessed on March 5, 2025.

7. Tanya Turner, telephone interview with Sylvia Ryerson and Judah Schept, March 3, 2020.

8. Tom Sexton, interview with Sylvia Ryerson, Whitesburg, KY, June 25, 2019.

9. Lill Prosperino, telephone interview with Sylvia Ryerson and Judah Schept, June 24, 2019.

10. Turner, interview.

11. Judah Schept, *Coal, Cages, Crisis: The Rise of the Prison Economy in Central Appalachia* (New York: New York University Press, 2022).

12. See https://abolitionistlawcenter.org and https://fight-toxic-prisons.org, accessed March 5, 2025.

13. Mitch Whitaker, interview with Sylvia Ryerson, Whitesburg, KY, June 28, 2019.

14. On the broad form deed, see Ronald D. Eller, *Uneven Ground: Appalachia since 1945*. (Lexington: University of Kentucky Press, 2008); and Eller, *Miners, Millhands, and Mountaineers: Industrialization of the Appalachian South, 1880–1930* (Knoxville: University of Tennessee Press, 1982).

15. Whitaker, interview.

16. Whitaker, interview.

17. Turner, interview.

18. Tarence Ray, "Hollowed Out: Against the Sham Revitalization of Appalachia," *Baffler* 47 (2019), https://thebaffler.com/salvos/hollowed-out-ray.

19. Whitaker, interview.

20. Dustin McDaniel, telephone interview with Sylvia Ryerson and Judah Schept, June 21, 2019.

21. For more on the backlash LGP members faced, see Tarence Ray, "A Way Out: An Activist with an Ulcer Asks, 'Why do Nonprofits Exist?,'" *Popula*, November 18, 2018, https://popula.com/2018/11/18/a-way-out.

22. Whitaker, interview.

23. "Prisoners File Unique Environmental Lawsuit Against New Federal Facility on Strip Mine Site in Kentucky," November 26, 2018, https://fight-toxic-prisons.org/2018/11/26/prisoners-file-lawsuit-against-new-federal-facility-on-toxic-strip-mine-site-in-kentucky.

24. Prosperino, interview.

25. Emily Posner, telephone interview with Sylvia Ryerson and Judah Schept, June 19, 2019.

26. Prosperino, interview.

11

Appalachian Transition Fellowship

Supporting Youth Leadership for a Long-Term Vision

ALICE BEECHER, ABBY HUGGINS, MAE HUMISTON, CAITLIN MYERS, SUSAN WILLIAMS, AND ELIZABETH WRIGHT

Highlander Research and Education Center's Appalachian Transition Fellowship was a leadership program in Central Appalachia that prioritized Appalachian people as experts of their own experiences, supported emerging and youth leadership, and increased capacity for just transition work on the ground. The seeds for the fellowship were planted in 2012, when the Center partnered with Rural Support Partners and the Appalachian Funders Network to organize listening sessions with regional stakeholders, young people, community allies, and philanthropic partners to examine the future of a just transition in Appalachia. The conversations highlighted the need for a leadership program in Central Appalachia, emphasized the importance of cross-sector partnerships, prioritized economic solutions independent of coal, and started to develop a concrete plan for an economic transition from extractive industries, ecological devastation, wealth and health disparities, and scarcity mindsets.[1]

The Beginnings: A Brief History of the Highlander Center

The Highlander Center (originally, the Highlander Folk School) was founded in 1932 to provide education and support for people in Appalachia and the Southeast through organizing for social justice and building local leadership. Highlander's skill-building and leadership development work supported the labor movement of the 1930s and 1940s, the Civil Rights movement of the 1950s and 1960s, and communities across the US South and Appalachia fighting for economic, environmental, and racial justice throughout the Center's ninety years.

From the 2008 economic crash through the COVID-19 pandemic, conditions facing Appalachian communities have intensified: lack of access to affordable health care, housing crises, food insecurity, high rates of addiction,

APPALACHIAN TRANSITION FELLOWSHIP

Appalachian Fellowship Transition Graphic, created by Beatriz Mendoza and AFT staff team, at a Highlander Seeds of Fire Camp, 2013.

unemployment, lack of broadband, human-instigated climate disasters, and racial and wealth disparities.[2]

The term "just transition" referred to our desire to create a more just, equitable, and sustainable future for the region by pursuing alternative possibilities. Highlander's just transition work centers solidarity economics, prioritizing people and the planet over profits. We developed "Mapping our Futures," a popular education curriculum that supports communities in assessing and shifting economics and governance systems and connects our region with international efforts animated by the same solidarity values. Solidarity economy principles call for an increase in community control, power in the hands of workers and directly impacted communities, and the protection of our region's natural resources. The AppFellows program applied these principles by supporting thirty-two emerging leaders from 2014 to 2019 in paid, yearlong fellowships with eighty-eight Appalachian organizations across sectors and issues, boosting capacity and connectivity for community-led projects that advanced just transitions.[3]

Fellows were emerging leaders with a demonstrated record of community work and a commitment to staying in Appalachia, collaborating with host communities in West Virginia, Kentucky, Ohio, Tennessee, Virginia, and North Carolina, in both urban and rural settings. Their day-to-day work included organizing community meetings, knocking on doors, water testing, researching land records, informing state and national policy, mentoring youth, facilitating popular education workshops, conducting oral history interviews, building relationships in their communities, and more.

Fellows gathered monthly for popular education workshops with Highlander staff, peer networking, and place-based learning in different communities across the region. Fellows and hosts came together each year for regional gatherings, exploring topics like scaling up local economies and people power, sharing our stories, and prison justice in Central Appalachia. The program was co-coordinated by members of the Education Team from Highlander with programmatic and administrative support from other Highlander staff. Detailed evaluations were conducted annually that explored each fellow's own personal gains, community benefits, and suggestions to improve the fellowship program. By 2019, AppFellows came to a close, having supported thirty-two emerging leaders and eighty-eight Appalachian organizations across sectors and issues, boosting capacity for community-led projects advancing a just transition. In 2021, Highlander released an overarching assessment and best practices for advancing this work through a report created in partnership with Dialogue and Design titled *Beyond Transition: Appalachia's Pathway to Justice and Transformation*.[4]

Selected AppFellow alumni offer their reflections below.

AppFellows on the Ground: Reflections on Successes and Challenges

Abby Huggins: Program Coordinator's Overview

The most successful outcomes occurred when smaller grassroots organizations were paired with larger organizations that had resources but allowed the work to be directed by grassroots players. This allowed for redistribution of resources and guidance by people who are experts in their own communities. For instance, in Martin County, Kentucky, where the community has been facing water crises or decades, Ricki Draper (2018–2019) worked directly with the Martin County Concerned Citizens (MCCC) to conduct water testing, hold community meetings, and advocate for affordable water at a state level. MCCC partnered with Appalachian Citizens Law Center (ACLC), which offered legal support and strategizing and helped write a report about this crisis. However, the work was directed by those in Martin County most affected by the environmental, infrastructural, and systemic challenges of a lack of clean, affordable drinking water.[5]

Some fellows remained with the host organizations or groups they connected with after their fellowship year. AppFellows Eric Dixon and Kenny Bilbrey (2014–2015) copublished a policy paper on abandoned mine land programs during their fellowship year. Eric continued to contribute to national policy related to abandoned mine land reclamation through the RECLAIM Act and is now a researcher with the Ohio River Valley Institute, providing research and resource support in the wake of the horrific flooding in eastern Kentucky in 2022. Kenny went on to become the inaugural coordinator of the STAY (Stay Together Appalachian Youth) Project.[6]

Many other fellows also remain in the region and continue to be leaders in the places they are making home. For instance, Willa Johnson returned to her home community to direct the Appalachian Media Institute and served as director of films at Appalshop, which experienced terrible damage in the wake of the flooding in 2022. Appalshop is working to recover archival films, to restore their building, and to provide support to the local communities through the Appalshop radio station, which was wiped out in the flood but quickly reorganized to broadcast in the wake of the flooding. Joey Aloi remains involved in health and food access in West Virginia; and Ricki Draper supported Martin County Concerned Citizens in raising awareness of the lack of affordable, clean water by coauthoring a report after the fellowship ended.[7]

Highlander also hired members of the second cohort in management positions to support programming of the third cohort. Over the course of the fellowship year and beyond, fellows developed strong relationships and an informal network of peer support. The first two cohorts formed an alumni advisory group that provided input to the next cohort. The AppFellows program belongs to a growing web of emerging and thriving leaders who now have deeper relationships and trust with each other as well as stronger connections with different organizations and sectors across Central Appalachia. Separate from the fellowship, but with much overlap, the STAY Project is a notable contributor to the growing family of youth leaders and relationships, rooted in the region.

While there are many successes to celebrate, the fellowship faced challenges related to ideological differences, clarity of purpose, intergenerational organizing, sustainability, time, and access. There was a tension between the radical history of social movements in Appalachia and Highlander and the mainstream nonprofits with whom the fellows worked. Fellows came from a variety of backgrounds and experiences, but many were progressive or leftist. At times, they struggled with a disconnect between a vision of justice and liberation and the limits of nonprofit work supported with foundation grants with specific but narrowly defined outcomes.

Fellows were sometimes frustrated by their mentors' lack of trust in their abilities and expertise. Mentorship was sometimes very hierarchical rather than focused on mutual learning across generation and seniority. We learned that in order to succeed in intergenerational organizing, we must all build skills in respectful communication so that youth can learn from elders while, at the same time, elders should show respect for the visions and support the leadership of younger generations. We also learned that one year was not enough time to have a deep and lasting impact, as it can take several months for someone to grow comfortable in a new role or community. The one-year time period was partly the result of limited resources, and, though nothing could be done to address that, it nevertheless represented a shortcoming of the program.

Finally, the fellowship program left us with a number of unanswered questions: How did our projects build power and provide benefits to cash-poor and working-class people? How are people of color, immigrants, and Indigenous people included and centered in a just transition? If we are not addressing white supremacy, poverty, gentrification, misogyny, xenophobia, homophobia, transphobia, disability injustice, and other oppressions, is it "just"? What are we transitioning toward, exactly?

Mae Humiston: An Appalachian Fellow's Assessment

About a year after my AppFellows term ended, a former fellow and I looked at each other and simultaneously exclaimed, "It worked!" The idea of developing Appalachian leaders through direct work with organizations doing work on the ground worked. Ours was the first cohort, so the concept was untested and fellows, hosts, and administrators alike experienced steep learning curves. But it worked.

The program placed me in Perry County to work on reviving a stagnated farmers' market as a fellow for Community Farm Alliance, the Foundation for

Appalachian Kentucky, and the Foundation for a Healthy Kentucky. Coming from an Appalachian timber and agriculture economy in western Virginia, I was new to the eastern Kentucky region and its relationship with King Coal. I came in with a focus on food and farm issues and an intention to bring what I learned back to my own little mountain community on completion of the fellowship. Five years later, I was still in Perry County building a model for more just and equitable consumer lending to transform the region's credit economy. My route from farming to finance was unexpected (most of all by me), but it is a powerful example of the impact of the AppFellows program, not just on me but on the area.

It began with the solidarity economy framework, which focused on community wealth, organizing, and community research. The framework not only introduced me to regional issues but also gave me the tools to fill the gaps in my knowledge. This space was critical for building my comfort and self-image as a community organizer—a label I had never identified with before but a label that transformed my thinking from the discrete project level to a systems perspective.

The systems-level emphasis of my training helped me network meaningfully with others working on the just transition, both personally and professionally. In this work, it became clear that the personal was often essential to the professional. My personal contacts frequently led to new relationships for my host organizations, relationships that persist today. The importance of personal trust and relationships is obvious in small towns. Perry County has experienced a revolving door of well-meaning volunteers for decades. The result is that many are fatigued after developing relationships and building hope only to have both dissolve when the volunteer's term ended. Aware of this, I concentrated on building local capacity for the community already wanted: to build a good, healthy, sustaining farmers' market. I did so using community engagement tools provided by AppFellows. Once the community saw my commitment and impact, their trust in me increased. This trust allowed me to share my ideas and perspectives on a variety of topics, including downtown revitalization, housing affordability, political accountability, and many other issues.

Having succeeded in revitalizing the farmers' market, building strong networks across sectors, and earning trust from the community, I moved to the world of personal finance with no real experience in finance. My lack of substantive experience mattered less than my ability to foster a project with community sensitivity and a commitment to equity—the very things my fellowship had developed in me.

Perry County seems more hopeful than when I first arrived in 2014. Of course, I don't attribute that entirely to AppFellows, but I think it played a role.

Once the community was able to see one dream come to fruition, other goals seemed attainable. The farmers' market gave rise to a food-focused nonprofit that has built equitable models for healthy food access and food-based community dialogue. This community dialogue has led to greater public conversation around change, challenges, and hopes, all of which changed the way our local politicians campaigned, which, in turn, led to a new administration. The new administration, experienced in community revitalization and food equity, has made changes that have inspired hope in the community.

In addition, Perry County hosted two other AppFellows who focused on the infrastructure and other systems needed to promote downtown revitalization. They provided capacity for InVision Hazard, a citizens group where people can bring concerns and ideas that require collective effort. InVision Hazard inspired new candidates to run for local government, which then initiated changes in local policy, including the hiring of a permitting and zoning officer, the reinstitution of its code enforcement board, and the introduction of property tax penalties on vacant and blighted buildings.[8]

There were certainly challenges to the AppFellows program. Taking risks on a new person or a new project is difficult because it requires allocation of already limited resources. It is challenging to open oneself to new perspectives and new techniques, especially when the existing perspective and technique have proven themselves useful for survival. Finally, it is difficult to build and maintain systems of communication and accountability across geographic and cultural divides. But if we were to weigh the challenges of AppFellows against the positive impacts, I'd say it was worth it. It worked.

Alice Beecher:
Supporting Place-Based Initiatives in Hazard, Kentucky

What makes young people radical? In *The Significance of Theory*, Terry Eagleton writes, "Children make the best theorists, since they have not yet been educated into accepting our routine social practices as 'natural.'"[9] In Appalachia, radical young people pose a threat to the prevailing social order that claims coal as king and good ol' boys as gods. Young people in Appalachia rebel against heteronormative and patriarchal social structures, against environmental devastation, against the many ways that capitalism deforms and swallows us. I have seen young people in Appalachia make magic out of this rebellion. I have seen teenagers in West Virginia form queer community out of backyard punk bands. I have worked with other twentysomethings in eastern Kentucky to organize against a proposed federal prison on a mountaintop removal site. I have stood freezing on the side of a mountain in southwest Virginia while my friends sat in trees to block the construction of a forty-two-inch natural gas pipeline. I have gathered alongside young-at-heart movement geniuses from all generations on a radiant hill in east Tennessee to scheme our visions for a world outside of capitalism.

Yet as a young person, I can say from both my experience in the Appalachian Transition Fellowship and from everyday life that the task of transforming the economy of this region to abide by the principles we hold dear can feel enormous. Our solutions—forming farmers' markets, organizing fiber worker coops, funding artists—often feel too small to impact the grand scale. Furthermore, the nonprofit industrial complex often reproduces the same oppressions we oppose. It is easy to give up. I have come to realize that the key ingredient to transformative social change is resilience. That conviction that we need to keep working for the impossible. That resilience is what I believe will ultimately catalyze a just transition in the Appalachian economy. And I believe with my whole heart that young people will be there, working on the front lines and in the fun dance parties of this struggle.

Caitlin Myers: The Clearfork Valley Goes Online

I never felt so lucky until I was chosen to be an AppFellow. In the position, I worked with grassroots organizers from rural areas in Hancock, Claiborne, Campbell, and Cocke Counties in East Tennessee. The group was riotous and intergenerational, and we had camaraderie and trust. Our little group met quarterly, and our meetings would last two days. When business was done on the first day, out would come the jar: big and full of smooth, clear moonshine. Somebody would start up the bonfire. And there we'd sit, passing the jar, singing, and laughing and joking until we dropped off, one by one, to go to sleep. It was work as I'd always hoped it would be: full of joy and camaraderie. Sustainable and Equitable Agricultural Development was our mouthful of a name, a.k.a. SEAD, and we started working to bring the internet to rural Tennessee because, simply enough, it would make life easier on a lot of people.

The Clearfork Valley, long a heartland in Tennessee of daring visions for economic justice, became the locus for this project. As documented in John Gaventa's book *Power and Powerlessness*, the Clearfork Valley has been host to radical projects over the years. Woodland Community Land Trust protects affordable housing from resource extraction and rent increases; a community-run utility keeps water prices low; and finally, Clearfork Community Institute, a community center housed in an old school, hosts day-care activities, movie screenings, educational events, and community meetings. It seemed like a natural extension of this network of community-centered projects to try to create something else new. Community leader Carol Judy called these "green pearls," the equal and opposite of the string of coal mines that companies have called "black pearls": healing instead of harming; creating, not destroying; born from the community and giving back to it rather than taking and taking and taking. It was the heart of what we call "just transition," a phrase whose meaning seems to get more muddled every year. To us, it means community ownership, decorporatization, deprivatization of land; it means handing back the reins of governance and power from wealthy people in faraway places to communities and allowing them to self-determine the future.[10]

It was Judy's idea to build the rural internet system in the valley, and we all encouraged it and helped it grow. Judy was an educator, amateur naturalist, and self-taught technologist who lived in Clearfork. Though the Clearfork Valley is beautiful, it is rugged and sparsely populated. As a result, big telecommunications companies do not choose to invest there. Judy would drive an hour to the nearest McDonald's to manage her various hustles alongside kids who couldn't do their homework at home, older adults looking for a way to FaceTime their families, folks seeking employment, folks just wanting to hang out on social media without interruption. That was a fact of life.[11]

We spent a long-time lobbying politicians for rural broadband, but over time that strategy seemed ineffective. Around the time Carol passed in February 2017, we took stock of our work and shifted it—fairly abruptly—to what she had always envisioned: the creation of a truly local network, run by and for her community. I think I am starting to see this shift as a tipping point: a move from one form of stasis to another form of stasis, from one reality to another. It changed our mode of being, our relationships to one another—and the going was often hard. Every day, we learned something new. As a fellow organizer remarked, "If we knew how to do this thing, we'd already have done it."

Some people have done this before, and we sought them out. The Detroit Community Technology Project (DCTP), run by Black and Latinx folks and addressing urban digital inequities, had trodden this path first; Red Hook Wi-Fi and several other neighborhood networks in New York City had done so. Often nonprofits, these groups organized their communities even as they set up line-of-sight towers on their neighbors' roofs; now that the networks are built, they hold parties to raise money, teach workshops, and train high schoolers in dish installation and setup. And above all, they prioritize marginalized people. DCTP developed the Detroit Digital Justice Principles; in digital justice work we need to prioritize access, participation, and healthy communities. They expand the definition of access to mean more than just simply having the internet: it means protecting ourselves from disasters when the state fails us, understanding privacy and protecting our information, owning the content we create for free, and knowing that affordable, high-speed internet is a utility providing a basic necessity.[12]

Inspired by endeavors like these, we succeeded in obtaining $400,000 of funding from Mozilla to establish an internet café in the Clearfork Community

Institute and to purchase internet hot spots and laptops for a lending program, administered through the Cocke County library system. In addition, AppFellows gathered community input on how to structure and operate a community-owned internet system. Community-owned internet would disrupt past relations of power and ownership in the region, democratizing them so that the community could own, manage, and consume the services provided. Such a project is daring because it transcends standard structures in the region and the nation while challenging regional stereotypes of a "backward" and "isolated" people who want nothing to do with the contemporary world. The internet is a part of the fabric of Appalachia, even if the digital divide disadvantages the region once again. Digital justice frameworks guide us to strengthen our communities and build trust with each other. Community networks in a digital justice framework allow Appalachia to speak to itself, unmediated—and perhaps to erode the power of monopolistic industry—on the road to liberation.

Exploring the Paths Ahead

In Appalachia, we have seen just transitions frameworks and initiatives deepen, expand, and push through growing pains as the economic conditions of our region shift alongside the political, economic, and social conditions nationally and globally. We know that our capitalist economy is rooted in institutionalized racism and builds wealth off the bodies, labor, and land of Black, Brown, and Indigenous people. This same strategy of extracting wealth and resources from communities and exploiting the labor of working people to build that wealth has shaped the Appalachian region. Although the root causes are the same, the symptoms look different in Appalachia.

Highlander explored these conditions to inform next steps from the AppFellows program through the 2021 assessment report *Beyond Transition: Appalachia's Pathway to Justice and Transformation*. We engaged leaders and organizers from Black, Brown, Indigenous, low- and no-income, young, and queer people in our region to achieve clarity about specific transition goals and how to reach them by enacting values and principles rooted in collective liberation.[13]

It is vital that Appalachians remember and carry forward the solidarity in linked struggles for collective liberation that are a key part of our rich radical history. As is true for all liberation work, we know that a just transition is a process and not a destination. We must fight to make sure that just transition work is truly collective and that it is a full transition from the profit-centered conditions we inherited to conditions that will allow all people to survive and thrive, moving beyond transition toward transformation. Our futures truly depend on it.

Notes

1. This chapter is dedicated to Elandria E. Williams (1979–2020) who lived in the future and shared her visions with people in Appalachia and across the country and the world. We also want to acknowledge the many, many people who made this program possible, from Highlander staff, Rural Support Partners, and the Appalachia Funders Network to all the fellows and hosts who devoted their precious time, energy, and imaginations toward conceiving and connecting possible presents and futures for Appalachia. Appalachian Transition Fellowship, Highlander Research and Education Center, https://highlandercenter.org/programs/appfellows, accessed September 3, 2024.

2. Highlander Research and Education Center, https://highlandercenter.org, accessed January 25, 2021.

3. Highlander Research and Education Center, "Mapping Our Futures: Economics and Governance Curriculum," https://highlandercenter.org/our-impact/economics-governance, accessed January 25, 2021.

4. Rural Support Partners, "Appalachian Transition Fellowship Evaluation (2017 Cohort of Transition Fellows)," https://highlandercenter.org/wp-content/uploads/2021/06/2017-AppFellows-Report_Final.pdf, accessed September 3, 2024.

5. "Martin County Concerned Citizens," Facebook, https://www.facebook.com/MartinCountyConcernedCitizens, accessed January 25, 2021; Mary Cromer and Ricki Draper, *Drinking Water Affordability Crisis: Martin County, Kentucky*, September 2019, https://aclc.org/wp-content/uploads/2020/08/Drinking-Water-Affordability-Crisis-Martin-County-Kentucky-1.pdf.

6. Eric Dixon and Kendall Bilbrey, "Abandoned Mine Land Program: A Policy Analysis for Central Appalachia and the Nation," AML Policy Priorities Group, Appalachian Citizens Law Center, Alliance for Appalachia, July 8, 2015, https://aclc.org/wp-content/uploads/2020/08/aml-policy-paper.pdf; The STAY Project, Stay Together Appalachian Youth, January 25, 2021, https://www.thestayproject.net.

7. Cromer and Draper, *Drinking Water Affordability Crisis*.

8. "InVision Hazard," Facebook, https://www.facebook.com/invisionhazard, accessed January 25, 2021; Mountain Association, "Supporting Strong Community Planning with InVision Hazard," May 1, 2020, https://mtassociation.org/training-ideas/supporting-strong-community-planning-with-invision-hazard.

9. Terry Eagleton, *The Significance of Theory* (Oxford: Blackwell, 1993), 34.

10. John Gaventa, *Power and Powerlessness: Quiescence and Rebellion in an Appalachian Valley* (Urbana: University of Illinois, 1982).

11. Malcolm J. Wilson and Jennifer Molley Wilson, "Carol Judy," Humans of Central Appalachia, January 22, 2016, https://www.humansofcentralappalachia.org/stories/2016/1/22/carol-judy?rq=carol%20judy.

12. Detroit Community Technology Project, "Detroit Digital Justice Principles," https://www.detroitdjc.org/principles, accessed March 13, 2021.

13. Highlander Research and Education Center, "Beyond Transition: Appalachia's Pathway to Justice and Transformation," March 2021, https://highlandercenter.org/wp-content/uploads/2021/06/Final-Highlander-Center-Report_3_18_21_smaller_res-2.pdf.

Conclusion

Strategies for a Regenerative Region and World

SHAUNNA L. SCOTT AND KATHRYN ENGLE

As scholars and activists working in Appalachia, we are mindful of the role that Appalachian industry has played in creating our current climate crisis and of our moral and political imperatives to find solutions to these problems. It is equally important to acknowledge that most Appalachian people, especially the workers, have also paid a high price in cutting the trees and mining the coal and minerals that fueled industrialization in the United States. As a region, we have suffered from poor health, environmental devastation, poverty, and loss of ownership or stewardship over our land and waterways. As a "resource curse" region, our governments have lacked transparency and democracy and been riddled with corruption. Here we emphasize the importance of democratic participation in policymaking and in the distribution of money, products, and services to achieve our goals of justice, equity, and regeneration. The participatory democracy we advocate, unlike representative democracy, involves citizens in actual policy- and decision-making rather than just voting for representatives to do that work.

In the United States right now, elected representatives do the bidding of the wealthy rather than their constituents, as Gilens and Page found in 2014. The United States, they concluded, is an oligarchy rather than a democracy. This conclusion is further supported by the corrupt and outsized role that billionaires played in the election and inauguration of Donald J. Trump in 2024–2025. Appalachia is accustomed to corrupt and oligarchic governance. It has been an energy oligarchy at least since the late nineteenth century. Oligarchy, however, will not support just transitions to regenerative communities because this form of governance is neither democratic nor locally controlled. In 2023, a majority of Americans believed that the government should do more to combat climate change, even after the 2022 Inflation Reduction Act invested $369 billion in climate change solutions. After decades of foot dragging and the first, disastrous Trump presidency, the Biden administration finally took a meaningful step by setting a target for reducing US emissions by 40 percent by 2030. Until then, however, US states and cities had more aggressively tackled climate change, with some cities and states on track to cut their emissions by 80 percent between 2005 and 2030.

A 2022 *New York Times* article called states like New York, Colorado, and Minnesota "laboratories for democracy," documenting how people with different ideologies had joined together to promote energy conservation and renewable energy.

Our country and region continue to be faced with endless war profiteering, imperialism, and mass incarceration. With Trump's second term, the prospects for just and democratic transitions have apparently dimmed, but hope should not be lost. Participatory democracy is more likely to succeed at local, state, and regional levels, where densely networked people can work closely together to identify commonalities and build trust. Every crisis, including Trump's economically disastrous ones, provides an opportunity to build something different. Of course, so-called "higher" authorities from outside the community sometimes oppose grassroots movements for justice and democracy, as Ostrom pointed out. Clearly, if outside authorities had respected the decisions of local communities, the citizens of Letcher County would not have to keep fighting against the construction of a prison. Ryerson and Schept have shown us, however, that the local community has been resilient; it has not given up, and thus far, it has prevailed. In January 2025, the Appalachian Rekindling Project, an Indigenous, women-led, community-building and land restoration group, purchased sixty-three acres of the land proposed for the construction of the prison. As a part of the larger Building Community Not Prisons coalition, which has been fighting FCI-Letcher since 2022, the group hopes simultaneously to block prison construction and rematriate the land according to just transition principles. The struggle continues.[1]

We also advocate for extending participatory democracy into the economy through employee-owned businesses and producer- and consumer-owned cooperatives, just as Billings has suggested. Employees should make hiring and promotion decisions and also decide how to allocate revenue—to salaries and wages, research and innovation, technology, education, local communities, and ecosystem regeneration. Workers have more practical knowledge about their workplaces than stockholders and billionaire CEOs. In addition, locally owned and employee-owned businesses provide better employee benefits, offer a more equitable salary structure, and act in a more socially and environmentally responsible way than national and multinational corporations do. In fact, Robert Reich and others advocate for employee ownership (and strong labor unions in conventional capitalist firms) as means to "*save* capitalism" (more about this below). Likewise, instead of wealthy philanthropists and their foundations donating money for purposes they have chosen, Smith argues that local Appalachian communities should decide how to disburse funding. Local access to and control over land are emphasized by Hansell and Shepherd-Powell. In a region with a high rate of absentee landownership, the lack of land to build housing, grow food, graze livestock, plant trees, and erect parks, community centers, stores, and other businesses is a serious barrier to just transitions in the region. DeVaughan reminds us of the continued impacts of colonialism and points to change through rematriation of land. Possibilities for just transitions through Indigenous practices and leadership promise opportunities for healing and different relationships between people groups and land.[2]

In addition to creating more democratic governance procedures, extending democracy to workplaces, and vesting more authority in local governance, we must reverse the privatization trends that were intensified in the neoliberal (now neofascist) period. Though some objects should be privately owned—underwear and toothbrushes come to mind—others are better managed with community oversight, such as public (schools, libraries, parks) or common (oceans and waterways, the air and climate) resources. In addition, collaborative consumption of "private" property like cars, washing machines, and tools would reduce waste, pollution, and "uneconomic" growth. (Uneconomic growth in production and consumption collectively costs us in resources, pollution, or lost ecosystem services more than it benefits us.) Some communities are starting "libraries" for tools that are not used every day. Cohousing and cooperative housing groups share laundry facilities, grounds, common spaces, and chores while still having private living quarters. As Engle et al. note, community gardens, community-supported agriculture, community kitchens, and local farmers' markets are just a few ways in which we can localize food systems. In short, there are many ways to configure the contours between private, public, and common property, and communities should have the authority to do so. We must look to Indigenous leadership on these issues and elevate Indigenous leaders and bodies of knowledge that show how to build community and steward the commons effectively.[3]

Life depends on biodiversity—a variety of species and genetic variations so that ecosystems can thrive and generate. But biodiversity also refers to diversity of culture, knowledge, skills, and perspectives. When communities embrace people across difference—regardless of gender, sexuality, race, ethnicity, age, religion, ability, or place of birth or residence—communities are stronger. In the United States and Appalachia, Indigenous peoples, African Americans and other people of color have historically been oppressed, marginalized, and erased, as Henderson notes. Appalachian youth, such as the Appalachian Transition Fellows and STAY (Stay Together Appalachian Youth) members, are at the forefront of movements to create more inclusive and welcoming communities in Appalachia. Young people are especially well positioned to consider the long-term consequences of policy decisions on the climate and the health of ecosystems on which their futures depend. Participatory democracy, by definition, must include everyone. This is why the current US oligarchic regime is so adamant to dismantle diversity, equity, and inclusion programs in schools, the government, and workplaces.

A primary goal of any just and regenerative society is to create healthy outcomes for humans and their mental and physical health, for our communities, for the soil, water, air, and climate, and for all the flora and fauna that inhabit the planet. To succeed in this, we must guarantee everyone access to the basic necessities of life: food, water, shelter, clothing, health care, vaccines, medicines, mental health care, social support, and meaningful work. This addresses a primary concern of Dixon and Scutchfield: the health of Appalachians who have suffered from the extractive, dangerous, and polluting industries of Appalachia and a high-cost, for-profit medical system that is tied to employment. The majority of Americans, in fact, believe that health-care costs are too high, and an increasing share favors a government-sponsored health-care system. A more democratic governance system is a necessary precondition to addressing health inequities in Appalachia and the world. The just transitions movement must include health and regeneration as central goals. Dismantling Medicaid and Medicare are moves in the wrong direction.[4]

While terms like "just transitions" and "regenerative economy" may not regularly appear in Appalachian conversation, the practices and values of justice, regeneration, and community participation are woven through the region's cultures and histories. This is evidenced by the labor union movement and resistance to strip mining, mountaintop removal mining, fracking, and pipeline construction. Appalachian communities sometimes push back against forces that commodify their home places and exploit them for profit. Practices of "making do," gardening, food preservation, moonshining, having yard sales, bartering, craftwork, and the forest commons history could inform a locally responsive and sustainable political economy, one that innovates, repairs, reuses, and collaborates. Furthermore, Appalachian communities—in small towns, rural hollers, and cities—are densely networked with social connections between family, church, neighborhood, and friendship. In addition, Appalachians have traditionally valued self-sufficiency, family, and neighborly reciprocity (mutual aid), and their "home places," values that are compatible with Ostrom's principles. Such values and practices must be revived to rebuild the social trust that has been eroded by centuries of exploitation and conflict; it could help local communities restore forest, streams, lakes, and grazing commons, which could (in turn) stabilize the global climate and ecological commons that we all share.[5]

To what extent is capitalism compatible with just transitions goals, including participatory democracy, an expanded commons with local control, healthy and regenerating ecosystems (with healthy, happy people), equity, diversity, and inclusion? That depends on your view of capitalism. As we defined it earlier, capitalism's characteristics are private property, the profit motive, the growth imperative, the tendency toward monopoly and centralization, increasing inequality of wealth, the exploitation of labor and nature, and the hyperexploitation of people of color and women. None of these characteristics is consistent with a just and equitable society. Proponents of capitalism, on the other hand, emphasize capitalism's competition, innovation, and high levels of production. They wish to salvage the positive aspects of capitalism through governmental regulations, a more progressive tax system, fairer bankruptcy laws, strong labor unions, protections for consumers, and support for cooperatives and employee-owned businesses—all goals that advance just transitions.

Even though we believe the proponents of "saving capitalism" are not sufficiently critical of capitalism's growth imperative (the expansion of production and consumption, which creates waste, pollution, and greenhouse gas emission), we could envision allying with such people in political elections, lobbying, social movements, and community organizing work. Perhaps we could make common cause with capitalism's reformers by introducing them to Flora and Flora's "community capitals framework," which includes: (1) natural capital (landscape, soil, biodiversity, etc.); (2) social capital (social relationships); (3) cultural capital (common language, symbols, beliefs, values); (4) human capital (knowledge, skills, health); (5) political capital (civic forums, leadership, influence, access to power, empowerment); and (6) built capital (stores, factories, utilities, infrastructure)—not just financial capital (money and institutions that lend money, such as credit unions, banks, microfinance schemes). Since we advocate for social institutions and practices that actually invest in and regenerate *all* types of capital, not just money, we could take the name of pro-capitalists. Likewise, if we wish to decentralize government and downsize the military, the police, and the carceral state, are we not advocating for "small government"? If we seek to slow climate change and save life on this planet as we know it, are we not "pro-life"?[6]

To be clear, we are not actually recommending such rebranding schemes, nor do we suggest spending much energy on political debates with opponents of democracy, climate action, and environmental justice. Instead, we propose finding common cause with our neighbors and forming alliances to engage in social action to pursue transformative social change. Although changing systems like racialized capitalism, neoliberalism, neofascism, and billionaire oligarchy seem to be an overwhelming task, revolutions have happened before. It is even possible to change the behavior of people without changing their minds. It only takes 25 percent of the population to create significant social change through the establishment of new norms. Furthermore, such transformations are more likely to succeed in times of crisis when people are most open minded and willing to reconsider the status quo. This has been made abundantly clear by how many US citizens are willing to normalize Nazi salutes at US presidential inaugural events and to reject representative democracy in favor of "strong executive" power and an alliance with Russia. The crisis is clearly upon us; we are headed in the wrong direction, and the consequences for inaction will be catastrophic.[7]

What to do next? First, it is important to become engaged in your communities. Individual actions like composting, gardening, taking reusable grocery bags to the store, recycling, and so forth will help but only if those norms become generalized. By participating in our communities—through mutual aid networks, volunteering, church activities, clubs, PTOs, protecting public libraries and schools, or whatever—we form networks through which to spread environmental and democratic norms; participation also builds community resilience and social trust, which will help us work together to avert, prepare for, and recover from disasters and other problems associated with climate change and to resist authoritarian control. Do not, as Timothy Snyder warns us, obey in advance to what we know to be unjust and unsustainable. It is important also to choose our careers, investments, and purchases wisely, to minimize our negative impact on ecosystems and to advance justice and community resilience. Equally important, we must become as politically engaged as we can—at least by educating ourselves on candidates and voting regularly. The contrast between the climate and social policies of US Republicans and Democrats is consequential, to state the obvious. To be more effective, we can run for office, engage in civil disobedience, and join social movements and community organizations that work toward political change, equity, fair taxation, and land ownership reform—for example, Landback and the Appalachian Rekindling Project. However, direct political participation does not suit everyone. Remember such efforts also need financial, legal, social media, and other types of support. Many organizations working in Appalachia incorporate just transition principles, such as STAY, Mountain Association, Foundation for Appalachian Kentucky, Community Farm Alliance, Southern Appalachian Mountain Stewards, and the Highlander Research and Education Center, which are documented here; but we do not have space to document the many groups that are doing this work. We can change social norms and even force regime changes with a relatively small percentage of engaged, organized citizens. Fear, apathy, hopelessness, and inaction are our enemies. We can do it, because we must. Future life on our planet requires it.[8]

Notes

1. Ronald M. Mason, *Participatory and Workplace Democracy: A Theoretical Critique of Liberalism* (Carbondale: Southern Illinois University, 1982); Elinor Ostrom, *Governing the Commons: The Evolution of Institutions for Collective Action* (London: Cambridge University Press, 1990); Thomas Piketty, *Capital in the Twenty-First Century* (Cambridge: Harvard University Press, 2014); Martin Gilens and Benjamin I. Page, "Testing Theories of American Politics: Elites, Interest Groups, and Average Citizens," *Perspectives on Politics* 12, no. 3 (2014): 564–81; Alec Tyson and Brian Kennedy, "Two-Thirds of Americans Think Government Should Do More on Climate," Pew Research Center, https://www.pewresearch.org/science/2020/06/23/two-thirds-of-americans-think-government-should-do-more-on-climate, accessed January 30, 2023; Maggie Astor, "As Federal Climate-Fighting Tools Are Taken Away, Cities and States Step Up," *New York Times*, July 1, 2022, https://www.nytimes.com/2022/07/01/climate/climate-policies-cities

-states-local.html; Melissa Barbanell, "Energy Provisions of the Inflation Reduction Act of 2022," World Resources Institute, October 28, 2022, https://www.wri.org/update/brief-summary-climate-and-energy-provisions-inflation-reduction-act-2022; Liam Niemeyer, "Indigenous Group Buys 63 Acres in Proposed Prison Site, Offers Different Vision for Eastern Kentucky Land," Kentucky Lantern, January 23, 2025, https://kentuckylantern.com/2025/01/23/indigenous-group-buys-63-acres-in-proposed-prison-site-offers-different-vision-for-e-ky-land/.

2. Ostrom, *Governing the Commons*; Michael Shuman, *The Small Mart Revolution: How Local Businesses Are Beating the Global Competition* (New York: Penguin Random House, 2006).

3. Edward J. Carberry, ed., *Employee Ownership and Shared Capitalism* (Champaign, IL: Labor and Employment Relations Association, 2011); Robert B. Reich, *Saving Capitalism: For the Many, Not the Few* (New York: Vintage, 2016); Carey Osen and John Case, *Ownership: Reinventing Companies, Capitalism, and Who Owns What* (Oakland, CA: Berrett-Koehler Publishers, 2022); Vandana Shiva, *Reclaiming the Commons: Biodiversity, Indigenous Knowledge, and the Rights of Mother Earth* (Santa Fe, NM: Synergetic Press, 2020); for more information on cohousing, see "CoHoUS: A Community of Communities," https://www.cohousing.org; for more information about tool libraries, see "Tool Lending Libraries," Urban Sustainability Directors Network, https://sustainableconsumption.usdn.org/initiatives-list/tool-lending-libraries, accessed January 31, 2023.

4. United Nations, "Handbook on Realizing the Human Rights to Water and Sanitation," https://www.ohchr.org/en/special-procedures/sr-water-and-sanitation/handbook-realizing-human-rights-water-and-sanitation, accessed January 30, 2023; Bradley Jones, "Increasing Share of Americans Favor Single Government Program to Provide Health Care Coverage," Pew Research Center, September 29, 2020, https://www.pewresearch.org/fact-tank/2020/09/29/increasing-share-of-americans-favor-a-single-government-program-to-provide-health-care-coverage; West-Health/Gallup, "2021 Healthcare in America Report," https://westhealth.org/resources/2021-healthcare-in-america-report/, accessed January 30, 2023.

5. Rhoda Halperin, *The Livelihood of Kin: Making Ends Meet "the Kentucky Way"* (Austin: University of Texas Press, 1991); Chad Montrie, *To Save the Land and People: A History of Opposition to Surface Coal Mining in Appalachia* (Chapel Hill: University of North Carolina Press, 2003); Herbert Reid and Betsy Taylor, *Recovering the Commons: Democracy, Place, and Global Justice* (Urbana: University of Illinois Press, 2010); Kathryn Newfont, *Blue Ridge Commons: Environmental Activism and Forest History in Western North Carolina* (Athens: University of Georgia Press, 2012); Matthias Schmelzer, Andrea Vetter, and Aaron Vansintjan, *The Future Is Degrowth: A Guide to a World Beyond Capitalism* (London: Verso, 2022); Naomi Klein, *This Changes Everything: Capitalism vs. the Climate* (New York: Simon & Schuster, 2015).

6. Robert B. Reich, *Saving Capitalism: For the Many, Not the Few* (New York: Vintage, 2016); Cornelia Butler Flora and Jan L. Flora, *Rural Communities: Legacy and Change*, 5th ed. (Boulder, CO: Westview Press, 2016).

7. Damon Centala, *How Behavior Spreads: The Science of Complex Contagion*, Princeton Analytical Sociology Series 3 (Princeton, NJ: Princeton University Press, 2018); Klein, *This Changes Everything*. On the other hand, crises can also provide opportunities for democracy's opponents to impose martial law and suspend elections and for corporations to drive smaller firms out of business, price gouge consumers, and take possession of foreclosed and

damaged properties; see Naomi Klein, *The Shock Doctrine: The Rise of Disaster Capitalism* (New York: Metropolitan Books/Henry Holt, 2007); Timothy Snyder, *On Tyranny: Twenty Lessons from the Twentieth Century* (Chicago: Turabian, 2017); Steven Levitsky and Daniel Ziblatt, *How Democracies Die* (New York: Crown, 2018); Masha Gessen, *Surviving Autocracy* (New York: Penguin Random House, 2020).

8. Snyder, *On Tyranny*, 2017; see also "Appalachia Cooperates Initiative," Ohio State University, Center for Food, Agricultural and Environmental Sciences, https://cooperatives.cfaes.ohio-state.edu/development-0/appalachia-cooperates-initiative, accessed January 30, 2023; Landback, https://ndncollective.org/landback/, accessed March 11, 2025; Appalachian Rekindling Project, https://www.appalachianrekindlingproject.org/, accessed March 22, 2025.

Acknowledgments

As with any project of this scope, more people and groups supported and inspired this work than can be listed here. Obviously, this book would not have been possible without the hardworking community organizations, activists, and citizens of Appalachia who are building a better future for our region. Many of those are the organizations described in this volume—for example, the Highlander Center, Appalshop, Mountain Association, Alliance for Appalachia, and Foundation for Appalachian Kentucky, to name a few. We are grateful to all the local, regional, and global organizations working toward just transitions, and we are committed to collaborating with them and lifting up this necessary work.

We also thank the editorial staff at the University Press of Kentucky, especially Patrick O'Dowd, who always believed in this book and shepherded us through much of the review and editing process, and Margaret Kelly, who capably stepped in to support us through the publication process when Patrick left the press. In addition, our anonymous reviewers provided valuable feedback, which improved the book. We thank them for their hard work to bring this volume to fruition.

More personally, the editors of this book owe debts to the mentors and colleagues who have guided our paths and encouraged us along the way. First, Irma Gall and Peggy Kemner, founders of the Lend-A-Hand Center on Stinking Creek in Knox County, Kentucky, shared their life's work with then–Appalachian studies college student Kathryn Engle. Words cannot convey Kathryn's appreciation to these two women, whose legacy of local action, mutual aid, and community service Kathryn has devoted her career to protect and advance. They have been an inspiration and guide especially in the work toward just transitions. Dr. Alan Banks, founder and former director of the Eastern Kentucky University Center for Appalachian Studies, and Pat Banks, Kentucky Riverkeeper, have been Kathryn's friends and mentors since her undergraduate days and have challenged her to think critically and creatively about class and the environment. Kathryn's UK colleagues and friends, including Drs. Jasper Waugh-Quasebarth, Zada Komara, Lindsay Shade, and Leah Vance-Berg have made up a vibrant and caring scholarly community. The late Dr. Tammy "Tambone" Clemons provided so much joy and so many visions and hopes for alternative futures. And lastly, Kathryn's pappy, Clarence Hoffman, a Pennsylvania coal miner's son, has been a constant supporter.

Shaunna Scott owes a long-standing debt of gratitude to her professor and academic adviser, Dr. Herbert Reid, who ignited her interest in studying Appalachia and secured for her an internship at Council of the Southern Mountains, where Cathy Stanley taught her how to use a 35 mm camera and Sally Ward Maggard showed her how to combine community activism with scholarship. Thanks also to her other academic adviser, Dr. Susan Abbott-Jamieson, who convinced her to add an anthropology major at UK, chaired her senior Honors thesis, took her to present at her first two academic conferences, and paved her way to doctoral work at the University of California, Berkeley, where Drs. Jack Potter, Dick Walker, Gerald Berreman, Aiwha Ong, Troy Duster, and Michael Burawoy oversaw her graduate education. Shaunna is grateful to Eastern Kentucky University sociologist Dr. Stephanie McSpirit for inviting her to collaborate on participatory action research projects in Martin and Pike Counties, Kentucky; these changed the course of her career. Also, Shaunna thanks Claire McCully, retired professor of environmental studies at the University of Ulster (Coleraine) for awakening in her a sense of urgency about global warming in the 1990s, when she was still naive and complacent that the existing institutional order would act in time. Her beloved granddaughters, Emma and Nola Barton and Stella Roberts, have kept Shaunna grounded in the present and focused on the necessity of regeneration for a just future. Last but not least, Shaunna thanks Keith Barton, her husband and partner in all life's endeavors, for his good counsel, companionship, cooking, and love, which makes all things possible.

We both have benefited from the mentorship and colleagueship of Dwight Billings, chapter author and editor of the Place Matters series in which this book appears. We also are grateful for University of Kentucky colleagues Betsy Taylor (currently director of the Livelihood Knowledge Exchange Network), Ann Kingsolver, Kathy Newfont, Shannon Bell (currently at Virginia Tech), Kopana Terry, and Doug Boyd, and all of our colleagues at the University of Kentucky Appalachian Center, the Nunn Center for Oral History, and the Department of Sociology, especially our chairs, Claire Renzetti, Patrick Mooney, and Jim Hougland.

Contributors

Alice Beecher served as an AppFellow in 2017 with the Mountain Association for Community Economic Development (now Mountain Association) and InVision Hazard in Hazard, Kentucky. She worked with community groups in Hazard to develop creative place making and civic engagement initiatives, including a summer performance arts series and the passage of several important city ordinances impacting Hazard's downtown. She is deeply committed to the struggle for racial, economic, political, and environmental justice in Central Appalachia and is currently participating in the Asheville Survival Program, a mutual aid network, and the Mountain Area Abortion Doula Collective that provides abortion care.

Dwight B. Billings, professor emeritus of sociology at the University of Kentucky, is the author, coauthor, or editor of six books and more than seventy-five articles and chapters on Appalachia and the American South, including *The Road to Poverty: The Making of Wealth and Hardship in Appalachia*, which he coauthored with Kathleen Blee. A past president of the Appalachian Studies Association and a past editor of the *Journal of Appalachian Studies*, he is the series editor of the University Press of Kentucky's Place Matters book series.

Ivy Brashear is a PhD candidate in communication at the University of Kentucky. Their work focuses on representation of Appalachia in the media, centering around the notion of reclaiming that narrative by queering it. Ivy was Appalachian Transition director at the Mountain Association in Berea, Kentucky, for nearly a decade, where they worked on shifting the narrative of Appalachia in eastern Kentucky as a critical aspect of just transition. They are a writer and journalist whose work has appeared in the *Huffington Post, Next City, Yes! Magazine, Scalawag, The Bitter Southerner, and Kentucky Lantern*. They are from the Left Fork of Maces Creek in Viper, Kentucky, and they currently live with their wife in Lexington, Kentucky.

Taysha DeVaughan is a UVA–Wise alumna who has lived in Wise County since 2011. She is a member of the Comanche Nation of Oklahoma, president of Southern Appalachian Mountain Stewards, and an appointee to the Virginia Council on Environmental Justice. She is a single mother to Aiden. She has advocated and volunteered for social and environmental justice for the last five years.

Rachel E. Dixon, a Kentucky native, works as policy officer in the Greater London Authority, United Kingdom. From November 2021 to July 2024, she also served as managing editor of the *Journal of Appalachian Health*, overseen by the College of Public Health at East Tennessee State University and published by the University of Kentucky. Prior to her work in London and at the *Journal*, Rachel successfully completed the MPhil in comparative social policy from the University of Oxford. Her dissertation work there explored transition-related social policies for coal-impacted communities in Alberta, Canada, and in West Virginia. She continues to engage with community-led approaches to well-being, health creation, and just transition, both in the United States and in the United Kingdom.

Elyzabeth W. Engle is department chair and associate professor of environmental studies at McDaniel College, where she teaches courses on environmental justice, food systems, and sustainability. She also coordinates McDaniel's new agrifood programs, including student-led organic gardens and a food forest. Elyzabeth received her dual-title PhD in rural sociology and human dimensions of natural resources and the environment from Pennsylvania State University in 2018. Her dissertation research was conducted in conjunction with the Grow Appalachia program, including field research sites in Kentucky, West Virginia, and Tennessee. Relevant publications include "'Coal Is in Our Food, Coal Is in Our Blood': Everyday Environmental Injustices of Rural Community Gardening in Central Appalachia," in *Local Environment*, and "Brokering Rural Community Food Security: An Organizational Network Case Study in Central Appalachia," in *Rural Sociology*.

Kathryn Engle is the director of the University of Kentucky Appalachian Center. For three growing seasons, Kathryn coordinated the Lend-A-Hand Center Grow Appalachia Gardening Program, working with home and community gardeners and helping establish the Knox County Farmers' Market. Engle currently serves on the boards of the Lend-A-Hand Center and the Knox County Farmers' Market. She is also involved in racial justice organizing with the Sunup Initiative in Corbin, Kentucky.

Tom Hansell is a filmmaker and author who examines the intersections of nature, energy, and culture in the Appalachian Mountains. Hansell teaches Appalachian studies and documentary studies at Appalachian State University in Boone, North Carolina, and has twenty years of experience at the Appalshop media arts center working with students and adults to create media about their communities.

Frances B. Henderson is associate professor of gender and women's studies at the University of Kentucky; her research includes Black feminisms and race in social movements in the United States. Her work, "Black Rural Lives Matter," appeared in *Transforming Anthropology*, and her writings on equity in teaching have been featured in the *Chronicle of Higher Education*. She is currently working on a manuscript about antiracist activism in East Tennessee and the ways in which this activism dovetails with Appalachian justice movements and the Movement for Black Lives.

Peter Hille retired in April 2025 after ten years as the president and CEO of the Mountain Association. He joined Mountain Association's board in 2003 and served as board treasurer and board chair before joining the staff in 2012 as executive vice president. Peter helped expand Mountain Association's work, making small business financing more accessible for start-up entrepreneurs and advancing clean energy solutions to make solar power more affordable for businesses and nonprofits serving low-income Appalachian communities. Previously, Peter was director of the Brushy Fork Institute of Berea College, working in leadership and community development throughout Central Appalachia for twenty-two years. He also served as a consultant to regional and national organizations and implemented community development projects internationally in Russia and Slovakia. Peter currently chairs the board of the East Kentucky Leadership Foundation and previously served on the Berea Human Rights Commission. He was founding board chair of the Kentucky Environmental Foundation and served in that capacity for more than two decades, during which time he helped to lead a successful international effort to ensure safe disposal of chemical weapons. A graduate of Swarthmore College, his background includes experience in grassroots organizing, consulting, woodworking, construction, and small-business management. He lives with his wife in a solar home they designed and built in the midst of fifty acres of forest near Berea, Kentucky.

Abby Huggins was a fellow in the second AppFellows cohort (2017). She collaborated with the Hindman Settlement School and the Appalachian Food Summit on the East Kentucky Food & Dance Trail, a project connecting stories and places where people gather to eat and dance. Abby then served as one of the program coordinators in the 2018–2019 fellowship year. Raised in Wilkes County, North Carolina, she currently makes her home in Durham.

Mae Humiston worked as an AppFellow with Community Farm Alliance, the Foundation for Appalachian Kentucky, and Foundation for a Healthy

Kentucky in Hazard, Kentucky, in 2014–2015. Mae engaged with low-income populations in eastern Kentucky communities to support the expansion of local healthy food initiatives in the state and by building support for localizing the food system. Mae reinvigorated the stagnating Perry County Farmers' Market by researching and visiting neighboring farmers' markets to learn and share best practices and by organizing farmers, craftspeople, and customers to redesign the market in their own vision. She also connected farmers to grant funding and managed Breaking Beans: The Appalachian Food Story Project, collecting stories along the supply chain to enhance policy advocacy, assist Appalachians in learning to share their stories, and build skills for community organizers. Postfellowship, Mae joined the staff of Community Farm Alliance as the development associate and later directed the start-up Community Development Financial Institution, Redbud Financial Alternatives Inc., in Hazard. Mae is now the nonprofit support specialist for the Foundation for Appalachian Kentucky, providing strategic planning, grant writing, and project management to limited-resource organizations in the region. During the July 2022 flooding response, Mae served as facilitator for interagency emergency response communications and managed the aggregation and public distribution of flood rescue and response information.

Caitlin Meyers is a writer and audio producer in Knoxville, Tennessee. She reports on climate, labor, and energy transition in Appalachia.

Candace Mullins is the director of Grow Appalachia, a strategic initiative of Berea College. Born and raised in Kentucky, she graduated from Berea College with a bachelor of science in business administration and has been working with Grow Appalachia for nearly a decade. In that time, she has collaborated with more than one hundred nonprofit leaders across the region, all working to build a vibrant, regional food system where healthy food is accessible to all.

Maggie Smith Mosely joined the Sustainable Agriculture & Food Systems Funders (SAFSF) team in June of 2021 and currently serves as the communications director. Formerly, Maggie worked for Community Farm Alliance, a statewide, policy-focused farm and food systems organization in Kentucky.

Martin Richards has a long history of working with communities addressing economic revitalization, sustainability, and resiliency, living and working in steel-towns, tobacco fields, and coal towns. With an educational background in architecture, he has extensive experience in agriculture, economic development, and land-use. Martin has been an active member of Community Farm Alliance for over twenty-eight years, serving on the board as chair and as executive director from 2010 to 2023. He was the first CFA fellow during the passage of HB 611 in 2000 that utilized Master Tobacco Settlement funds to create the Kentucky Agricultural Development Fund. Besides having served on numerous boards and councils, Martin has served on the Planning and Zoning Commission and the Board of Adjustments in Berea, Kentucky, and the Bluegrass Regional Planning Council. During the Biden administration, Martin participated in the task force to inform the White House's National Strategy on Hunger, Nutrition, and Health and testified before the US Senate Subcommittee on Food and Nutrition on Food is Medicine. He also presented at the Tufts University Food is Medicine National Summit and represents CFA on the National Produce Prescription Collaborative.

Sylvia Ryerson is an assistant professor in the Department of American Culture at the University of Michigan and a postdoctoral scholar in the Michigan Society of Fellows. Her work is guided by participatory media and research praxis, building from her time at the Appalshop media arts center in Whitesburg, Kentucky. In 2023, she directed the short documentary film *Calls from Home*, and she is currently working on a manuscript that examines the intertwined histories of incarceration, extraction, and resistance in Central Appalachia.

Judah Schept is a professor in the School of Justice Studies at Eastern Kentucky University. He is the author of *Coal, Cages, Crisis: The Rise of the Prison Economy in Central Appalachia* (New York University Press, 2022) and *Progressive Punishment: Job Loss, Jail Growth, and the Neoliberal Logic of Carceral Expansion* (New York University Press, 2015) and coeditor of *The Jail Is Everywhere: Fighting the New Geography of Mass Incarceration* (Verso, 2024).

Shaunna L. Scott is an associate professor emeritus of sociology at the University of Kentucky. She is a former editor of the *Journal of Appalachian Studies*, former president of the Appalachian Studies Association, and former director of Appalachian studies at the University of Kentucky. She is the author of *Two Sides to Everything: The Cultural Construction of Class Consciousness in Harlan County, Kentucky* and a coeditor of *Studying Appalachian Studies: Making the Path by Walking*.

F. Douglas Scutchfield, MD, FACPM, was the Peter P. Bosomworth Professor Emeritus of Health Services Research and Policy at the University of Kentucky. He was responsible for establishing two new schools of public health, at San Diego State University and at the University of Kentucky. Previously the editor of the *American Journal of Preventive Medicine*, Scutchfield coedited

Scutchfield and Keck's *Principles of Public Health Practice, Contemporary Public Health: Principles, Practice, and Policy* (fourth edition) and *Appalachian Health: Culture, Challenges, and Capacity.*

Julie Shepherd-Powell is an assistant professor and graduate program director in Appalachian studies at Appalachian State University. As an anthropologist, Julie's research interests include community-based activism around coal extraction and natural gas pipeline development in Appalachia. She investigates the complicated intersections of everyday lives, economic uncertainties, and environmental destruction in mountain communities.

Lora Smith-Tovar is a writer, cultural organizer, and mother from eastern Kentucky. Lora currently works as the director of investment partnerships at Justice Funders, where she facilitates the Just Transition Integrated Capital Fund, a fund governed by movement partners that move foundation endowment dollars to BIPOC-owned and controlled projects. She is the cofounder and former executive director of the Appalachian Impact Fund at the Foundation for Appalachian Kentucky, where she directed grant-making and impact investing strategies for eastern Kentucky. She is a past cochair of the Appalachian Funders Network and served on the Community Advisory Council of the Federal Reserve. Lora's work as a cultural organizer has included being a founding member of the Waymakers Collective, a democratically controlled fund making grants to Central Appalachian artists and arts organizations. In 2022, she cofounded and launched the Lige Clarke Liberation Fund with Clarke's family to support LGBTQIA+ artists, movements, and people in eastern Kentucky. Lora is a founding organizer of the Appalachian Big Ideas Festival, a three-day event focused on arts, culture, and social movements in the mountains. Lora's writing has appeared in the *Oxford American, Bon Appetit, NPR's The Salt, Nonprofit Quarterly,* and other national outlets. Her first book, a collaborative collection of essays about Appalachian foodways, was published by the University of Ohio Press in 2019. Lora is currently a M.F.A. candidate in the Creative Writing program at the University of Kentucky.

Stay Together Appalachian Youth (STAY) is a network of young people, aged between fourteen to thirty, who are committed to supporting one another to make Appalachia a place we can and want to STAY.

Betsy Whaley is the director of Strategic Initiatives for Mountain Association. In that role, she works to leverage the resources of Mountain Association and its partners to support communities in eastern Kentucky. She is invested in developing collaborative relationships and building strong networks to support communities, nonprofits, and businesses in eastern Kentucky and Central Appalachia. She serves in a leadership capacity with What's Next EKY?! and the Central Appalachian Network.

Susan Williams has worked for four decades as a community organizer, a popular educator, a participatory researcher, and a librarian/archivist in East Tennessee. She organized with Save Our Cumberland Mountains for ten years and then came to Highlander Center as a staff person in 1989 to work on economic and environmental issues, including ten years working to build the Tennessee Industrial Renewal Network and organizing to confront factory closings and free trade agreements. As the education team coordinator for many years, she participated across Highlander's educational programs and supported the Appalachian Transition Fellowship program in its first cycle. She contributed to the development of the Mapping our Futures: Economics and Governance curriculum. She served as a librarian and archivist at Highlander, working with past Highlander staff to develop a project to digitize, narrate, and make available a Highlander ninetieth timeline project, providing context and examples of the educational work of the last fifty years. She enjoys hosting visitors and groups to the new Septima Clark Learning Center at Highlander Center. She has a master's degree from the UT School of Information Science as well as knowledge acquired from decades of interactions with amazing people coming to Highlander. Susan retired in March 2025 after thirty-six years at the Highlander Center.

Elizabeth Wright is a lifelong Tennessean who is an organizer, strategist, and educator for social change, a writer and storyteller at heart, and a garage-band musician who brings a punk rock and a do-it-together ethos to her life and work. She is the communications strategist at the Highlander Research and Education Center, where she also served as the education team coordinator after first coming to the organization as an intern. She is the cofounder of KnowHow, an organization that supports leadership development and community engagement among Knoxville's youth, celebrating art, culture, and media as vital tools to amplify their power, agency, and voices. Elizabeth holds a master's degree in social work from the University of Tennessee and has worn many hats in nonprofit and grassroots groups, including advancing progressive tax policy while serving as executive director of Tennesseans for Fair Taxation and as editor of the *Knoxville Voice* community newspaper, which is rooted in solidarity journalism.

Index

Italicized page numbers indicate illustrations.

A. Donald E. McEachin Environmental Justice for All Act (2023–2024), 60
Abolitionist Law Center, 165, *167*, 168
Ag Legacy Initiative, 100
Agarwal, Arun, 93
agriculture, 29, 55–56, 136, 180; community-supported, 96–97, 188; local, 96–97; regenerative, 4, 60–61; sustainable, 6, 73–74. *See also* food system
Agriculture, Kentucky Department of, 107
Agriculture, US Department of, 91, 100, 155
AIR Institute of Berea College, 152
Akers, Everett, 85
Alberta, Canada. *See* Coal Workforce Transition Program
Alliance for Appalachia, 29, 195
American Public Health Association, 135
Appalachia Proud, 97
Appalachia: Rich Land, Poor People (documentary film), 25
Appalachia(n): demographics by race, 43–44, 47–48; economy, 70, 96; health, 117, 129; identity, 48; migration, 41–47, 51–52, 89, 120; racial erasure, 37–52; stereotypes, 1–2, 32, 62, 110, 184
Appalachian Center, University of Kentucky, 99
Appalachian Citizens Law Center (ACLC), 178
Appalachian Community Fund, 76
Appalachian Food Summit, 97
Appalachian Funders Network, 151–52, 175
Appalachian Homestead Act, 90–93
Appalachian Impact Fund, 73

Appalachian Land Ownership Study, 87–88
Appalachian Regional Commission (ARC), 29, 48, 68, 91, 96, 108, 129, 155; Local Food Local Places Technical Assistance Program, 98, 109
Appalachian Resource Conservation & Development Council, 96
Appalachian Sustainable Agriculture Project (ASAP), 96
Appalachian Sustainable Development (ASD), 96
Appalachian Transition Fellowship, 10, 155, 175–85
AppalCEED (Appalachian Communities Encouraging Economic Diversity), 61
Appalshop, 85, 132, 149, 162, 178, 195
AppHarvest, 122
appropriation, 1, 3–6, 24–26, 32, 51, 117
Arthurdale, WV, 88–91
Aspen Institute, 72

Bell, Derrick, 38
Bell, Shannon E., 130–32
Beloved Asheville, 75, 78
Berea College, 41, 101, 106, 152
Berea Kids Eat, 104
Berlant, Lauren, 31
Berry, Brian, 19
Beshear, Stephen, 166, *167*
Biden, Joseph R., 7, 17, 29, 186
Bilbrey, Kendall, 178
biodiversity, 1, 4, 188, 190
BitSource, 127
Black Appalachian Network, 47, 147
Black Appalachian Young and Rising, 74
Black By God West Virginia, 78
Black in Appalachia, 78

Black Lives Matter (BLM), 163
black lung, 59, 115–19, 129–31
Black Lung Clinics Program, 129
Black Lung Disability Trust Program, 59
Branscombe, James, 90–93
Brushy Fork Institute of Berea College (Leadership Summit), 152, 156
Bureau of Prisons, US, 9–10, 166
Bush, George W., 131

Cado Nation (Hasinia Band), 55–56
CANE Kitchen, 74
carceral state, 160–68, 190
capital: built, 190; cultural, 190; financial, 190; human, 190; political, 190; social, 96–97, 190
capitalism, 10, 17–18, 23–26, 50, 66, 81; definition, 23–25; extractive, 66; types of, 2–3. *See also* economy
Carson, Ron, 117
Catawba people, 82
Caudill, Harry, 129
Central Appalachian ArtPlace America, 76, 78
Central Appalachian Family Farm Fund, 100–101
Central Appalachian Network (CAN), 100, 147, 149–57
Cherokee (Eastern Band), 3, 5, 55–56, 82. *See also* Trail of Tears
Chickasaw people, 82
Chorus Foundation, 69
civic engagement, 4, 67, 69, 73. *See also* community participation
Civilian Conservation Corps, 124
class, 9, 51, 59, 118, 161, 163; exploitation, 4; forgotten, 42; hierarchy, 45; identity, 42; justice, 8, 18, 23, 25, 28–29, 32; middle, 39–40, 51; processes, 24–25; upper, 41; working, 38–41, 50, 78, 179
Claude Worthington Benedum Foundation, 68
clean coal: rhetoric, 131–32; technology, 134
Clean Power Plan, 134
Climate Justice Alliance, 57, 63, 73

Coal Mine Health and Safety Act of 1969 (US), 115, 130
coal severance tax, 161
Coal Workers' Health Surveillance Program (CSHWP), 115
coal workers' pneumoconiosis (CWP). *See also* black lung
Coal Workforce Transition Program (Alberta, Canada), 133–34
Collins, Kristin Walker, 72
colonialism, 4, 55, 58, 63–65, 81
colonization, 64, 94; of Appalachia, 3–4, 92; of lifeworld, 23
collaborative consumption, 188
Comanche people, 55–56
communal (collective): access to common-pool resources, 3, 9; gardening, 103. *See also* collaborative consumption; land ownership: communal (collective)
commons, 3–6, 8, 86, 93–94, 188–91; Commons Community Act, 88, 91–92; definition of, 3; forest, 4, 91, 189; privatization of, 17; tragedy of, 92–93. *See also* communal (collective): access to common-pool resources
communicative action, 18–22, 26–32
community participation, 82, 189
community foundation, 71–75; Leslie County, 73
Community Farm Alliance (CFA), 97–101, 111
community garden, 7, 97–101, 108, 154, 188. *See also* communal: gardening
community-supported agriculture (CSA), 97
cooperative, 7, 26–29, 58, 77, 187–90
COVID-19 pandemic, 74, 101, 112, 119, 125, 147, 175
Cree people, 82
critical race theory (CRT), 37–38, 49–52
commodity (commodification), 2, 184, 189
community foundation, 71–72
company towns, 45–48

Dakota Access Pipeline, 6
decolonization, 57–58
Delgado, Richard, 38

democracy, 4, 8, 10; class justice and, 27–28; communicative action and, 26; deep, 58–61; liberal, 22; local, 171; participatory, 22, 86, 186; political justice and, 21; regenerative economy and, 61; representative, 186
democratic governance. *See* democracy
democratic participation, 186. *See also* democracy
DeMartino, George, 23–25
Department of Health and Human Services, US, 129
Department of Labor, Division of Coal Mine Workers' Compensation, 130
deprivatization, 183
Detroit Digital Justice Principles, 183
discourse, 45; capital-centric, 24; "forgotten man," 39–40; just transition, 117; media, 172; political, 24, 172; race, 43; rational, 20–24
discourse ethics, 18–20
discourse principle, 21
discursive: entry point, 23; formation, 49; process, 21–22
disparity: economic (including income and wealth), 66, 94, 129, 175–76; food, 98; health, 96, 117–118, 129, 133, 135, 175. *See also* racism: racial health disparities
distribution, 24–26, 38, 46–47, 60, 62, 75–76, 92, 150, 186; of surplus value, 24–25. *See also* redistribution
diversity: cultural, 65, 188; economic, 58, 61, 91, 120; racial, 49
Dixon, Eric, 178

Eagleton, Terry, 181
Eastern Kentucky Food System Collaborative (EKY FSC), 99
economy, 90, 98, 110, 198; agricultural, 103; capitalist, 2, 4, 17, 184; cooperative, 27; democratic, 32; diversified, 93; extractive, 2, 57, 66–68, 74, 81, 175, 188; political, 2, 27, 189; postcapitalist, 23; post-coal, 157; postindustrial, 88; regenerative, 2, 57, 60–61, 189; solidarity, 176–80; sustainable, 153, 171, 189; undiversified (mono), 56, 147. *See also* capitalism
economic diversification, 9, 17, 63, 90, 93, 147. *See also* economy: undiversified (mono)
EKY Farm Table Program, 100
EKY Mutual Aid, 74–75, 79. *See also* mutual aid
Emission Gap Report (2022), 4
employee-owned enterprises, 184
Energy Regulatory Commission (Federal Energy Regulatory Commission), US, 6
Environmental Impact Statement (study), 6, 162, 165
environmental justice, 63, 118; health and, 120, 136; religion and, 18, 190
environmental justice movement, 50, 57–65
environmental racism, 50
equity, 1, 98, 110, 150–51, 154, 180, 186, 188–89, 191; food, 181; health, 121, 129–36; racial, 78

farmacy program, 136
farmers' markets, 97–99, 105–7, 111, 136, 180–82, 188. *See also* Knox County Farmers' Market; Letcher County Farmers' Market; Perry County Farmers' Market; Seniors Farmers' Market Nutrition Program (SFMNP)
Farris, Mary Rice, 47
Federal Emergency Management Agency (FEMA), 62, 75
feminism, 61
First Step Act of 2019, 170–71
flooding: general, 9, 119; July 2022, 5, 28, 62–63, 74–75, 81, 85, 100–101, 112, 147, 161, 173, 178
Flora, Cornelia Butler, 190
Flora, Jan L., 190
food hub, 97, 100
food security, 102–4, 124; initiatives, 107
food system, 4, 9, 57, 103, 188; community, 100; eastern Kentucky, 99; equitable, 101; health impacts of, 120; local, 97–98, 107, 109, 111; regional, 96, 107; resilient, 112

Foundation for a Healthy Kentucky, 180, 199
Foundation for Appalachian Kentucky, 71–74
framing (theory), 111, 135, 164–72
framework, 99, 102, 111, 131, 173; antiracist, 49; capitalist, 4; community capitals, 190; digital justice, 184; just transition, 50, 57–59, 63, 68–69, 77, 135, 147, 152, 184; solidarity economy, 180
Freedman, Allen, 38
Friends of the Lilley Cornett Woods and North Fork River Watershed (FOLC), 170
Frost, William, 41

Garret, Thomas, 92–93
Gerwig, Kathie, 117–18
Global South, 3, 86–87, 92–94
Gore, Al, 131
Gramsci, Antonio, 32
grassroots, 29–30, 60, 67–70, 73–77, 108; decision-making, 164; dialogue, 97–99, 101; institutions (organizations), 101, 177; movement (organizing), 100, 119–20, 131–35, 187; network, 152–57; power, 67
Greater Kanawha Valley Foundation, 68
Green New Deal, 8, 17–18, 28–32, 89–92, 134, 135
Grow Appalachia, 97, 101–12

Habermas, Jürgen, 18–23, 31
health, 178–90; disparities, 96, 116–18, 129, 133, 135
Healthy Food and Farm Innovation Fund, 101
Hemphill Community Center, 74
Heron, Cassia, 98
heteronormativity, 8, 181
Highlander Research and Education Center (Highlander Center), 10, 50, 94, 155, 175–79, 184, 191
Hillbilly Elegy (Vance), 39
hillbillyness, 44
Hip Hop from the Hill Top & Call from Home (WMMT 88.7 radio show), 162–63

Hispanic people, 48
H.O.M.E.S. Inc., 75
homestead, 85, 88–94. *See also* Appalachian Homestead Act; Homestead Act of 1862
Homestead Act of 1862, 90
Housing Development Alliance (HDA), 74–75
Hurricane Helene, 5, 28, 62, 75

identity: Appalachian regional, 3; class, 42; cultural, 98, 131; gender, 82; politics, 39–46; racial, 42
identity entrepreneurism, 40, 50; definition of, 53
immigration, 41, 44, 67–68
Indigenous Environmental Network, 8, 57
Indigenous people, 6, 50, 76, 88, 90, 93–94, 179, 184; Appalachian, 3–5, 56, 86; communities of (including organizations and groups), 63–65; culture, 55; knowledge, 8, 57; leadership, 58, 188; sovereignty/control, 65, 87; voices of, 60; youth, 68. *See also specific tribe names*
inequity, 40, 50–51, 68 94, 99–101, 125. *See also* equity; justice; racism
Inflation Reduction Act of 2022, 29, 186
infrastructure, 133, 181, 190; "critical," 6–7; health, 134–36; human, 101; philanthropic (nonprofit), 67–77; physical, 63, 75, 101, 103, 119; social, 17, 101
Infrastructure Investment and Jobs Act of 2022, 92
injustice, 64, 78–79; racial, 79, 116. *See also* justice
Intergovernmental Panel on Climate Change (IPCC), 4
internal colony, 92
Invision Hazard, 181

justice, 1, 8, 10, 55, 179, 186–87, 189; climate, 17–18, 23, 31–32, 134; criminal, 163; definition of, 2, 17; digital, 183; economic, 107, 112, 182; food, 98; health, 117; prison, 177; racial, 32, 48–51, 67, 90, 175; reproductive,

68; social, 175. *See also* environmental justice; injustice
Just Transition Alliance, 2
just transition(s), 10, 39–40, 75, 175, 177; cultural preservation and, 98; decolonization and, 57–58; food and, 97, 99, 102–4, 111–12; health and, 131, 135–36, 189; historical trauma and, 56–57; land ownership and, 86–88, 94, 187; local control and, 85, 89 150, 186; definition, 1–2, 57–58, 153, 176, 182–83; 17, 23, 28–30; as discourse, 117; in philanthropy, 78; framework (model), 62–63, 69, 77, 147–48, 152; liberation and, 81; movement (coalition), 9, 68, 77, 156–57, 161, 168, 171–72; networks, 151, 180; "philosophies," 120; policies/plans, 7, 92, 118, 121, 132–35; practices/work, 8, 37, 129, 184; principles, 5, 58, 63–64, 90–91, 173, 191; race and, 47–52, 68, 179; rematriation and, 63–65; role of democracy, 189–90; role of youth, 182; for workers, 17, 23, 28–30
just transition movement, 37, 69, 77, 161, 168, 171. *See also* just transition(s)

Kennedy, John F., 43
Kennedy, Robert F., 47
Kentuckians for the Commonwealth (KFTC), 149
Kentucky Agricultural Development Fund (KDAF), 101
Kentucky Black Farmer Fund, 100
Kentucky Broadband Initiative, 136
Kentucky Coal Association, 131
Kentucky Department of Corrections, 160
Kentucky Double Dollars, 101
Kentucky Food Action Network, 101
Kingdom of the Happy Land, 88
Klein, Naomi, 2–3
Knox County Cooperative Extension, 110
Knox County Farmers' Market, 97, 107–11

land ownership, 9, 85–94; 191; absentee, 9, 85–94, 187; communal (collective), 88–94; history of, 85–88. *See also* communal: access to common-pool resources

land reform (redistribution), 88, 93
Latinx people, 5, 51, 76, 183, 201. *See also* Hispanic people
Lend-A-Hand Center, 108
Letcher County Farmers' Market, 104
Letcher County Planning Commission, 163–64
Letcher Governance Project (LPG), 162, 168
Lewis, Helen M., 78
Lexington Herald-Leader, 93
LGBTQIA+ people, 6, 9, 82
Loyal Land Company, 87
Lumbee Tribe, 78

Manchin, Joe, 7
Margaret A. Cargill Philanthropies, 69
Marguerite Casey Foundation, 69
Marshall Plan for Middle America, 123
Marxian theory, 23–24, 32
Marxism, 18, 23–25
Mary Reynolds Babcock Foundation, 68
McDaniel, Dustin, 168
micromobilization, 131–33
Miller, Tom, 87
Mine Safety Health Administration (MSHA), 115–16
Mondragon, 27–28
Moneton people, 82
Mountain Association, 99, 132, 148–57, 191
mountaintop removal mining, 18, 58–62, 119, 181, 189
Mountain Valley Pipeline (MVP), 6
Movement Generation, 68
Muscogee/Creek people, 82
mutual aid, 77, 189, 191

narrative: Appalachia as "big black hole," 67; Appalachia as victim, 42, 61–62; Appalachian as degenerate and lawless, 42; Appalachian as white, 42, 47; Appalachian coal country, 38; Appalachian transition, 69; Appalachian youth, 82; Black Appalachian, 37, 46; change, 149, 153–54; community, 111; "forgotten man," 40; form, 5; hillbilly, 44–45; just transition, 76; poor white

narrative (*continued*)
  Appalachian, 39; post coal, 37; racial, 50; storytelling and, 156. *See also* discourse; story
National Committee for Responsive Philanthropy, 67
National Dislocated Worker Grants, 134
National Energy Policy Development Group, 131
National Environmental Protection Act of 1969 (NEPA), 162
National Industrial Recovery Act of 1933, 88
National Institute for Safety and Health (NIOSH), 115–21, 130
Native Americans. *See* Indigenous people
neofascism, 187, 190
neoliberalism, 2–3, 28, 94, 187, 190
network(s), 2, 60, 110, 156, 180, 182; agriculture and food, 97, 99; building, 107, 109, 111; commons, 5; of communities, 152; community, 184; of community leaders, 153; cooperative, 27; coordinator, 155; formal, 149, 157; friend and familial, 44; funder-driven, 151–52; grassroots, 153; just transition, 147; local, 183; opportunities, 110; mutual aid, 191; organic (informal), 148–49, 151, 178; organizational, 102; of organizations, 102; peer, 177–78; regional, 111; rural, 154–55; social, 66, 106; structured, 148; theory, 152. *See also* Appalachian Funders Network; Black Appalachian Network; Central Appalachian Network (CAN); Kentucky Food Action Network; Rural Development Philanthropy Network; Stay Together Appalachian Youth (STAY)
Neves-Graca, Katja, 93
New Deal, 9, 32, 88, 124

Obermiller, Phillip J., 43–44
Occupational Safety and Health Act of 1970, 115
Occupational Safety and Health Administration (OSHA), 115

oligarchy, 8, 186
On Our Own Land (documentary), 85
opioids, 75, 81, 129
Osage people, 82
Ostrom, Elinor, 5–8, 92, 132, 187–89

patriarchy, 8, 39, 58, 61, 181
Pelosi, Nancy, 31
Perry County Farmers' Market, 179
philanthropy, 8, 58–59, 151; community-controlled, 66–79; disaster, 74–75; private, 100; as a tool of capitalism, 66–67
Pine Mountain Settlement School, 105–6
planning: community (local), 118; economic, 51, 171–72; production, 104; program, 106; strategic, 109–10. *See also* Letcher County Planning Commission; Saving Our Appalachian Region (SOAR)
PODER Emma, 78
politics, 32, 153; of climate change, 21–22; coalition, 51; of health advocacy, 129; identity, 39; solidarity, 169, 171, 173
Posner, Emily, 171
poverty, 3–4, 56, 67, 79, 98–99, 120, 136, 186; generational, 40, 147; health and, 118, 128; mountain (Appalachian), 90, 129. *See also* War on Poverty
POWER+ plan (Partnerships for Opportunity and Workforce and Economic Revitalization), 134–35
prison abolition, 68. *See also* prison construction: negative impacts of
prison construction: as economic development, 9–10, 160–61; negative impacts of, 10, 118, 125, 169–70; opposition to, 81–82, 125, 161–72, 181, 187
Prison Ecology Project/Fight Toxic Prisons, 165
private ownership (private property), 2, 93–94
privatization, 3, 17, 22, 56–187. *See also* deprivatization
production, 9, 23–31; cost of, 2; of surplus value, 24–25

progressive massive fibrosis. *See* black lung
Prosperino, Lill, 163, 170, 172
protest(s), 58; against injustice, 7; anti-racist, 49, 166–68; environmental, 6–7. *See also* prison construction: opposition to
public policy, 17, 67, 88, 93, 97–101, 111
Puckett, Anita, 20–21

racialized: Appalachia, 37, 40–46, 50; capitalism, 2, 190; class war, 161; mass incarceration, 173; state violence, 169. *See also* Appalachian: stereotypes; capitalism: types of; equity
racism, 5, 37–39, 42–44, 47, 50–51, 116, 176; racial division, 59; racial health disparities, 116–18; racial hierarchy, 3–4, 38, 45, 50–51; racial segregation in coal towns, 45–46; racial stereotypes, 46; racial structure, 51; racial violence, 44, 49. *See also* justice: racial; inequity
Rawls, John, 19
Ray, Tarance, 168
RECLAIM Act of 2017, 59, 91–92, 178
Reclaiming Appalachia Coalition, 29
Red Bird Mission, 105
redistribution, 60, 75–79, 88–91, 178
regenerative economy, 57, 60–61, 189
regulatory capture, 129–31
ReImagine Appalachia, 124
Rekindling Project, 65, 78, 187, 191
rematriation, 55, 64–65, 187
Reich, Robert, 187
resilience, 182; community, 62, 98, 105, 191; ecological, 2; local, 106; of indigenous people, 56
Resnick, Stephen, 23
resource curse, 6, 186
resource extraction, 1, 56, 59, 62, 86, 171, 182. *See also* economy: extractive
Roberts, Cecil, 30
Rogers, Harold "Hal," 162–68
Roosevelt, Eleanor, 90
Roosevelt, Franklin D., 39
Rural Action, 96
Rural Action Plan of 2020, 129–31

Rural Development Philanthropy Network, 72
Rural Health Policy, US Office of, 129
Rural Health Service Center, 129
Rural Support Partners, 154, 175

Sanders, Bernie, 28–29
Scotts Run, WV, 88
Sen, Amartya, 19
Seniors Farmers' Market Nutrition Program (SFMNP), 100
Shaping Our Appalachian Region (SOAR), 96, 153, 166–69. *See also* planning
Shawnee people, 82
Smith, Barbara Ellen, 43
Smith, Tony, 19, 21, 23
SNAP (Supplemental Nutrition Assistance Program), 100, 108, 110–11
Snyder, Timothy, 191
social determinants of health (SDOH), 117, 120, 134–35
solidarity, 8, 22, 27, 46, 62, 68, 169; economy, 176–84; politics, 169–71
Southern Appalachian Mountain Stewards (SAMS), 8, 58–59, 61–63
speech pragmatics, 19–22
Standing Rock Sioux, 6
Stay Together Appalachian Youth (STAY), 8, 74, 81–82, 149, 178, 188
Stiglitz, Joseph, 19
Stoll, Steven, 91. *See also* commons: Commons Community Act
story, 55–65, 76, 116, 164; story-based communication strategy, 99; storytelling, 60, 156. *See also* discourse; narrative
Stronza, Amanda Lee, 93

Trail of Tears, 41
trauma (historical), 55–59
tropes, 39; Appalachian, 39; "forgotten man," 40
Trump, Donald J., 17
trust (mistrust), 60, 63, 75, 78, 132, 179–80, 184; governmental, 30; social, 4, 105, 154–56, 187–91
trusts: community, 7; land, 88, 182

Try This West Virginia, 153–54
Tsoyaha people, 82
Turner, Tanya, 162–64
Turner, William H., 44–45

Universal Displaced Worker Program (US), 134
United Nations (UN), 192. *See also* Intergovernmental Panel on Climate Change; Emission Gap Report (2022)

Vance, J. D., 39
Villanueva, Edgar, 78
Virginia Council on Environmental Justice, 60

Wagner, Thomas E., 43–44
Walker, Kristin Collins, 71–72
Walker, Thomas, 87
War on Poverty, 42, 46–47, 90
Waymakers Collective, 75–78

Werner, Tammy I., 41
West Virginia Center on Budget and Policy, 87–88
West Virginia Food and Farm Coalition, 96
What's Next, East Kentucky?! (WNEK), 147, 152–57
Whitaker, Mitch, 165–73
white supremacy, 2, 4, 8, 43–50, 58, 81, 168, 179
Williams, Elandria, 94
Wolff, Richard, 23
Women, Infants, and Children (WIC), 100, 109–11
Woodland Community Land Trust, 182

Young Appalachian Leaders and Learners (Y'ALL), 9
Yuchi people, 55

Zegeer, David, 25

Place Matters: New Directions in Appalachian Studies

Series Editor: Dwight B. Billings

This series explores the history, social life, and cultures of Appalachia from multidisciplinary, comparative, and global perspectives. Topics include geography, the environment, public policy, political economy, critical regional studies, diversity, social inequality, social movements and activism, migration and immigration, efforts to confront regional stereotypes, literature and the arts, and the ongoing social construction and reimagination of Appalachia. Key goals of the series are to place Appalachian dynamics in the context of global change and to demonstrate that place-based and regional studies still matter.

Appalachia in Regional Context: Place Matters
Edited by Dwight B. Billings and Ann E. Kingsolver

Engaging Appalachia: A Guidebook for Building Capacity and Sustainability
Edited by Rebecca Adkins Fletcher, Rebecca-Eli Long, and William Schumann

Literacy in the Mountains: Community, Newspapers, and Writing in Appalachia
Samantha NeCamp

Appalachia Revisited: New Perspectives on Place, Tradition, and Progress
Edited by William Schumann and Rebecca Adkins Fletcher

Toward Just Transitions: Visions for Regenerative Communities in Appalachia
Edited by Shaunna L. Scott and Kathryn Engle

The Arthurdale Community School: Education and Reform in Depression-Era Appalachia
Sam F. Stack Jr.

Sacred Mountains: A Christian Ethical Approach to Mountaintop Removal
Andrew R. H. Thompson

Power and Place: Preservation, Progress, and the Culture War over Land
Melinda Bollar Wagner

Rereading Appalachia: Literacy, Place, and Cultural Resistance
Edited by Sara Webb-Sunderhaus and Kim Donehower

Religion and Resistance in Appalachia: Faith and the Fight against Mountaintop Removal Coal Mining
Joseph D. Witt